THAT THEY MAY BE ONE

THAT THEY MAY BE ONE

A Study of Papal Doctrine
(*Leo XIII* — *Pius XII*)

by

GREGORY BAUM, O.S.A.

1958
THE NEWMAN PRESS
WESTMINSTER, MARYLAND

© 1958 by Bloomsbury Publishing Co. Ltd.

Imprimi potest: P. Fr. Hermenegild M. Biedermann, O.S.A.
  Provincialis
Nihil obstat: Daniel Duivesteign, S.T.D.
  Censor deputatus
Imprimatur: Georgius L. Craven
  Epus Sebastopolis, V.G.
Westmonasterii, die 3a Februarii, 1958

PRINTED IN GREAT BRITAIN BY
BARNICOTTS LIMITED AT
THE WESSEX PRESS, TAUNTON
AND BOUND BY KEMP HALL
BINDERY, OXFORD

CONTENTS

		Page
Introductory Note		vii

Chapter 1	THE UNITY OF THE CHURCH	1
	THE UNITY OF GOD'S PEOPLE	2
	The People's Mission	2
	The Social Body	6
	Unity of Faith	8
	Unity of Government	11
	THE UNITY OF CHRIST'S BODY	16
	The Completeness of Redemption	17
	The one Holy Spirit	19
	The one Head	20
	The Completion of Christ	24
	A NOTE ON MEMBERSHIP IN THE CHURCH	27

Chapter 2	DISSIDENT CHRISTIANS	33
	THE DIVINE PATRIMONY	35
	THE DISSIDENT CHRISTIANS OF THE EAST	35
	THE DISSIDENT CHRISTIANS OF THE WEST	37
	The Sacrament of Baptism	38
	The Virtue of Faith	40
	THE SEED OF DISSENTION	47
	THE ORIGIN OF DISSENTION	48
	In the East	49
	In the West	50
	THE DYNAMISM OF DISSENTION	51
	In the East	51
	In the West	52
	THE RESULTANT SITUATION	55
	The 'Faith' of Protestants	57
	The Relation of Dissident Christians to the Catholic Church	59

Chapter 3	DISSIDENT CHURCHES	65
	THE NATURE OF SEPARATED CHURCHES	65
	The Dissident Churches of the East	69
	THE SUPERNATURAL GOOD IN DISSIDENT CHURCHES	73

		Page
Chapter 4	**CATHOLIC ECUMENISM:**	
	ITS FOUNDATION	77
	ECUMENISM OR MISSIONS	78
	THE CATHOLICITY OF THE CHURCH	82
	The Catholicity of God's People	83
	The Catholicity of Christ's Body	85
	Two Aspects of Catholicity	86
	THE MOTHERHOOD OF THE CHURCH	88
	THE CHURCH, MOTHER OF DISSIDENTS	89
	The Sacraments	90
	The Holy Scriptures	91
	A NOTE ON OUR LADY	94
	CATHOLIC ECUMENISM	97
Chapter 5	**CATHOLIC ECUMENISM:**	
	ITS EXERCISE	102
	THE ECUMENICAL WITNESS	102
	THE WORLD COUNCIL OF CHURCHES	103
	THE ECUMENICAL ATTITUDE	108
	The acknowledgment of the Christian elements in other communities	109
	The refusal to proselytize	111
	The sincere search for truth	113
	The anticipation of the benefits of reunion also for the Catholic Church	117
	The faith that the Catholic Church is the home of all Christians	120
	ECUMENICAL CHARITY	123
	The Holiness that Unites	124
	Prayer for Unity	127
Appendices	NOTES TO THE TEXT:	
	to Chapter 1	135
	to Chapter 2	143
	to Chapter 3	151
	to Chapter 4	155
	to Chapter 5	161
	BIBLIOGRAPHY	172
	THE BOSTON LETTER	177
	INDEX	180

INTRODUCTORY NOTE

THE instruction of the Holy Office "On the Ecumenical Movement" demands that Catholic theologians study the movements for Christian unity in the light of the doctrine and principles set forth by the Holy See[1]. In recent years several such studies have been published[2]; not all of them however, even when they intended to present exclusively the Roman standpoint, were based on a sufficient number and an adequate knowledge of the official documents. There is, we believe, room for a more thorough investigation of the papal teaching on Christian unity. In the following pages we shall study the official documents of the Holy See in modern times, beginning with the pontificate of Leo XIII, or more precisely with his encyclical *Praeclara Gratulationis* (1894) which is said to have inaugurated a new period in the history of the Church's relationship to other Christian confessions[3]. Our purpose, however, is neither to set up a chronology of the Roman encounters with separated Churches, nor to give an account of the decisions and directives by which the Holy See has regulated Catholic reunion movements. Our concern is theology. We shall try to present the doctrine of the papal writings on Christian unity.

Since many of the papal pronouncements on the unity and disunity of Christians are simply pastoral or disciplinary in character, it is at first sight by no means obvious whether our plan to present doctrine can be followed through. If however, in addition to the explicit teaching of our documents, we also consider the principles and the conclusions implied in them, we do find enough doctrinal material to outline a theology of Christian unity. In this study, then, we shall limit ourselves to the Roman documents; we shall not say all that has been said, or that can be said, on Christian unity from the viewpoint of Catholic theology. Our aim is simply to present and expand the principles taught in the recent documents of the Holy See; expanding these principles, however, we shall not go further than is sanctioned by the documents themselves. Our study will thus be a sort of exegesis of the papal writings, and when we quote them as much as we do—and to some it may indeed appear excessive—it is to authenticate our interpretation and to convince the reader of our consistency.

This study intends to be a contribution to the ecumenical dialogue[4]. Because the Catholic Church considers herself as the one true Church of Christ and all other Churches as in error, it is sometimes thought (by Roman and non-Roman Christians) that religious dialogue is incompatible with her nature. The office of the Church is to teach, it is said, as it is the duty of "the others" to listen. We believe, however, that in spite of the unique claims of the Catholic Church, the view of Christian unity presented in the papal documents renders a dialogue not only possible, but necessary. In the writings of the modern popes, dissident Christianity is never considered as a mission field where the task of the Church is simply to preach. The witness of the Church in separated Christianity has a different theological quality; it must always include the acknowledgment of the Christian elements surviving in the precarious state of separation. In the course of this study we shall come to the conviction many times that a Catholic speaking to non-Catholic Christians must first listen, and listen carefully. While the popes decry anything that looks like dogmatic compromise or even tends to make Catholic truth appear relative, they do not want to discourage that contact with dissident thought which is essential for shaping the Catholic ecumenical witness. The reunion of Christians is not only the task of non-Catholics; it is also, and in a special way, the task of the Catholic Church. To understand the theological character of this quest is a particular concern of this study.

At the very beginning we must set down the definition of a term which is constantly used in these pages: a Christian. *By a Christian we mean a man who acknowledges Jesus Christ as God and Saviour.* This definition excludes many who like to think of themselves as Christians, but in denying that the eternal Word has become flesh in Jesus Christ they do not step out of the circle of what may at best be called a human wisdom. Christians we shall call only those men who acknowledge Jesus Christ as the Son of God, the one Mediator, true God and true Man. This definition includes, at least theoretically, all members of communities belonging to the World Council of Churches; for the official basis of this Council is the common faith in Christ, God and Saviour.

About our sources and method of citation a few remarks will suffice. While in our text we always cite the Roman documents in English translation, in the footnotes we refer to the corresponding place in the official Latin source and, for important quotations, also give the Latin original. The English translations are mostly our own, but even when we follow a printed version, we have always compared and sometimes corrected the passages from the Latin, hoping thereby to make them more precise and more readable. The principal sources from which we quote are the *Leonis XIII Acta* (LA)[5] and the *Acta Apostolicae Sedis* (AAS); these are the official collections and the most easily available. Citing from them we give the volume and the page; between these two numbers we insert in parentheses the year to which belongs the body of the documents contained in the particular volume[6].

We do not wish to close this introductory note without expressing our gratitude to Rev. Heinrich Stirnimann OP, professor at the University of Fribourg, for the pains he took in directing this study, and to Rev. Lawrence C. McHugh SJ, who was kind enough to read the manuscript and suggest corrections in the language, which is not native to the author.

---

[1] See Chapter 5, note 42.
[2] See Bibliography, section C, p. 175.
[3] ROGER AUBERT, *Le saint-siège et l'union des Eglises*, Brussels 1947, p. 31.
[4] For our use of the word 'ecumenical', see p. 78.
[5] *Leonis XIII Pontifici Maximi Acta*, vol. 1–23, Rome 1881–1905.
[6] We note that for the *Leonis XIII Acta* the date of publication of a volume is always one year posterior to the documents which it contains. Thus, for instance, *Praeclara Gratulationis* was written in 1894, while the volume containing it was published in 1895. Yet for the sake of a better chronological orientation, we refer to a volume of the LA by giving, not its year of publication, but the year of the documents collected in it.

CHAPTER ONE

THE UNITY OF THE CHURCH

THE Roman Catholic Church is united to Jesus Christ, the Saviour of the world, as his mystical Body. This must be called a certainty of faith(1). Christ could have founded a Church with the sole function of preaching the gospel and congregating the faithful without identifying himself more closely with his purchased people. He could have founded a Church which was to be a witness to him without being a bearer of him. It was however the intention of the Son of God to unite the community of believers to himself as his own body of which he was the head, and in doing so he made the Church at once a society of men and an organism of grace. The Church, by the hidden and mysterious unity of its visible and invisible components, is an object of divine faith. *Credo unam Ecclesiam.*

The Church of Christ is one. 'She is an indivisible whole because Christ himself with his Church is undivided and indivisible'(2). From whatever angle we may look upon the Church, we shall discover her unity. Just as every cross-section of a sphere is circular, though perhaps of different dimensions, so every view of the Church reveals her indefectible unity under various perspectives.

In this chapter we shall begin considering the Church as the People of God and describe her unity as it proceeds from the foundation and the call of Christ. Then, considering the Church as the mystical Body, we shall develop her unity as a sharing in the life of Christ made accessible to man on the cross. In the first section it will be mainly Leo XIII in his encyclical *Statis Cognitum* who will be our guide, in the second we shall follow the doctrine given by Pius XII in the encyclical *Mystici Corporis*. It is not our intention to give a complete account of the papal teaching on the Church's unity; this would take us far beyond the purpose of this study. We shall present the official doctrine rather briefly, singling out certain perspectives which will contribute to our understanding of Christian unity and lend themselves to ecumenical thinking. For this reason, also, we have divided our consideration into the unity of God's People and the unity of Christ's Body. The official documents of the Holy See do not pretend to be a complete source of theology, but we shall try to show without going further than is warranted by these documents that the Christian community is one by reason of its destiny (the affirmation of the Ecumenical Movement), and that the Christians' incorporation into Christ is manifested by an historical unity (the doubt of the Ecumenical Movement). Finally, in order to collect the necessary theological equipment, we shall append a note on membership in the Catholic Church.

THE UNITY OF THE PEOPLE OF GOD

The Church is God's own people. 'You are a chosen race, a royal priesthood, a holy nation, a purchased people; that you may proclaim the perfections of him who has called you out of darkness into his marvellous light. You who in times past were not a people, but are now the People of God' (1 Pet. ii. 9–10). While Christ was walking on this earth, he called and elected men to enter into fellowship with him. Yet he did more. Having chosen a group of apostles he sent them into the world as he had been sent by the Father, that through their word men might believe and enter the new community by means of baptism. The apostles were to teach, to consecrate, and to rule in order to separate the faithful from a world headed for destruction. Need we emphasize that the young Church was a visible reality? It is hardly necessary, for the New Testament knows of no other Church than the perceptible People of God, 'the Israel of God' (Gal. vi. 16), 'the congregation of the truly circumcised' (Phil. iii. 3), 'the twelve tribes that are in the dispersion' (James i. 1) (3). Just as the people of Israel had been a visible and definable group in history, so the new Chosen People in whom the promises made to Israel are fulfilled is a visible community of men manifest before the world. The faithful of Christ are bound into one, not only by their spiritual union to the Saviour, but also by the perceptible links of appointed offices and sanctioned rites. The People of God is one; it is *one* in the sense that there is and can be only a single Church, and *one* in the sense that the faithful constitute a united human family of which God is the Father.

The People's Mission

The unity of Christ's purchased People is generally admitted by all Christians. In *Mortalium animos* Pius XI writes, 'None of those who call themselves Christians will deny, we think, that Jesus Christ founded a Church, in fact, one sole Church' (4). But, he continues, as to the exact nature of this Church, there is not the same agreement. The principle, however, according to which unity in the Church must be determined is perfectly clear: it is the positive will of Christ. 'One must know above all what Christ had in mind and what he actually did'. It is not a question of 'what form of unity the Church might have had, but rather what unity was intended by her divine Founder' (5). It is a question of fact, of history, and the only way to find an answer is to return to the sources, to the Scriptures and to the records of antiquity. Hence the papal documents on the unity of God's People are primarily concerned with the exegesis of Scripture and the testimony of Tradition.

The return to Christ's original intention also prevails in non-Catholic ecumenical thought, particularly as it finds expression in the documents of the World Council of Churches. The myth of an invisible Church has been abandoned. 'We all believe that the Church persists in continuity throughout history through the presence and power of the Holy Spirit' (6). But what is the nature of this Church? According to the testimony of the New Testament, it is one. Unity then is not something to be created; rather is it the gift of Christ and realized by perfect obedience to him. We read in the Report of the Advisory Commission for the Evanston Assembly: 'We are not at one concerning the form which the corporate unity of the Church should take . . . We trust our common Lord to continue to guide us towards that fulness of unity which is His will for His people' (7).

The Church, then, is the People of God, and its unity is determined by the will and intention of him who has called and predestined it. But what was the intention of Christ in calling his Church into existence? The answer is given by a single phrase in the Vatican Council, and all the subsequent formulations in the Roman documents are commentaries on this statement: 'It was in order to *perpetuate his work of redemption* that the eternal Pastor and Bishop of our souls decided to build a holy Church in which, as in the house of the living God, all the faithful might be bound together by the link of one faith and charity' (8). At greater length, we read in *Satis Cognitum:*

'Jesus Christ wanted this one thing: to transmit to the Church for perpetuation the mission and office which he had received from the Father. This he resolved to do, and this he actually did. "As the Father has sent me, I also send you." "As thou hast sent me into the world, I also have sent them into the world." Now the mission of Christ is to save "what was lost", that is to say, not some nations or peoples but the whole human race without distinction of time or place . . . Hence the redemptive work of Christ and all the graces emanating from it must be fully communicated and transmitted by the Church to all men and through all ages. For this reason, according to the will of her Founder, she must be one in all lands and in all times. If we were seeking room for another Church, we would have to leave the confines of this earth and think up a new and unknown race of men' (9).

The People of God received the commission to continue the work of Christ, to act as his instrument in reconciling all things to the Father. Hence the Church is not simply the congregation of the faithful; she embraces also the totality of the means of salvation which the Lord has brought. She is a supernatural organism rather than an organization. Even considered as a social body, she has a character of her own, different from all other societies. This difference becomes plain at her very foundation. While human societies are set up and determined by a constitution and the appointment of leaders, the Church only received its beginning, its substructure, its organization from the law of Jesus Christ. 'The divine Redeemer *began* to build the mystical temple of the Church when he was preaching and giving his commandments; he *completed* it when he hung in glory on the cross; he *manifested* and promulgated it by the visible mission of the Holy Ghost to his disciples' (10). Through the power of the cross and the communion of the Holy Ghost, the fullness of Christ was given to the Church; and on account of this fullness she can perpetuate the work and office of the Saviour throughout history. The People of God is more than a congregation of men; it is called upon to mediate grace, to be an instrument of salvation. How are we to understand this?

It would be an error to think that the role of the Church was to apply and distribute the effects of Christ's redemptive work as if she were a channel, a long mechanical conductor by which a gift made at a distance is delivered here and now. It is true, the Church is said to mediate the effects of Christ's death and resurrection, but not by interposing the many centuries which separate us from Calvary and reaching with a long arm, as it were, to a gift which at that time had been confided to her treasury. No, the Church is mediatrix of grace by making present Christ, the free bestower of his grace. In her and through her signs, Christ wants to be present to all generations.

It was the intention of Christ to remain present in his People in such a way that through its activity he continues to save men. This is the teaching of our Roman documents. 'It is indeed Christ who lives in his Church, and through her teaches, governs, and sanctifies' (11). 'At every liturgical act is present, together with the

Church, her divine Founder' (12). The presence of the Lord in his People is most apparent in the sacraments: 'When the Church by external rites administers the sacraments, it is Christ himself who produces the effect in the soul' (13). It is less apparent but nonetheless real in all manifestations of her supernatural life. 'We must learn to see in the Church Jesus Christ himself' (14). Because of the commission which he gave to the apostles and by sending his own Spirit, Christ lives in the Church and the Church lives in Christ. This is the fulfilment of the prophecies of the Old Testament: the Lord living in his People. 'Behold, I am with you always', Jesus said. As King he rules from above and as Saviour he obeys in the hearts of the faithful. Christ is the subject to whom all expressions of supernatural life are ultimately referred and attributed. The visible People subsists mysteriously in its Lord who, without destroying the individual existence of the members, becomes its hidden and transcendental Personality.

Expanding through time and over the continents the Church embodies the presence of Christ in history. According to the remarkable phrase of the Faith-and-Order Conference at Lund, 'The Church is called to continue the mission of Christ to the world, so that the way of Christ is the way of the Church' (15). The Church, then, is the People of God purchased and acquired by Jesus Christ, following her Master through a land of exile to the Heavenly Jerusalem by drawing with her all mankind, even all of creation. The way of the Church is a return, a pilgrimage; it is not an idle waiting but a going forward to meet the Lord coming in his glory. The Church has an active part to play in the extension of the Kingdom, in making Christ grow on earth and thus preparing his return. She is called upon 'to fight the good fight' (1 Tim. i. 18 vi. 12; 2 Tim. iv. 7), to imitate the Lord by working and suffering for the salvation of men.

To understand the significance of the battle to which the People of God are called, we recall that the faithful of Christ are not surrounded by a world friendly or even neutral to them. On the contrary, sharing the fate of their Lord they are exposed to the powers of darkness, the enemies of God who spread their destructive influences, 'seeking whom they may devour'. It is a battle not against flesh and blood but against 'principalities and powers'. In this perspective God's peaceful People can be likened to a fighting contingent, to 'a well-arrayed army', to an invincible host following 'the Word of God whose garment is sprinkled with blood' (Apoc. xix. 13). The community of love an army? Yes; for we have the testimony of Scripture. The Church of God is a reality which cannot be described by a single concept; we need many images and notions to express her role in the divine economy. Seeing her against the background of satanic enmity, the Church is an army and the Christian is 'a soldier of Christ' (2 Tim. ii. 3).

The Social Body

The People of God, we have said, is a unique society because into its founding went, in addition to a legal act, the life-giving sacrifice of Christ on the cross and the mission of his invisible Spirit. Compared to human societies, civil or otherwise, the Church is a society only in an analogical sense.

'God made the Church a society far more perfect than any other. The end for which the Church exists is as much higher than the end of other societies, as divine grace is above nature, as things eternal are above things temporal. Therefore the Church is a society, divine in its origin and supernatural in its end and in the means which lead to the end. A human society it is only in as much as it is composed of men' (16).

Because the faithful of Christ have the same final end, the same common concern, because they are called upon in various ways to help one another, because they employ the common means they have received, they constitute a social body. But the structure of this holy society is completely dependent on the will of the Lord who fashioned the instruments of grace as he wished. It is true, the popes occasionally emphasize strongly that the Church is a perfect society, yet it is not their intention to establish a parallel between ecclesiastical and civil society. From the constitutions of human societies it is never permissible to draw conclusions about the essential structure of the Church of God. Even here, our only source of knowledge is apostolic testimony and apostolic tradition. Certain laws and properties of human societies have, by divine institution, obtained validity in the Church, but they must be understood in an elevated and accommodated sense, adapting them to a spiritual end.

Very frequently the papal documents speak of the Church as 'a perfect society' (17). This is a technical term current in traditional Catholic theology which signifies that the Church, due to her exalted aim, which is holiness, is independent of all other social bodies in supporting and propagating herself. If the Church had not the means of realizing her essential purpose, there would be no place on earth where she could find them. But being appointed to reconcile the world in the name of Jesus Christ, she was equipped with inexhaustible fountains giving her spiritual self-sufficiency and power with respect to the world. Stressing the Church as a 'perfect society' vindicates her independence from the state and from government interference. It is not meant to relegate the Church into the species of perfect human societies, of which she would be the most perfect. 'The Christian Commonwealth differs profoundly from all kinds of political realms. Even if it should bear a certain resemblance to civil society, it is distinguished from it by its origin, its principle, and its essence' (18). The People of God constitute a society in an analogical and elevated sense.

There are Catholic writers who consider the Church a society in a univocal sense: she is the most perfect society among others of the same specific nature. S. Tyszkiewicz sets up the following parallel: just as Christ has a perfectly integrated physical body, so the Church has an external structure which is a perfectly integrated society, the most perfect of its kind (19). Now it is true that the Church is made up of an invisible life and a visible structure, which come together in a union similar to the union between soul and body in a human nature (20). But the above parallel, strictly drawn as it is, must be misleading. While Christ has a visible body in a univocal sense, we maintain that the Church's visible body is a society in an analogical sense.

Christ's physical body is specifically like other human bodies. Even though more perfect, it remains flesh of our flesh, made up and functioning like our bodies. It has the same bone structure, the same organs, the same nervous system. The body of Christ was not only *in* this world; it was also *of* this world. More than that, the body of the Lord was destined to share the glory of his eternity. In heaven Christ has the same body with which he was nailed to the cross. The People of God, on the other hand, is *in* this world without being *of* it. Its social structure does not include all that a perfect human society normally includes. 'The role of the Church is not to comprehend and somehow embrace, like a huge empire, the whole of human society' (21). On the contrary, her organization embraces only a minimum of the world, only as much as is necessary to perpetuate her existence in the world (22). Even in her earthly life, the Church is ever a sign pointing to the age that is to come; she is not at home on earth, not even as a society. 'On her way to her eternal destination the Church adapts her pace to temporal conditions, but the ages she has passed and is expecting are for her like a single day' (23).

Even if the eschatological aspect of the Church is not particularly emphasized in the writings of the popes, the Christian dogma of the *Parousia* is never absent from their minds. The Church is a pilgrim society which awaits the end of its lowly state. Her external structure is marked by an eschatological yearning since it is destined to pass away on the Last Day. The Church is not an incarnation of a spiritual life into a visible framework which is to last for ever. On the contrary, the order of faith, of sacrament and jurisdiction is a token of her pilgrimage; they imply, to the extent that they are necessary, that the presence of the Lord in his People is not yet consummated. For in the holy City that is to come 'there shall be no temple. The Lord God almighty and the Lamb shall be the temple thereof' (Apoc. xxi. 22). The Church militant longs to be transfigured into the Church triumphant, not indeed by hoping to perfect its earthly structure, its hierarchy and sacraments, but by abandoning all its lamps. For in the final stage of the Church 'there is no need for lamps or the light of the sun; the Lord God shall shed light upon it' (Apoc. xxii. 5).

The popes specify above all two visible links by which the wayfaring People of God are held together in unity: faith (which here includes the sacrament of faith, which is baptism) and obedience to the legitimate hierarchy.

Unity of Faith

'Faith is the first bond between God and men' (24). It separates men from the world dedicated to perdition and, in union with baptism, makes them brothers of Jesus Christ. By faith man is given a new orientation towards the merciful God who reveals himself as the Lover and Saviour of mankind. Faith is the gift of God by which we adhere to him and his saving Word; it is also the principle of a new life of obedience to the same Word. However, faith is not merely in the private order of God and the soul. The end towards which faith directs and destines us as individuals is at the same time the common end of the whole community of believers. Faith determines the orientation of the People of God on its pilgrimage. Hence, by its ordination towards Christ, faith integrates us into the People of God, not by authorizing our entry by an external label, but by making us participate in the common destiny of Christ's chosen People.

Faith must be one. This is the explicit doctrine of Holy Scripture. The well-known phrases of St Paul, such as 'one Lord, one faith, one baptism' and 'one mind and one judgement', are frequently quoted in our documents. But the unity of faith is seen more clearly from the wider consideration of the end and purpose which God has set down for his Church. The sublime and eminently spiritual end, the perpetuation of Christ's redemptive work, requires a unity of minds which exceeds anything that is known in a natural community. Every Christian is called upon 'to have the mind which is also in Jesus Christ', to see the world and to look up to God with the eyes of Christ; and this happens on earth through faith. Hence just as there is one Christ, there must be one faith.

Leo XIII was of the opinion that 'all Christians are agreed that faith must be one' (25). But in what exactly does this unity consist? He gives us the Catholic principle: 'We must investigate which is the unity of faith Christ has commanded' (26). We must let ourselves be guided by divine Revelation. To seek a concept of faith beginning from the dilemma of existing divisions may be very tempting on account of its apparent realism, but it would conceal the essential nature of Revelation. For God has spoken, and it is up to us to listen. Therefore, whenever the Roman documents define the unity of faith, they derive it from the biblical sources.

There is no need to go into a detailed exposition, for the popes give but the accepted exegesis of the Catholic tradition. God has spoken his full and final Word in Jesus Christ, and it is by faith in this Word of God that man shall be justified. 'God who in times past has spoken to the fathers by prophets, last of all in these days has spoken to us by his Son' (Heb. i. 1). 'But to as many as receive him he gave the power of becoming sons of God,—yes, to all who believe in his name' (John i. 12). Seeing that faith means clinging to God's Word as spoken in Jesus Christ, 'adhering to God as the source of truth' (27), it must of necessity embrace all that God has communicated to men. 'The things that I speak, I speak as the Father has bidden me' (John xii. 49). Man must hear in total obedience. 'My brethren are they who hear the Word of God and act upon it' (Luke viii. 21). Before God's Word man does not remain free to follow his own preference. Should he reject a part, even a very small part of that which God has revealed, he would make a choice against the sovereignty of the Lord. 'He who hears *my word*' says Christ 'and believes in him who sent me, has life everlasting' (John v. 24). The word of Christ, word in the singular, is the message of salvation which he revealed to us; the word of Christ is one thing, it has no parts, it is either wholly accepted or not accepted at all.

In the technical language of theology we say that faith is *one* because it is uniquely determined by its formal motive (*id quo creditur*), the authority of God the Revealer, and by its formal object (*id quod creditur*), the divine message of salvation. In other words, faith is uniquely defined by the Word of God which is both its authority and its content. And just as the Word of God is one, so is the faith which is its echo. Faith embraces all that God has revealed (28).

Since faith comes from hearing, Christ has appointed apostles to preach what he has revealed to them, and he enjoins all men to believe the preachers whom he has sent. 'Go ye into the whole world to preach the gospel to every creature' (Mark xvi. 15). 'He who hears you hears me, and he who rejects you rejects me' (Luke x. 16). 'These two commandments, the one to teach, the other to believe unto salvation, must be fulfilled. But they cannot be understood unless the Church proposes the evangelical doctrine completely and understandably, and in proposing it is immune from all dangers of error' (29).

This is the traditional doctrine of the Christian community: with respect both to the teaching and the believing, the Church is infallible. Only in the Church do we hear and encounter the Word of God in its integrity. Only she transmits Christ by commission, only she believes him in all fullness. The Church does not teach in her own name, rather does she give testimony to divine Revelation. Hence 'all that the ecclesiastical magisterium proposes as divinely revealed in the Word of God, written or unwritten, must be believed', not indeed because of the Church but 'because of God the Revealer who cannot deceive or be deceived' (30). Leave the divinely established rule of faith, and you will jeopardize the sovereign and absolute nature of divine Revelation. Man will be forced to have recourse to his own interpretation, and this own, this *proprium*, will introduce the human into what is altogether from God. Faith then is one in its formal object as it is proposed by the testimony of the Church.

In the World Council of Churches we find the wide-spread conviction that divisions in doctrine are the result of sin. 'There is diversity which is not sinful but good because it reflects both the diversity of gifts of the Spirit in the one body and the diversities of creation by the one Creator. But when diversity disrupts the manifest unity of the body, then it changes its quality and becomes sinful division' (31). The Church of Christ must preach one and the same message. But the documents of the Council are reticent about the teaching office of the Church. Admitting that it is through her testimony alone that Christ is communicated to men, they do not try to specify the qualities which Christ has attached to her testimony. This is, alas, exactly the point which separates us. The witness of the Church is for the Catholic the *regula proxima fidei*, the immediate criterion of faith, infallibly laying down what is to be received as divinely revealed, determining which of the ancient books are the inspired Word of God, and in some cases giving authoritatively the interpretation of scriptural texts which is in harmony with her indefectible life.

If Christian faith were merely the pledge of friendship between God and the soul, it would not be unreasonable to consider it independent of an external criterion. It was however the will of Christ that faith integrate men into his chosen people, that by faith they participate in the common orientation of the exile community. Hence the faith of the whole people must become the rule of faith for all believers who enter the household of God. Because faith is a matter at once individual and social, because it determines the personal orientation towards God as well as the end of the whole people, faith must have the same objective content in all members and coincide with the faith of the Church.

Unity of Government

The People of God is not a self-directing body; it is governed by a supreme authority. Jesus Christ who called, redeemed, and established his People is also its King and Master. But there is a question as to whether the ecclesiastical community needs a visible authority, a governing organ on this earth. Since the Church is 'a perfect society', it would seem that she must necessarily be equipped with a supreme authority to make and enforce her laws, and to steer the community in its daily course. But, we continue to ask, does the notion of perfect society as it is analogically applied to the Church really include a visible authority? This question can be resolved only by a return to Scripture and to the understanding which the Church has had of her own role.

When the documents of the Holy See broach the question of governmental authority in the Church, they often refer to the fact that she is a 'perfect society' and 'hence unthinkable without a supreme governing power' (32). But scrutinizing the context we discover that this argument is only used as a *ratio convenientiae*. In *Satis Cognitum* Leo XIII makes specific mention that the Church as a perfect society demands a supreme authority, but a few lines farther down he continues, 'The nature of this supreme authority can be determined only by inquiring into and determining the will of Jesus Christ' (33). All the official documents derive the jurisdiction of the hierarchy from divine Revelation, from the intention of Christ as recorded in Scripture and handed down in the Christian community. 'When Christ was about to leave this world and return to the Father, he entrusted to the Prince of the apostles the visible government of the whole society which he had founded. Such was *his wisdom* that he could not leave the social body of the Church without a visible head' (34). The visible government of the Church is of divine institution; arguments from the exigencies of a perfect society appeal to the wisdom of Christ, to the harmony and fittingness of his decrees.

The Catholic position is well known; the papal documents merely confirm the common doctrine. The People of God are ruled by the apostles and their appointed successors. The Church of Christ has an hierarchical structure: jurisdiction is held by the bishops, supreme and direct jurisdiction resides in the pope, bishop of Rome, successor to St Peter. This is dogma. The Church teaches that the episcopal constitution was given to her by Christ; accepting it, the Catholic accepts Christ.

This is also the doctrine of Holy Scripture—as it has been and is understood in the living Christian community. Abstracting from the tradition of the Church, it may be difficult to produce a cogent demonstration from scriptural testimonies for apostolic succession and the extent of jurisdictional power. In the Report of the Faith-and-Order Conference at Lund we read that several distinct Christian bodies try to justify their ministry by an appeal to the New Testament (35). The popes have recourse to the Petrine passage of the 16th chapter of Matthew's as the principal biblical testimony for ruling authority in the Church:

'And I say to thee, thou art Peter, and upon this rock I will build my Church, and the gates of hell shall not prevail against it. And I will give thee the keys of the Kingdom of heaven; and whatever thou shalt bind on earth shall be bound in heaven, and whatever thou shalt loose on earth shall be loosed in heaven.'

To a Catholic this passage is very clear; it seems to him that in biblical images the presence of a spiritual government in the Church could not be expressed more forcefully. Since the passage not only testifies to jurisdiction in the Church but also to the primacy of Peter, it is not so perspicuous to dissident Christians, and perhaps a little embarrassing to them.

In the recent papal documents, particularly in those of Leo XIII, we find an unusual stress on the supreme and singular position of the bishops of Rome. These writings still echo the doctrine of the Vatican Council, and were largely designed to defend and justify it before the world. They do not, however, obscure the essential structure of the Catholic Church by presenting it, as they have been misconstrued, as a multitude of individual Christians subject to the sole authority of the pope. The Catholic Church is a family of episcopal Churches under the supreme jurisdiction of the Roman pontiff. Even if in the encyclical *Satis Cognitum* many pages are devoted to the primacy of Peter and his successors, while the power of bishops is mentioned quite briefly, nevertheless the episcopal structure of the Church is clearly and forcefully expressed. We quote:

'But if the authority of Peter and his successor is plenary and supreme, it is not to be regarded as the sole authority. For He who made Peter the foundation of the Church also "chose twelve whom he called apostles"; and just as it is necessary that the authority of Peter be perpetuated in the Roman pontiff, so the bishops who succeed the apostles must inherit their ordinary power. Thus the episcopal order necessarily belongs to the essential constitution of the Church. Although bishops do not receive plenary, universal or supreme authority, they are not to be looked upon as mere representatives of the Roman pontiffs. They exercise a power truly their own and are ordinary pastors of the people which they govern' (36).

That there be unity in the Church, bishops must be in communion with the successor of Peter, who is the foundation. 'Bishops who deliberately secede from Peter and his successor are deprived of the right and power to rule' (37).

The apostolic authority of the pope does not impair but strengthens the jurisdiction of bishops (38). We have here neither delegation nor competition; we have two genuine apostolic powers, one of them supreme, blending in a living harmony. This doctrine supplies us with the principal means of understanding the organic unity of particular Churches in the one universal Church of Christ.

A particular, episcopally governed Church is the community of the faithful gathered about a successor of an apostle, receiving from him the rule of faith and the obedience to Christ. Through the apostolicity of their bishop the local Churches enjoy unity of faith and government, and even if this unity becomes catholic and therefore complete only through the communion with the See of Peter, the single Churches realize in themselves the essential structure of the unique and universal Church. Their ecclesiastical character is not simply a participation in the nature of the universal Church; this would be true if bishops were teachers and rulers only as representatives of the pope. In the continuity of the whole Church, local Churches possess the authentic faith, sacramental fullness, and apostolic power—and this is what we mean by ecclesiastical character—from the apostolic succession of their own bishops. In structure and quality local Churches resemble the universal Church of which they are members. Yves Congar writes, 'In the language of the schools the one and unique Church is a homogeneous body, that is to say, it is made up of parts which reproduce the nature of the whole' (39). These local Churches are organically united under the supreme apostolic power of the Roman pontiff, under a plenary power extending to the single Churches as well as to each of their individual members, without invalidating the ordinary jurisdiction of the bishops. The Roman Catholic Church is a family of apostolic Churches under the supreme authority of the bishop of Rome.

The governing power which Christ has conferred on his Church is ordained to rule for the sake of eternal life. It is not power in the secular sense. 'Ecclesiastical power' we are told 'is essentially different from civil power' (40). 'Whatever in things human is of sacred character, whatever pertains to the salvation of souls or to the worship of God . . . is subject to the power and judgment of the Church' (41). Other matters do not belong there. Only in this perspective are the words *potestas* and *jurisdictio* divested of their worldly and perhaps ambitious overtones. 'The Church does not covet power', writes Leo XIII (42). 'The Church is not an empire', explains Pius XII; its main realm is in the heart of man, and from there proceeds its visible influence (43). Jurisdiction in the Church is wholly dependent on faith; we believe in its divine origin which consists in Christ's commission to the apostles, and we believe in its end and purpose which is growth of holiness and salvation.

If he had wanted, Christ could have left the community of the faithful without any governing authority save his own sovereign kingship. He could have established them as a family of men having the same ideal, bound by the ties of love alone without any additional legal relationship. Why did he do more? The reason must be sought in the peculiar mission of God's People: to continue Christ's battle against the powers of darkness. 'Jesus had prophesied that the hostility and hatred of men, which he himself had experienced, would likewise be shown towards the movement founded by him . . . Therefore it was his intention not only to train disciples of his doctrine but to unite the faithful into a society . . . and give them the mission to fight for the salvation of mankind like "a well-arrayed army" ' (44). Since, even after Christ's irrevocable victory on the cross, sufficient power is left to Christ's enemies to sift his followers, to send them tribulation, to expose them to false prophets, the Church must be a city built on a rock against which the gates of hell shall not prevail. The authority in the Church is power against power. It has been conferred on the apostles not to govern the world but to help separate from the world whatever can be spared from the judgment of God (45).

Jurisdiction in the Church is not a symptom that she has become a secular society; on the contrary, it is a mark of her pilgrimage. The power to rule is for the protection of the faithful in the little while that the Lord tarries; and it will become increasingly necessary as the Last Day draws closer, for not only will the realm extend from Jerusalem to the ends of the earth but tribulation also will increase, taking on new and terrible forms. Thus in the present age the Church awaits the dissolution of her governing power; she longs for the day when her way of the cross shall be relieved by the glory of the returning Christ, when, all enemies being subdued, she will no longer need the external help of a visible government.

Even if power in the Church is qualitatively different from secular power, it is not therefore less binding. If she wishes to do so, the Church can command in matters belonging to her mission more firmly than any human authority. She can command with the force of love. 'Just as the end of the Church is the highest of all ends, so her authority must be the most exalted on earth' (46). Jurisdictional power in the Church takes its character from her final end, which is holiness (47). The Church does not govern to protect a common good belonging to this world, but she binds and looses on earth for the sake of an imperishable good that is to come. The People of God are apostolically governed in order that they remain one, holy, and catholic until the Day of fulfilment.

* * *

The People of God are linked together by the fundamental unity of faith and communion. This unity, though invisible and mysterious in its nature, is visible in the sense that it can be determined by observable signs: faith becomes visible in the creed professed, and communion in obedience to the hierarchy. This double bond produces the unity of orientation towards the common goal of the whole People.

If we consider only these two visible elements of unity and leave aside the more profound and spiritual bonds uniting the members of Church, even then it is evident that anyone who refuses to walk with the People of God shall not be spared from the judgment of God. 'Whoever lives apart from the Church does not fulfil the will and the command of Christ. Having left the path of salvation he is on the way towards perdition' (48). That is the language of Scripture, of tradition and of our documents: those who do not follow Christ belong to the world which is in darkness. Having died for the whole human race Christ calls all men without exception; yet it seems that not all of them hear his voice, and some who hear it will not follow him. Since the People of God is an exile community engaged in combat, it is not sufficient to be called; one must also follow and take part in 'the good fight'.

The two bonds of faith and communion are the basis of a more profound, more spiritual and more intimate union among the brethren of Christ. 'The nobler the end towards which the common aspiration is directed and the more divine the source from which it springs, the more sublime will also be its unity' (49). This sublime unity, which lives in the People of God and surpasses all that nature can boast of, is charity. Charity reigns in the Church. She is the community of love, the family of God, the Christian fellowship. This however is not the place to show how, in the eyes of the popes, social charity grows on the foundation of faith and communion. Suffice it to recall that without divine charity in the heart, a member does not belong to the Church in a healthy, full-grown and normal way. 'It is not sufficient to be accounted a member of the Church; one must be a living member of her in spirit and in truth' (50). Charity is the life of the Church.

Together with the charity which proceeds from faith and communion, there are other manifestations of unity in the Church. There is above all the sacramental worship of the triune God which Christ has bestowed on the Christian community. But beyond all visible and invisible links which bind the Church into unity, there is the source and pattern of unity which is Christ himself. 'The personal unity of Christ is the hidden and mysterious model to which he himself wanted to conform the unique structure of the Christian community' (51). The Church is one because Christ identified himself with his People.

THE UNITY OF THE BODY OF CHRIST

On the cross Jesus Christ completed his work of redemption. His physical body being wounded and broken, he took unto himself a new body; he grafted the community of believers into his own flesh to be an organism vivified and ruled by his own life. On the cross was born the Church, the mystical Body of Christ. More than once the popes refer to the comparison used by the Fathers (52): As Eve, the mother of the living, was taken from the side of the sleeping Adam, so the Church was born from the opened side of the second Adam, Jesus Christ, asleep on the cross. This is more than a metaphor. From the cross flows the Spirit and the abundance of Christ's grace on the community of believers, forging them into a living body of which Christ is the principal member, the vital source and the directing mind—in the other words, the head.

'Because the Church is a body', writes Pius XII, 'she must be something unique and undivided' (53). A body, though made up of various parts, is one by reason of its invisible life principle. However perfect the organization, however uniform the manifestations of life, the ultimate reason for unity is spiritual. Hence studying the Church's unity we must investigate the unity—its origin and its nature—of the invisible force which produces her life. This unit will surpass anything that is known in the realm of nature. As the last word summing up all that God has done in his merciful intervention in creation, the Church will reflect a oneness which is known only in the Triune God.

In this section we shall speak of the unity of the Church in its root, the one sacrifice of Jesus Christ. Then we shall describe the bonds that hold together the living Body acquired on the cross: the one Spirit poured forth in the Church, the one Head responsible for her life, and the hidden Personality of the Church which is Christ himself.

The Completeness of Redemption

'On the cross Jesus Christ completed his work' as Saviour of mankind (54). Ratifying and abolishing the old Law he sealed the New Testament in his blood; he reconciled fallen humanity to God the Father, and acquired for it a new life of grace. 'On the cross Jesus Christ not only made reparation for the injured justice of the Eternal Father but also merited for us, his brethren, an unspeakable abundance of graces. These graces he might have bestowed directly upon the whole human race, but he actually willed to do this by means of a visible Church, in which men would be united' (55). When they were still enemies of God, Christ died for all men. Through his sacrifice of love on the cross he achieved once and for all the salvation of mankind. He acquired, irrevocably, the fullness of life which he was to communicate to this brethren, and this not only singly, one by one, but to all of them united as his Body, as he foresaw and elected them on the cross. Having finished everything Christ committed the plenitude of his grace to his purchased People; in other words, the fullness of Christ is alive in the Church.

We wish to emphasize this. 'Dying on the cross he bestowed upon the Church the boundless treasure of redemption without any co-operation on her part' (56). Jesus Christ has done everything that can be done for the salvation of man. Because of him, there is nothing left unpaid, unrepaired, unreconciled; because of him, there is no want of mercy, no lack of grace. The Church in a sense is complete on the cross. It is fully constituted, it has received all its members. 'It was on the tree of the cross that he purchased his Church, that is, all the members of his mystical Body; for they would not become united to that Body by baptism, were it not for the saving power of the cross on which they had *already* become in the fullest sense the property of Christ' (57). With the cross of Christ all is fulfilled. *Consummatum est.* This must be said clearly, though this is not all that must be said. For, as we shall see later, 'Christ wills that from his divine fullness flow the abundance of gifts into the Church that she may *quam maxime*, in increasing measure, be conformed to him' (58).

The Body of Christ, then, is *one* because it is constituted by one act of Jesus Christ: his glorious death on the cross. No man can find his way back to God, except in the power of the cross; conversely no one on earth can be so far removed from God by sin as to exhaust the saving power of Christ's death. By the one sacrifice and through the unique and unlimited fullness of grace, Christ gave birth to the Church as the extension of his own human flesh which he built about himself as he hung upon the cross. 'We are the flesh of the Crucified' (59), writes Pius XII, quoting a famous passage from Leo the Great. Since 'our Saviour so shares with his Church the gifts that are especially his own' (60), the one Body contains all that Christ has done for mankind. It is his fullness.

The converse of this proposition is also true. 'Whoever is not united to this Body . . . is not in communion with Christ, the Head' (61). 'Scattered and separated members cannot possibly cohere with the Head so as to make one Body' (62). This is the constant doctrine of the popes. To receive grace and salvation from Christ must mean to approach and enter that mystical Body to which he has communicated all that is communicable. To say that some people are united to Christ by means of his Body while others are directly linked to him without being members of the Church is, according to the papal pronouncements, in contradiction to Holy Scripture. Pope Leo XIII reasons as follows (63): It is the teaching of St Paul that Christ is the head of all the faithful. Being their head, they are his body; 'Although many they form only one body' (1 Cor. xii. 12). All those who are linked to Christ receive from him an influx of grace which builds them into one organism; 'From him the whole body is closely joined and knit together' (Eph. iv. 16). To say that there is no salvation outside the Church is to claim that apart from Jesus Christ crucified no man can find the true life.

The Church then is one on the cross; it is fully established through the one event apart from which God cannot be found in the darkness of the world. But can we determine what supernatural bonds of unity Christ bestowed upon the community of his followers?

The One Holy Spirit

In a significant paragraph of *Mystici Corporis* Pius XII shows that it was really through Christ's death on the cross that his Spirit, the Holy Spirit, was communicated to the Church, even if the visible descent of the Spirit occurred only after Christ had ascended to the Father. Summing up, Pius XII writes, 'At the hour of his precious death Christ willed his Church to be enriched with the most copious gifts of the Paraclete' (64).

The Spirit living in the soul of Jesus Christ without measure is now communicated to the members of the mystical Body 'according to the measure of the giving of Christ'. The Spirit of Christ not only moves and directs men in their salutary actions in order to sanctify them as individuals, but he so moves and directs them as to increase the union of all parts of the Body with one another and with their common Head. Since it is by his Spirit that Jesus Christ builds up his Church to full stature, he gives the Spirit in various measures according to the place and function which he assigns to each member in the Body. It is the Spirit 'who is present in all the members and divinely acting in each, though he also acts in the members set below through the ministry of those set above' (65). Since the vivifying action of the Spirit pervades the whole Body, since he is the Source of all supernatural life, since he draws together the members into a living unity, he is called in a phrase which is more than a metaphor though less than a definition—the soul of the Church. Soul he is, not of course as intrinsic, form-giving principle but as extrinsic, transcendental and infused Principle responsible for the Church's supernatural life.

The One Head

Together with the Holy Spirit, Christ communicates to his Church the created gifts and graces (*gratia capitis*) produced in his own soul by the same Spirit who is now to be their Author in the souls of the members. On the cross, therefore, by the selfsame gift the community of believers received as Soul the Holy Ghost and became conformed to Christ himself as its Head. 'Although the Saviour was appointed Head of the human family already while in the womb of the Virgin, it is only by virtue of the cross that he exercises his headship in the Church in all fullness' (66).

Christ is the Head of the Church not only because he is her Founder and Saviour, but also because he shares with her the created life which gives to his soul its sublime holiness and perfection. He becomes one organism with his Church. He retains, of course, a position of singular pre-eminence in the Body; he is the God-Man of whose fullness we have all received. Sharing his life, he still remains Master, Sovereign, Lord.

At the same time it must be said—'and this is a tremendous mystery' (67)—that Christ requires the help of his Body, the co-operation of all his members one by one. 'The head cannot say to the feet, "I have no need of you" ' (1 Cor. xii. 21). Certainly, Christians are in absolute dependence upon their mystical Head but, in a sense far different though still proper, Christ wants to be dependent upon the co-operation of his members. 'This is not due to any insufficiency or need in him' (68). Christ needs his brethren not because his sacrifice on the cross was incomplete, not because his work of redemption was revocable and conditioned; to claim this would be blasphemy. Christ needs the help of his members not for his own sake but for theirs. 'It is for their greater honour' (69). So much does he share his life with them that they participate even in his task of saving and sanctifying the world. He could have done less, but he wanted to raise his members to such similitude with himself that a co-operation and mutual assistance would be possible.

'Dying on the cross he bestowed upon the Church the boundless treasure of redemption without any co-operation on her part; but in the *distribution of this treasure* he not only shares his work of sanctification with his spotless Bride but wills it to arise in a certain manner from her labour' (70). Like formulations are frequently found in the Roman documents and in traditional Catholic theology.

However the image of 'distributing the treasure' is not easy to understand. It is obviously taken from material things which can be earned, entrusted to an institution, stored in safe keeping as a treasure, and finally distributed in small amounts. Grace however is not a thing; whether considered as a transient help or as an inhering form, it has no substantial existence. In the language of philosophy it is an 'accident'. It is always the result of an encounter with Jesus Christ; it is he who sends his grace-bestowing Spirit every time. Moreover the image of 'distributing the treasure' might give rise to the idea that Christ's redemptive work was the acquisition of the treasure, while the distribution was left to human effort. This would gravely misrepresent Catholic teaching: for Christ has done everything. He has merited the treasure and its application. Christ uses the co-operation of his members not as a co-ordinated help (two men lifting a stone together) but as a subordinated help (a man and his lever lifting a stone). Christ means the activity of the Church to be an effort which springs from his own vivifying influence in his members, a labour which is an echo to his call.

How then must we understand the theological image of the Church 'distributing from the treasury' bequeathed to her by Christ? The Church mediates grace by making present the crucified and risen Christ, who is the bestower of his grace; this she does by the power of the cross, that is, in virtue of that dispensation which Christ freely established as well as bloodily earned for us on Calvary. The Church is said to 'distribute', in order to indicate her active part, the labours and sacrifices which Christ demands of her in making his saving power spread in the world. She is said to possess 'a treasury' because Christ bequeathed to her that by which she could extend and continue his life on earth. He put into her hands, not grace, but the signs of grace—some efficacious (the sacraments), others only producing a disposition in various degrees (the gospel, preaching, the liturgy)—to render present the power of the cross. More than that, he poured forth into the hearts of the faithful his own grace and his own love so that the life of the whole People should be an imitation, nay, a continuation of his own. While it was his wish to justify Paul without any intermediary, he wanted to save Cornelius through the preaching of Peter and Augustine through the prayers of his mother Monica. These acts of assistance which the members offer to their Head are rooted in the cross; they are not helps to Christ in as much as they are of human origin, but precisely to the degree in which they are the fruit of his grace. In this sense the Church 'completes what is lacking to the suffering of Christ' (Col. i. 24).

From these remarks it becomes clear that the Church by her co-operation does not pretend to go beyond the gift of Christ, does not add anything to it which is not of Christ. By her co-operation the unity of the Church does not increase, because the one act by which Christ acquired this unity included the intention to have his work 'completed' by the activity of the Christian community.

Jesus Christ is also called Head of the Church because 'he is the sole ruler of the Church' (71). Not only does he impart a new and superior life principle to his Body, he also governs sovereignly the members of his Church. 'He governs directly the society which he founded; he reigns in the minds and hearts of men, bending and constraining even rebellious wills to his decrees' (72). The Church is thus the beloved Spouse who ever pleases and obeys her Lord.

But it would be against the testimony of Holy Scripture to suppose that Christ rules his Church only in an invisible manner. Because he is absolute and supreme Lord of his faithful, even in their free co-operation, he could entrust the visible government of his Church to the apostles and the supreme leadership to Peter, Prince of apostles, without letting the rule slip out of his hand. The appointed bishops, who rule the Church as successors of the apostles, are the visible links by which the faithful are subjected to the government of Christ, a government which envisages along with the sanctification of the individual the building up of the whole Body. The principal visible link effecting obedience to Christ is the pope, successor to St Peter. He may be called the visible head of the Church. Together with Christ he constitutes but one head. Peter is not Christ's successor (Christ never relinquished the government of his Church) but his representative or vicar in the visible government of the Christian community. It would be altogether false 'to create an opposition between Christ, Head of the Church, and his Vicar on earth, to see in the affirmation of Christ's lordship a denial of the Vicar's right to rule' (73). Precisely because Christ is Head, Master, and Ruler of the Church, he can appoint a visible government without thereby introducing the sway of chance into his realm on earth. The appointed shepherds are in the all-powerful hands of the Good Shepherd, and when they demand obedience, it is not human power which we obey but the Word of God which was spoken into the world in Jesus Christ.

Believing as we do that Christ entrusted the supreme visible authority in the Church to one man, to one single office, we may well ask what was the fittingness of his decree. 'If the personal unity of Christ' writes Pius XI 'is the hidden exemplar to which he wanted to configurate the unique body of the Christian society, then . . . it must arise from one faith, one hierarchy, and one supreme teacher' (74). Christ wanted his mystical Body to be conformed as much as possible to his own image; he decreed that the Church on earth appear to the world as a living body having one head and one visible structure, a head which commands and a body which co-operates. This is undoubtedly the mind of the popes: through the supreme bishop as visible head, the Church is made more like the image of Christ. 'If we remove the visible head and break the perceptible bonds of unity, the mystical Body of the Redeemer is so obscured and disfigured that it becomes impossible . . . to recognize and discover it' (75).

This brings us to another reason why Christ is called in a proper sense the Head of the Church: Christ desires to conform his Body in ever greater likeness to himself. Through baptism and the grace which at the cross flowed from the fullness of Christ to the Body, man is imprinted with the likeness of Christ; but this likeness must grow, both in the individual Christian and in the whole Church. For just as Christ at the moment of the incarnation was fully constituted as Saviour and Mediator and yet had to become in all fullness Head of the human race at the last moment of his earthly life, so also the Church being constituted with all its members on the cross must grow in an ever greater likeness to Christ—until the day when the Lord returns. 'Then we shall be like unto him' (1 John iii. 2).

The Church's similitude to her Saviour is at one and the same time something already given and something to be further attained. It is both a gift and a task. The Church possessing full perfection must still 'advance in wisdom and age and grace before God and man'. In this light of growing similitude can be seen all of the Church's activity. 'This likeness is seen with evidence when, following the footsteps of her divine Founder, she teaches, governs, and offers the divine sacrifice' (76). Like Christ the Church must be 'a sign lifted up among nations', like him she invites men to believe in God's Word by the testimony of her holiness, her unity, and her marvellous history (77). But like Christ the Church must also be 'a sign of contradiction' in the world, like him she will suffer persecution and denigration. But the conformity to Christ consists above all in charity. Just as the Christian increases formally in the likeness of Christ by love, so the Church is ever more transformed according to the image of Christ by that charity which binds the members to one another, unites them to their divine Head, and embraces all of humanity in the unbounded love which Christ has brought down from his Father. Because the Church is the hearth on which burns the fire which Christ has cast on the earth 'that it be enkindled', she cannot be assigned simply the role of a prophet. United to Christ by a faith living in charity she can transmit—even apart from the sacraments—much more than the message of salvation; she can transmit it in power, in the power of that love which Jesus has engendered in her on the cross in order to conform her *quam maxime* to his own image. Thus the Church testifying to the Word of God offers to all men the charity of her own life, knowing that communion with her mediates the possession of God in Jesus Christ. 'That which we have seen and heard we declare unto you that you may have communion with us. And this communion is also with the Father and with his Son Jesus Christ' (1 John i. 3).

The headship of Christ impresses on the Church a visible-invisible unity of an altogether singular character. The oneness of life which exists in the Head and the Body raises the members to a real co-operation with Christ, to perfect obedience to his rule, and to an increasing likeness to his image. This is the visage of the Church's unity.

The completion of Christ

Summing up the Church's relationship to Christ we shall quote a sentence from Pius XII of extraordinary comprehensiveness.

'Due to the communication of the Spirit and due to the graces . . . which, existing eminently, abundantly, and efficiently in the Head, stream into all members of the Church and in them are perfected daily according to the place of each in the mystical Body—due to all this the Church becomes as it were the fullness and completion of the Redeemer, Christ in the Church being in some sense brought to complete fulfilment' (78).

The verbal reference is to St Paul's Epistle to the Ephesians: 'And God gave Christ as head over all the Church, which is his body, the completion (*pleroma*) of him who fills all with all (i. 23) (79). Not only is the Church the fullness of Christ in the sense that he gave to her, on the cross, all that he possessed in a communicable way, but having given her to share in his own life he is able, through her, to love all men and draw them to himself. In the Church and through the Church—yes, through her labours and sacrifices—mankind becomes integrated with Jesus Christ so that in her the Saviour grows and is completed. Jesus Christ and his Body is, in a sense, more than he is alone. In the words of St Augustine so often quoted by the popes, Head and Body together are the whole Christ, *totus Christus*.

This takes us to the profound mystery which we have remarked when discussing the aim and office of the People of God: the mission of the Church is to make present and to bear Christ through history. Christ the Lord has so much identified himself with the Church, has so much penetrated her life and is so completely and sovereignly Head that he may be called her hidden Personality. Because of his commission to the apostles and because of the mission of the Spirit, the Author of Christ's own life in the Body, it is to Christ that all its supernatural activity must be attributed. In the words of *Mystici Corporis*, Christ *sustentat* and *sustinet* (80), that is, upholds and bears the Church in such a way that together they form but one mystical Person, Jesus Christ. The personality of each member of the Church remains free, indeed is given a new freedom, but Christ is so much Master even of our free acts that through the Church he grows in history as he wills, that through her he works for the reconciliation of mankind which on the cross has by rights become his. The unity of the Church, then, is measured by the unity of Christ himself. 'The Church possesses in God, in the God-Man Jesus Christ, the invisible but unshakable principle of its unity and indefectibility, that is, in the unity of Head and members in the fullness of its own life' (81).

'The Church is an indivisible whole because Christ himself with his Church is undivided and indivisible. According to the profound phrase of St Augustine, Christ with his Church constitutes "the whole Christ". This wholeness of Christ signifies according to the holy Doctor the indivisible unity of Head and Body in *plenitudine Ecclesiae*, in that fullness of life of the Church which embraces and unites all lands and all ages of redeemed humanity without exception' (82).

The Church is drawn into a unity which is far beyond the possibilities of nature, a unity which emanates from the Triune God. In this light the Church appears as a reality which is more closely related to the divine missions than to the order of creation. She is the temple of the Holy Trinity. In virtue of their mission from the eternal Father, the Son and the Spirit give being and life to the

Church; they do not divide her because they are one God. We have the word of our Lord himself that the ultimate exemplar of the Church's unity is the mystery of the invisible God: 'That they may be one as Thou, Father, art in me and I in thee.'

*   *   *

We have described the unity of the Church from two different starting points, the Church as society and the Church as organism. Considering the sociological aspect, we discovered that there is a divinely established visible unity of faith and communion on which is built a spiritual and living unity which, progressing through the bond of charity, seeks to draw all creation into the peace of perfect reconciliation. The People of God are one because they have received the mission to bear Jesus Christ through history until he returns in glory. Beginning with the organic aspect, we saw the unity of the Church rooted in the unique historical event of Christ's triumphant death by which redeemed humanity was irrevocably grafted into the flesh of Christ as his acquired Body. The mystical Body of Christ is one by reason of its life-giving principle, the Holy Ghost, and in virtue of Christ's own grace which the Spirit communicates; extending from the spiritual to the visible order, the union between Head and Body is so perfect that together they form but one mystical Person in Jesus Christ.

These two approaches describe the same gift of unity which the Lord has given to his Church. Yet they have supplied the various elements which constitute this unity under different perspectives. We shall briefly trace these elements by way of comparison.

In the first context the Church's unity is visible because Christ has acquired for himself a people in this world, in the second context because it belongs to the nature of a body to be visible (83). *Faith and baptism*, the fundamental elements of Christian unity, appear on the one hand as the call and orientation towards the new and gratuitous end of the whole People, on the other as the incorporation into Christ, the living Vine. Ecclesiastical *communion* is in the first connection the guarantee of the People's unity of action, in the second the visible manifestation of the Body's conjunction to the Head. The two ways of regarding the Church are equally well adapted to make plain its *hierarchical structure*, for both in a society and in a body there must be members of higher and lower function. While the *invisible* and more profound component of unity appears in our first consideration as the result of the Church's mission to perpetuate the redemptive work of Christ through time, it appears in the second as the bonds by which Christ renders the faithful similar to himself and transforms them into his Body. The Church, in both cases, is the presence and *continuation of Christ in history*. It is the Lord in the midst of his People merging spiritually into one Person; it is the Head singularly united to the Body forming but one mystical Person.

The People of God and the Body of Christ signify one and the same divine gift. Yet the conceptual distinction has the advantage that it underlines the peculiar character of the Church in the 'little while' between Christ's Ascension and his Second Coming. Calling the Church the People of God, our immediate attention is fixed upon her pilgrim state on earth, and only on reflection we recall that the Lord is present in the midst of his people by anticipating the future glory. Calling the Church the Body of Christ, the first thought which comes to the mind is the marvellous incorporation of mankind into Jesus Christ, and only as an afterthought do we remember the crucified state in which the Body exists at the present age. If we take the two biblical images together, the body and the people, then we can never forget that the Church in history knows both fulfilment and expectation, the possession of God and the loneliness of exile.

A NOTE ON MEMBERSHIP IN THE CHURCH

The Church which the Lord has founded and united to himself as his mystical Body is the Catholic Church with its visible centre at Rome. It is this Church which possesses the unity established by Christ on the cross, the unity of the Holy Ghost, of faith, hope, and charity, of sacramental communion and ecclesiastical obedience. Who, we now wish to ask, belongs to this Church? Who is incorporated into the Body of Christ? Only Roman Catholics? Since it is Catholic doctrine that outside the Church no salvation can be found, the question is of primary importance for the religious understanding of the world and, more especially, for our problem of Christian unity. From recent official documents of the Holy See we shall derive the principle, which has long been classical in theology, that apart from integral and complete ecclesiastical membership there is another way, incomplete but salutary, of belonging to the Catholic Church. In this note—for we shall try to be brief—we shall confine ourselves to a commentary on two significant documents, the first setting out the problem with remarkable precision, the second giving the clues to the solution.

In an important passage of *Mystici Corporis* we read: 'Only those are to be accounted *reapse* members of the Church who have been regenerated in the waters of baptism, who profess the true faith, and who have not detached themselves from the structure of the Body unto their own undoing or been cut off for a great crime by legitimate authority' (84). Members of the Church *reapse*, that is really and truly, are only those Christians who are distinguished by the triple mark of baptism, creed and ecclesiastical communion. We notice however that Pius XII does not say that in this triple mark *consists* the unity of the Catholic Church. The visible threefold mark records ecclesiastical unity without constituting it; and inferring from the verbal references to 1 Cor. xii. 13 and Eph. iv. 5 which follow, the unity of the Church is conceived even in this context principally in terms of one Spirit, one Lord, and one Body. 'Through this one Spirit and in this one Body,' continues the Pope in a very severe phrase, 'they cannot live who are divided from one another in faith or government' (85). Taken by itself and isolated from the rest of the encyclical, this sentence could imply that no man living outside the canonical boundaries of the Catholic Church can belong to the Body of Christ in a salutary way or possess the grace of the Holy Spirit.

Returning to the same subject in a later paragraph of the same encyclical, the Pope entreats those who do not belong to the visible structure of the Catholic Church 'to yield their free consent to the inner stirrings of God's grace and to extricate themselves from a state in which they cannot be secure as to their eternal salvation; for though they may be orientated (*ordinentur*) to the mystical Body of the Redeemer by an unconscious yearning and desire (*voto*), they are deprived of many spiritual gifts and graces which can be enjoyed only in the Catholic Church" (86). What exactly is this relation or orientation towards the Body of Christ which, according to the encyclical, men outside the Church may possess? Is it a relation brought about by forces which remain *exterior* to the Church, by a sort of natural preparation in outsiders produced by a human longing for salvation? Or is it a relation established by forces which properly speaking are *interior* to the Church, by gifts of the Church which await their fulfilment at the source from which they have come? In the first case, these men would not hold any pledge of salvation from the mystical Body of Christ; their relation to the Church would be due to a natural bent quickened by transient graces. In the second case, they would already live by the Church and her gifts; their ordination towards Christ's Body would be supernatural and

THE UNITY OF THE CHURCH

salutary. Our question comes to this: Is the orientation toward the Church, of which Pope Pius speaks, extrinsic, or is it intrinsic? In other words: Can we account him who is *voto* orientated toward the Church properly speaking as *membrum in voto?*

From the severe sentence cited above, which seems to deny the life of grace to all who are not united to the Church by full membership, it would appear that only an extrinsic relationship to the Church is possible. This however would be a wrong interpretation, contrary to the doctrine of the encyclical and Catholic theology in general. Nature knows no positive ordination towards grace. The unconscious yearnings and desires of nature are not of such a kind as to produce a real relationship to the Church; and even actual graces, which effect a transient orientation to the Church, cannot produce a lasting relationship. A relatively permanent ordination towards the Church must be effected by stable elements connatural to her, which mark the soul with an inhering modification. It follows that an *in voto* orientation towards the Church constitutes a membership *in voto*.

Nevertheless the terminology of the encyclical was such that doubts remained in the minds of theologians about the papal doctrine on Church membership; this is amply demonstrated by the theological literature of the years following the encyclical (87).

Less than a decade later, an heretical opinion of an American priest, Leonard Feeney, elicited a dogmatic letter from the Holy Office, addressed to the Archbishop of Boston in 1949 and published in the *American Ecclesiastical Review* in 1952 (88). Unfortunately the text is not reprinted in the *Acta Apostolicae Sedis*. This important letter of extraordinary clarity is a perfect crystalization of the traditional doctrine of the Church; it settles a number of questions which to some extent had remained open and even controverted in theology. We shall append the official English translation of the Boston Letter to this study.

The unorthodox opinion of Feeney was a false interpretation of the doctrine: No salvation outside the Church. He preached the terrible view that apart from Catholics and their catechumens no man could possibly be saved. To this error, contradicting the constant Catholic tradition, the Holy Office replied in the abovementioned letter that the dictum *Extra Ecclesiam nulla salus* was indeed Catholic dogma, but that it had to be received in the sense which the Church gave to it. This sense the letter proceeds to explain.

Jesus Christ intended to reconcile mankind to God by incorporating it into his Body which is the Church. Belonging to the Church is thus necessary for salvation, *necessitate medii*; Christ has instituted the Church as the universal medium of atonement. To the apostles he said: 'Go into the whole world and preach the gospel to every creature. He who believes and is baptized shall be saved, but he who does not believe shall be condemned' (Mark xvi. 16). Belonging to the apostolic community of believers is of equal necessity to salvation as the baptism by which we enter it. However, just as for baptism, so as regards Church membership, the merciful God who wishes all men to be saved grants under certain conditions the effects of salvation to the *desire*, effects which ordinarily are bestowed only on the *fact*. Just as there is a baptism of water and under certain conditions a baptism of desire, so there is a full membership in the Church (with the triple mark of baptism, creed, and communion) and under similar conditions a membership of desire. In the former case we speak of belonging to the Church *in re*, in the latter of belonging to her *in voto*.

For membership *in voto* the Boston Letter uses the expression *adhaerere Ecclesiae*, to adhere to the Church. This carefully chosen term, rich in theological implications, explains and specifies the more distant *ordinari ad Ecclesiam* which we read in *Mystici Corporis*. Adhering to the Church suggests the idea of being attached to her, living from her life, clinging to her with deepening roots, and yet remaining outside, grown as it were onto the surface (89). It calls to mind the image of a living body with some parts fully incorporated as members and others merely adhering to the outside in a loose but vital manner. In the official English translation of the letter we note that *adhaerere Ecclesiae* is rendered more strongly by 'being in union with the Church', a term denoting a spiritual solidarity where an actual participation is impossible. It is an expression which must be used with some care in order to prevent the wrong impression that a person in union with the Church already belongs to her unity. But whatever the terminology chosen, and it seems that great freedom is left to us in this regard (90), the doctrine is perfectly clear. There are more ways than one of belonging to the Catholic Church: either one is united to her in fact, or one is in union with her by desire.

What are the conditions under which God joins men to his Church without incorporating them fully? To this the letter also gives us the answer. Assuming that there is guiltless ignorance about the mystery of the Church, it is necessary for salvation that there be at least the *votum*, the wish or intention of becoming a member of the organism of grace, of employing all the means which the Lord has ordained for salvation. It suffices if this *votum* is unconscious and remains implicit in the desire for mercy from the all-just God who reveals his grace in Jesus Christ. But what is absolutely necessary is that this desire shall be founded on a living supernatural faith, and in consequence be supernatural itself. The human conviction, however explicit, that God exists and is a merciful Judge cannot possibly suffice to be accounted as initiating salvation. Not even the human approval of the good sense and the truth in the gospels can avail anything for eternal life. Our justification is from God and not from ourselves. In order to belong to the Church of God in an initial way, even by the most remote desire which prompts God to concede the effects of membership, there must be faith, the gift of divine faith 'without which it is impossible to please God' (Heb. xi. 6).

Is supernatural faith possible apart from Christian Revelation? Certainly not ordinarily. Faith comes from hearing, says St Paul, from hearing the preaching of the Church. However the God who wishes that all men be saved will not suffer that anyone be condemned without cause. Even if a man never had the occasion to hear the gospel of Jesus Christ, he may be led by God to follow 'the law that is inscribed in his heart" (Rom ii. 15), and come to discover that 'God exists and is a rewarder of those who seek him' (Heb. xi. 6); and if God so decides, he may inspire his elect to embrace this fundamental truth with supernatural faith (91). This faith would be Christian by implication, since it contains the gospel of Christ implicity in the supernatural readiness to receive the whole salvific message from God. Where and how often this occurs, we do not know; but it may happen that God reveals himself in the heart of a pagan and, in view of the crucified and exalted Christ drawing all things unto himself, makes him holy by the gift of a living faith and an unconscious desire of belonging to the Church, the organism of salvation.

From the Boston Letter we have established with certainty that in addition to complete membership there are other ways of belonging to the Body of Christ. In fact, there is a whole range of possible ways in which men may be in union with the Church; between the totally implicit desire of the 'holy pagan' and the explicit intention of the catechumen to enter the Church, the varieties are unlimited. It would be incorrect, therefore, to suppose that the usefulness of the distinction between membership *in re* and *in voto* applies only to the unsearchable cases of people beyond the reach of Christian preaching. On the contrary, we shall make use of these theological concepts to determine the relationship to the mystical Body of dissident Christians, of those Christians who have received the Word of God without wanting to listen to the voice of the Church.

CHAPTER TWO

DISSIDENT CHRISTIANS

THERE are many Christians in the world who do not belong to the Catholic Church; and nobody will deny that they present a problem to Catholic thought on the Church's unity. If we take them to be friends of Christ, we seem to divide the Church; and we insist on the visible unity of the faithful, we seem to account their faith as void. The religious situation of separated Christians is not easily assessed; more delicate still is it to determine their relationship to the Catholic Church. We shall try to give an answer to these problems from the recent official documents of the Holy See, to which we have confined our study. Unfortunately there is no one place in these documents where we find a theological doctrine on separated Christians. We have no other choice than to read with great care the various relevant passages which we find, and develop the theological teaching which they imply. From the words addressed to our separated brethren and from the remarks made about them, we must extract the principles on which these statements rest and the conclusions towards which they point. Our task will be one of interpretation.

In this chapter we are, of course, not speaking of schismatics and heretics (1). The judgment of the Church on men who stubbornly reject her authority, be it in matters of government or of doctrine, has been constant. The attempt to rend the unity of the Church has always been considered a tremendous crime; the New Testament is quite clear on this point. 'If anyone does not abide in Me (the mystical Vine), he shall be cast outside and wither' (John xv. 6). 'The lying teachers, who bring in destructive sects and disown the Lord who purchased them, will bring upon themselves speedy perdition' (2 Pet. ii. 1). 'The factious man . . . condemns himself' (Tit. iii. 10). Knowing what God has done for mankind in Jesus Christ and rejecting the fullness of Christ in the Church is a paramount sin, for which it would seem the author of Hebrews foresaw no forgiveness (cf. ii. 1-3, vi. 4-7). Those who knowingly cut themselves off from the Church, the living Body of the Lord, will perish. About this there can be no doubt.

In this chapter, however, we shall deal with another group of men, with separated Christians, with what our documents call *fratres dissidentes*, with those Christians who were born and guiltlessly remain outside the Catholic fold. They are separated by an abysmal gap from schismatics and heretics, whom they may resemble externally. Like them, they are Christians who refuse to listen to the Church; but unlike them, they are deaf without guilt. In order to avoid all misunderstanding, we define once and for all that *by dissident or separated Christians we mean all men believing in Jesus Christ as God and Saviour who remain apart from the Catholic Church in good faith*. The multitude of dissident Christians we shall call dissident Christianity.

It is not an easy task to draw a picture of separated Christians from the many texts and cursory remarks referring to them in our documents. Dissident Christians appear as if made up of two contradictory elements; we get the impression that two alien streams come together in them which can never mingle. They are marked by a fundamental ambiguity. Approving their loyalty to Christ, we can never concede them the right to alter the divine message; and while we are aware of their double heritage, we cannot be certain where exactly runs the dividing line between the authentic and the false. That there should be men who wish to belong to Christ without seeing clearly how to embrace him totally, is painful and theologically embarrassing. The dissident Christian, as he appears in the papal documents, stands in a flickering, unsettled light; sometimes he is so hidden by shadows of darkness that he can hardly be recognized as a Christian, at other times a ray of light illuminates his face, revealing the traits of a brother. His presence is disturbing—and more than disturbing; it is a scandal and a source of grief that there can be divisions among those who believe in Christ, that there can be barriers to fellowship where there may be unity in grace.

The references to non-Catholic Christians are frequent in the papal documents of our period (2). The popes doubtlessly reveal a pressing concern for the problem of Christian unity. According to Roger Aubert (3), this attitude of the Holy See is comparatively new. The author shows that, from the days of Leo XIII on, the popes have become increasingly aware of the Church's obligation to work for the reunion of Christians; moreover, and this is the new element, they have manifested a greater readiness to take into account the good will of dissidents, and have sought a return to unity by creating an atmosphere of benevolence and honest search for truth. The contemporary papal literature on Christian unity is certainly extensive. Leafing through the Acts of the Apostolic See, we continually hit upon texts dealing with separated Christians; yet while the material is ample, the theological content frequently remains undeveloped. The statements are often brief, sometimes vague, always inspired by the intention to do justice to a complex situation; and while care is taken to dispel a satisfaction in a Christianity which falls short of Catholic fullness, there is a conscious attempt to avoid insulting formulations.

We wish to determine theologically the nature of dissident Christians. By referring to the official texts, we shall describe the fundamental ambiguity to which we have alluded, first the supernatural heritage of dissidents, and then the seed of discord of which they too are heirs. Finally we shall attempt a synthesis by determining their relationship to the Catholic Church.

THE DIVINE PATRIMONY

The Christian communities separated from the Church of Rome have retained a part of the Christian heritage, a supernatural 'patrimony' (4) which they took away with them into their solitude. While in a Christian who knowingly rejects the authority or the doctrine of the Church all supernatural elements simply die, the situation is quite different for a Christian who finds himself in separation from the Church by birth. The patrimony which a heretic carries away is a patrimony only materially; by reason of his bad will, it is dead for him. But the patrimony which he passes on and which dissident Christians receive in a spirit of obedience to Christ, may be for them a living supernatural reality. This is amply testified to in the Roman documents, not only for Orthodox Christians but also—even if not with equal insistence—for the Christians of the Reformation.

THE DISSIDENT CHRISTIANS OF THE EAST

It is a well-known fact that the kinship of Orthodox Christians (5) to Catholic Christianity is very close. 'The difference that separates the Eastern Churches from us is not so great,' writes Leo XIII. 'Nay, with few exceptions we are so entirely at one that in defence of the Catholic faith we often have recourse to reasons and testimony borrowed from the teaching, rites, and customs of the East. The principal subject of contention is the primacy of the Roman pontiff' (6). But it is not a memory of a glorious past which is attributed to the Orthodox; they are credited with the Christian life in the present, the supernatural following of Jesus Christ in the unity of the sacraments instituted by him. 'They have faithfully preserved such a great part of divine Revelation; among them is found a sincere obedience to Christ, a special love of his holy mother, and a utilization of the sacraments' (7). The Orthodox Christians are 'part of the Lord's flock' (8), or 'a part of the Christian people' (9). 'By the blood of the Saviour and by baptism they are elected into the fold of the Lord' (10). Speaking of the work for the reunion of Christians, Pius XII pleads with Orthodox and Catholic Christians for a sincere and heartfelt benevolence from which should grow a greater mutual knowledge and esteem. 'This esteem and high regard is due to all that the Eastern peoples have received from their forefathers as their spiritual patrimony, their sacred liturgies and hierarchical orders as well as the other ways of the Christian life, as long as they are in full harmony with genuine faith and just norms of conduct' (11).

In spite of the tragic consequences of the discord, Orthodox Christians of good faith—and the popes seem to assume that collectively they may be spoken of as in good faith—remain in some way united to the Church. Writing to separated Armenian Christians, Leo XIII characterizes them as 'worshippers of Christ' and as 'having entered the society of the Christian life by baptism' (12), in other words as being united to Christ by faith and the sacraments, even though they are 'miserably' separated from the See of Peter, the centre of unity. 'Miserably separated'—how often this phrase occurs in the Roman letters! Yet however great the evil, and we shall discuss the full extent of this misery further on, it does not prevent the official documents from referring to separated Eastern communities as *Ecclesiae* and to their clergy as *ecclesiastici* (13). The dissident Christians of the East who are suffering persecution and death for the 'constancy of their virtue and the profession of the Christian faith' (14) are more than once called martyrs (15). Considering the extraordinary dignity which the Church attributes to martyrdom and the ancient opinion that outside the Church martyrdom is fanatical and hence not acceptable to God, the recognition of martyrdom among Orthodox Christians is of great theological significance, to which we shall have occasion to return.

In the minds of the popes it is above all the effect of the holy Eucharist, celebrated with so much devotion in the separated Churches of the East, which draws them into the Church by its own sacramental grace. To understand the nearness of Orthodox Christians to us in Christ, we only need recall the doctrine of Scripture that the Bread which we break is the bond of unity, and the constant tradition of the Church that the proper fruit of this sacrament is the unity of the mystical Body (16). The popes of our period are particularly conscious of the communal effect and significance of the Eucharist, and they repeatedly remind Eastern Christians of the living bond which unites us (17), that is, Christ himself who transforms into his own Body those who eat his flesh. 'Because there is only one Bread, we the many are only one Body, all of us who partake of the one Bread' (1 Cor. x. 17).

We see that the popes readily acknowledge the presence of living faith and sacramental charity among the dissident Christians of the East. There is no hesitation on this point. Orthodox Christians belong in some way to the Church of Christ, whose visible centre is at Rome. When Pius XII on one occasion restates the oft-repeated guarantee that the traditions of the East, their liturgies, laws, and customs, will always enjoy a holy freedom in the Catholic Church, he addresses himself to two groups of Eastern Christians, to those 'who already live in the bosom of the Catholic Church' and to those 'who by wish and desire are on their way to her' (18). This text implies that Orthodox Christians are members *in voto* of the Church; this however is not saying enough, since, as we have shown, they adhere to the Church with a considerable degree of reality. Some Orthodox may indeed possess *in re* all the elements making up the Church's unity save one, communion with the See of Peter, which they possess only *in voto*.

THE DISSIDENT CHRISTIANS OF THE WEST

For the separated Christians of the West who differ so widely in doctrine and practice both from us and among themselves, the question of a Christian patrimony is much more complicated. Even if there is perfectly good faith, the determination of the supernatural elements is not easy because so much of the deposit of faith has been changed. And who knows how deeply the changes have penetrated into the substance of Revelation! Calling somebody a Protestant does not give much information about his beliefs. Nevertheless, for the sake of brevity, we wish to ask the reader's permission to call all dissident Christians of the West simply 'Protestants', even though many of them, particularly in the Church of England, have retained a strong ecclesiastical tradition and do not think of themselves as Protestants (19).

Speaking of or to Protestants, the papal pronouncements never voice the approval and supernatural sympathy which they exhibit towards the Christians of the East. A notable exception is perhaps Leo XIII's letter to the English *Amantissimae voluntatis* (1895), where he expresses a real appreciation of the spiritual fruits of religion in England (20). Often, however, the words addressed to Protestants become so vague and non-committal that such a benevolent observer as Oliver Thomkins can write that he is never quite sure whether the popes consider Protestants as real Christians or only as brethren of the one human family (21). Even some Catholic writers seem to be in doubt whether it is in perfect harmony with papal teaching to recognize and appreciate a living supernatural heritage in the Christian communities of the Reformation. Certainly these writers will claim that a Protestant may be saved by the faithful disposition to receive the divine pardon, which God offers to all men who by his grace are of good will, but they will not consider this faith as in any way mediated by the separated Christian communities. While the Catholic is said to have his faith communicated by the very Institution to which he belongs, the Protestant may have faith by fortuity, because the Spirit blows where he wills, that is, not as an heir to the promises of Christ in whom he is taught to believe, but by the unsolicited bestowal of God. A Protestant, then, would not differ essentially from the good pagan whom God has determined to save for the sake of Christ. We believe that this view, which seeks to deny to all Protestants a living patrimony of grace, cannot be defended from the Roman documents of our period. On the contrary, we shall show that in the eyes of the popes grace continues to flow in the vessels which were visibly disjoined from the Church at the time of the Reformation.

The Sacrament of Baptism

A great number of Protestant communities have retained the baptism of the Catholic Church, the baptism of water and the Spirit in the name of the Holy Trinity. It is common Catholic doctrine that through baptism we are incorporated into Jesus Christ or, which is saying the same thing, are made members of his Church (22). 'Those who were born to this mortal life are regenerated from the death of sin and made members of the Church by baptism; they also receive a spiritual character which enables them to receive the other sacraments' (23). It makes no difference who administers baptism, be it even an apostate from the faith; as long as it is administered *cum intentione faciendi quod facit Ecclesia*, with the intention of doing what the Church does (24), it is a true and valid baptism. Any Christian body which in accordance with its constitution administers the sacrament of baptism to its members, communicates an enormous treasure, even if strictly speaking the treasure does not belong to it.

Since a child is baptized not in his own faith nor in that of his godparents but in the faith of the Church, and since through this sacrament he becomes united to this faith (25), it is the full Catholic profession of faith (with the acknowledgment of the divinely established hierarchy) that is implied in every infant baptism. A child, therefore, baptized in the name of the Holy Trinity anywhere at all becomes thereby a member of the Catholic Church in the full sense, and he will continue to belong to it as long as he does not cut himself off by some form of infidelity or incur the censure of excommunication. In the case of an adult baptized validly in a Protestant church and possessing a pure intention and faith in Christ, we must also recognize an incorporation into Christ, though according to the terminology of *Mystici Corporis* he cannot be called *reapse* a member of the Church. We have seen that to be a member of the Church really and truly there must be the triple bond of faith, baptism, and ecclesiastical communion; hence a believing Protestant who is baptized is in union with the apostolic community only implicitly. He is a member of the Church only in an initial way.

So great is the effect of baptism that, in reference to all baptized and separated Christians, we read in a sentence written by Leo XIII, and quoted 25 years later by Pius XI: 'Those who have been validly cleansed by the waters of baptism belong by right to the Church, *si spectetur ius*, even if error keeps them apart or disagreement severs them from fellowship' (26). For baptized Christians to remain dispersed and separated is not only a taint but an anomaly, for by the character of baptism they are destined to belong to the Church of Christ. Baptism is the act of naturalization whereby is conferred the citizenship of the People of God, and a joint commission to fight the battle of God against the powers of evil. Writing to the dissident Christians of the East, Pius XII refers to this abnormal situation: 'Against the confederate forces (of anti-Christians) there cannot remain disjoined and separated those who by the sacred character of baptism have been appointed to fight the good fight of the Saviour' (27).

This doctrine is in perfect agreement with Holy Scripture: baptism unites men in the Body of the Lord. 'All who have been baptized into Christ have put on Christ. . . . For you are all one in Christ Jesus' (Gal. iii. 27, 28). 'In one Spirit we are all baptized into one body' (1 Cor. xii. 13) (28).

In the language of the *Codex Juris Canonici*, 'Baptismate homo constituitur in Ecclesia Christi persona' (can. 87) (29). The Church is always aware that separated baptized Christians participate in her sacramental life, that they by right belong to her, and that as such they are subject to her legislative authority (can. 12). However, in most cases she refrains from using this authority; it is usually taken for granted that the Church does not wish to oblige dissident Christians by her universal laws. There are however exceptions. Can. 1099 §2 exempts non-Catholics from the 'form' of marriage prescribed for Catholics, so that they are validly married by mutual consent. As a consequence of this legislation, the marriage between two baptized dissidents is a valid Christian sacrament in the eyes of the Church (can. 1012 §2), even if the religious confession to which these persons belong does not recognize it as such. Quite generally we can say that by the character of baptism dissident Christians are rendered capable of receiving the other sacraments, even if according to present law Catholic priests are forbidden to administer the sacraments to them (can 731 §2). Only in danger of death may a priest give sacramental absolution to a dissident Christian (30).

These brief considerations suffice to show that the dissident Christians of the Reformation still have a share in the sacramental life of the Church. Through baptism validly administered, they receive at least an initial membership in the Catholic Church, the indelible character of being a Christian, and—if they do not set up an obstacle—the living gifts of Christ. We cannot deny that this sacramental reality is mediated, at least materially, by the Protestant Churches which still insist on Christian baptism; it is mediated not by anything proper to them, but by an element inherited from the Catholic Church.

The Virtue of Faith

Of even greater importance is the question whether Protestants of good will have a share in the supernatural life proper to Christ's mystical Body. The full fruit of baptism is not the sacramental character but the living grace of belonging to Christ. Since the adult cannot receive sanctifying grace unless he has faith, let us put the question simply: Can those who are separated from us in faith have the faith which justifies? Or, removing the equivocation from the question: Can Christians who differ from us in creed nevertheless possess the virtue of faith?

There have been Catholic theologians who denied that members of any community originating in a movement of heresy can have the gift of faith. Augustine Gibbon, an Augustinian theologian of the 17th century, taught that apart from the infallible magisterium of the Church no man can accept the Word of God in that absolute and unconditional sense which is required in divine faith (31). Even if a Protestant acknowledging the Scriptures should be psychologically certain that he believes the Word of God, the relationship of his creed to divine Revelation would remain arbitrary. If his creed, that is, his interpretation of the Bible, does happen to correspond to the divine Word of salvation, this would not be due to a necessary and divinely-given criterion but to the preference, either personal or inherited, of private choice (heresy). This however is not the view of modern theologians, and we find nothing in the Roman documents of our period to encourage such an opinion. On the contrary, we believe that it is in accordance with our official sources to say that Protestant Christians may believe the Word of God with divine faith. We shall discuss the problem in greater detail.

That divine faith is not intrinsically bound to the testimony of the Church, we see demonstrated in the saints of the Old Covenant. But even for the New Dispensation, we have an ecclesiastical document speaking of the possibility of faith outside the Church. In the Boston Letter, we read that the salvation of a man outside the Church depends on his *votum* to belong to her, on a *votum* which must be based on a truly supernatural faith and be alive with perfect charity (32). Hence there are cases—and judging from the erroneous opinion to be corrected, the Boston Letter envisages mainly Protestants—where the virtue of faith, *virtus fidei caritate formata*, is bestowed by God outside the visible boundaries of the Catholic Church. This takes us to the important question: What is the role of the Church's teaching office in the genesis of Christian faith?

According to the Vatican Council the *motivum formale fidei*, the proper and fundamental reason why and on account of which we believe, is the sovereign wisdom of God the Revealer. Referring to this doctrine of the Council and citing verbally from the official text, Leo XIII writes: 'Christian faith rests not on human but on divine wisdom; for what God has revealed "we believe not on account of an intrinsic evidence of truth which our reason discovers in revelation, but on account of the authority of God the Revealer who can neither deceive nor be deceived". From this it follows that whatever things are manifestly revealed by God must be received with an equal assent. To refuse to believe one of them is equivalent to rejecting them all' (33).

The Pope continues by explaining the role of the Church in engendering our faith in God's Word. 'It belongs to the magisterium of the Church, to whom God has entrusted the safekeeping and interpretation of his utterances, to determine which are the doctrines divinely revealed' (34). The Church gives testimony. She makes known and communicates to men that which God has revealed. But the witness of the Church (which is created) cannot be contained in the formal motive of faith (which is uncreated); hence we do not believe because of the Church, but rather because of God, whose message is proposed to us by the Church.

The Church, then, is the divinely appointed voice by which the gospel of salvation is mediated to mankind in all its integrity. In the normal economy of grace, Christ wants men to find faith in him through the testimony of those whom he has sent. Thus, whether the message is written or orally delivered, it is on the Church's testimony that the faith of the Christian world is dependent. Her witness, in fact her infallible witness, is *ex parte objecti* the necessary condition for supernatural faith, since only through her is the Word of God audible in the world.

Ex parte subjecti, however, that is, from the point of view of the individual, the necessary condition for faith is not the full weight of the Church's infallibility, but a slightly lesser aspect of her preaching: the rational credibility of divine Revelation. God wished that his intervention in the history of mankind be recognizable by definite signs, which make the acceptance of the gift of faith both reasonable and pleasing. The Vatican Council teaches that the fact of Revelation, that is, the divine origin of the Christian religion can be demonstrated from records and facts accessible to historical study (35). 'God desired that to the interior graces of the Holy Spirit be added external arguments for his Revelation, divine facts, especially miracles and prophecies (recorded in the Scriptures) . . . which are the signs of divine Revelation, signs of great certainty accommodated to all minds, *omnium intelligentiae*' (36). It follows that any man hearing or reading the biblical account of the life, death, and resurrection of Jesus Christ can discover sufficient credibility for the Word of God, so that the act of faith becomes possible and reasonable. We must conclude that rational credibility which *ex parte subjecti* is the necessary condition for the gratuitous gift of faith can be obtained outside the Catholic Church, even if not completely independent of her testimony. It can be found above all in the gospels, the divinely inspired records of apostolic preaching, which contain the main evidence by which God wants to awaken faith. 'Therefore (on account of the signs vouching for the truth of Revelation), all those who put faith in the gospels do not believe rashly as though following fictitious tales, but by a reasonable consent subject their intelligence to an authority which is divine' (37).

We must add, however, that all the signs authenticating divine Revelation were given to the Church—to be proclaimed together with the good news. 'To the Church and to her alone belongs *all* that God has disposed in so many wonderful ways to make evident the credibility of the Christian faith' (38); hence the biblical arguments which warrant faith are strictly speaking never detached from her witness. The gospels are never outside the Church since they were divinely committed to her preaching. The Church is the home of all motives of credibility.

To the Catholic the Church is even more. She is the *custos et magistra verbi revelati* (39), the divinely appointed rule of faith, infallible and indefectible. But this is not the basis of his faith but a consequences; in embracing the revelation of Christ in the total obedience of faith, the Church which Christ has founded is also believed, that is, she also becomes an object of faith. *Credo Ecclesiam.* A Catholic cannot depart from the teaching of the Church and retain Christ.

A man however who is approaching Christ through the biblical account without a full understanding of the divine commandments can find faith in Christ, even without the abundance of credibility which the Church offers him. If then he does not perceive that the Church is a part of the revealed mystery, his divine faith will not be taken from him for this reason alone. Hence we must admit that a separated Christian community which teaches that the Bible is the book of salvation and places it in the hands of its members must be said to mediate, at least in a material sense, sufficient credibility for faith in the Word made flesh.

We must make a small digression. Catholic theology confirmed by the Roman magisterium recognizes the possibility of a supernatural faith which is not dependent on the testimony of the Church (40). A man who is guiltlessly ignorant of Christian preaching may come to believe with a divinely given purity of heart that 'God exists and that he is a rewarder of those who seek him'; and God who is free to reveal himself to whomever he chooses may raise this human belief to a supernatural faith, to a faith resting on his own divine authority, to a faith which justifies. Can this faith be called Christian? Yes, since even in this case the saving gift is bestowed by God in view of the cross of Jesus Christ; but the Christian message is not contained in it, except by a remote implicitness.

How does this undeveloped faith of the 'holy pagan' (as we have called him) compare with the faith accessible to dissident Christians? Of course, they have the same formal motive, the authority of God who reveals himself. Essentially, all justifying faith is one. But the faith of the holy pagan is not mediated by the preaching of the Church. It remains ignorant of Christ. More than likely, the man thus enlightened by God will not be aware of the supernatural character of his religious belief. In any case it is given apart from the normal genesis of faith which comes from hearing, from hearing the envoys of Christ. The faith of the holy pagan is *ante praedicationem;* it is not brought about by any of the visible means which God has established through his Son Jesus Christ. Gratuitous and unpromised, it is due to the Spirit who blows where he wills.

The faith accessible to dissident Christians, on the other hand, is not apart from, at least not totally apart from the signs which God has established to prepare and announce the Christian faith. It is *post praedicationem*. Having heard the words 'Repent and believe in the gospel' (Mark i. 15), their faith is gratuitous but not unpromised. The believing Protestant has received the testimony of Jesus Christ, and he is conscious (in a way similar to the Catholic) of whether or not he believes in him as God and Saviour. His faith is generated by the preaching of the Church as it is accessible to him in the Bible. It would be a theological error as well as an injustice to Protestant Christians, were we to regard their virtue of faith as one with the elusive and unprofessed faith of the chosen pagan, which does not knowingly feed on the cross of Christ.

We conclude that dissident Christians who receive the Bible from their Churches may have the faith which justifies, and this not only accidentally, by an extraordinary election of God, but rather according to the normal genesis of faith which presupposes the divine credentials offered by Jesus Christ.

* * *

If we were to stop at this point, our interpretation would be incomplete, if not altogether false. So far we have said nothing of the weight of discord which burdens the heritage of our separated brethren. However, before dealing with this seed of dissention, we must confirm what we have said about faith among Protestants from the direct testimony of the Roman documents.

We have defined dissident Christians as believers in Christ who are separated from the Church in good faith. All the remarks we have made about their sacramental life and their virtue of faith presupposes that they are guiltlessly ignorant of Christ's design for his Church. But is this a reasonable assumption? Good will being an invisible attitude of the heart, it is known to none but God; yet there are innumerable situations in life—in the Church, in society, in the family—where we are obliged to make a judgment on the good will of our neighbour, proceeding from the signs which he gives us, from his words and his actions. Hence it is not unreasonable to ask whether the multitude of Protestants in our century can be credited with good faith.

Here we are concerned only with the Roman estimate. In an address delivered to the German *Katholikentag* on the day after the close of the first General Assembly of the World Council of Churches in 1948, Pope Pius XII said that 'the Church embraces the separated brethren with unfeigned chartiy, and with the fervour of prayers for their return to the Mother from whom *God knows how many* live apart without personal guilt' (41). It is to this God knows how great a multitude which Leo XIII refers when in his letter to the English he writes of 'their minds so well disposed' (42) and in a letter to the American hierarchy he speaks of those 'dissenting from heritage rather than from choice' (43), or which Pius X had in mind when in a letter to the Canadian hierarchy he expresses the belief that 'in great part non-Catholic Canadians are in good faith' (44). According to these passages, it seems to be the personal conviction of the popes that the multitude of Protestants in our day must be considered as separated from the Church without personal fault.

However, examining the volumes with great care we found only these four quotations, which are slight evidence over so many years. Fortunately, there is another indication, more certain and more frequent, that these passages do not mislead us. The Roman documents contantly refer to separated Christians as *fratres dissidentes;* there is no need to give references since it is the accepted terminology. 'Separated brethren' cannot designate schismatics or heretics, who have been severed from the Church by their own choice or by ecclesiastical censure. They are not brethren. The term undoubtedly refers to Christians outside the Church of whom the greater part must be considered as our brethren in Christ, as our brethren, because they have received of the gifts of Christ into their broken vessels (45).

Yet the good intention of dissidents and their consequent access to faith cannot obscure the unmitigated claim of the Catholic Church that her creed is the only true one. In reserving for the Church the unique and infallible testimony to the Christian gospel, we note however that the Roman letters clearly imply, by carefully chosen adjectives, that one can fail against this truth not only by outright contradiction but also by lack of integrity. Catholic truth, we read, is 'the perfect and absolute truth' (46), 'the whole of Christian wisdom' (47), 'the integral and genuine doctrine' (48), 'the full profession of the Christian law' (49), 'the uncurtailed, full and open profession of faith" (50). Separated Christians, we read, "lack the integrity of the Christian faith' (51). We are exhorted to pray "that they may know the truth in all its fullness and embrace the designs of God in single and entire faithfulness' (52).

The mutilated faith of Protestants notwithstanding, we read remarkable characterizations of the Christianity which is still left to them. 'They acknowledge Jesus Christ as Redeemer and rejoice in the Christian name' (53), 'they are initiated in the Christian religion' (54), they are not 'altogether void of the Christian faith' (55), 'they are introduced into Christianity' (56), 'they acknowledge Jesus Christ, Son of God and Saviour of mankind' (57), 'they set on Christ all their hope of salvation, both for themselves and for the human family' (58), 'they are worshippers of Christ' and 'believers in Christ, through separated from the Church' (59). While not belonging to 'the visible structure of the Church', they are united to us 'by the love for the person of Christ or belief in God' (60) or, more explicitly, 'by faith in God and Jesus Christ' (61). In a letter to the Scottish hierarchy Leo XIII writes, 'Of the Scottish separated from us in faith so many love the name of Christ from their heart, endeavour to obey his rule of life, and by imitation seek to follow his holy example' (62). In his letter to the English people the same Pontiff writes, in a context which indicates that he is referring to all religious men of England, 'The highest credit is due to those who fearlessly and unceasingly proclaim the rights, the laws, and the charter of God Almighty and his Son Jesus Christ; for in these the divine kingdom endures on earth'. A little farther down, still speaking of separated Christians, he claims 'to have observed the frequent and manifest signs of grace in their midst' (63). These passages are too clear to leave any doubt; however tragic and abnormal the situation of our separated brethren may be, there is no attempt in the official documents of the Holy See (of our period) to deny that they have access to the faith which justifies, to the supernatural and living faith in Jesus Christ, Son of God and Saviour of the world, which in all its integrity is found only in the Catholic Church.

This conclusion, which is disturbing as well as consoling, raises a difficult theological problem. Have we not said that divine faith is an undivided whole which does not suffer partition, which is either accepted completely and without reserve or does not exist at all? How then can we claim that someone who does not share the full

Christian profession of faith may still have the virtue of faith? Benedict XV writes, 'The nature of Catholic faith is such that nothing can be added or subtracted. Either all is received or all is rejected' (64). This is a problem which we must discuss. But first we shall describe the other, negative aspect of separated Christians as we find it expressed in our documents.

THE SEED OF DISSENTION

We would be unfaithful to our sources, were we to speak of dissident Christians only in terms of grace and their orientation towards Catholic fullness, without laying bare the seed of dissention which lives in them, and which stems from the schismatic or heretical origin of their Churches. Divine Revelation is a living unity—it is due to the one act of God by which he spoke to men—and a defect in its integrity will initiate grave distortions. If elements are torn away from a system of thought or a discipline of life, it will thereby become incomplete and unfinished, but if a living organic unity such as the Christian religion loses its wholeness, it is thrown into terrible convulsions by its own dynamism. Hence we cannot speak of our separated brethren in terms of light without immediately adding that they are menaced by darkness. They may be in grace individually but they are at the same time exposed to the forces of destruction.

In the following section we shall not be obliged to give as many verbal quotations; for so well known is the intransigence of the Catholic Church that any reprobation or condemnation of separated Christian bodies on the part of the Holy See will be believed only too readily. The Catholic Church considers herself as the one true Church of Christ. Hence the claims of any other Church or denomination are simply false. Hence, also, the creed which is not Catholic is simply not true. To discover the supernatural among dissident Christians we had to take into account their subjective situation. Objectively they are in error.

Looking upon our Orthodox brethren simply as a group of Christians who deny that Jesus Christ founded his Church with a visible unity of government, they are, in spite of their kinship and similarity to us, 'wandering off the right path' (65), 'apart from the unity of the mystical Body' (66), 'unable to share in the fullness of Christ which cannot be enjoyed save in the Church "which is his Body"' (67). In the severe phrase of Pius XI, 'they walk apart from the unity of the Church and consequently from Jesus Christ' (68). Our Protestant brethren, considered simply as

Christians denying that Christ founded an infallible Church, are in grave error and destroy the divine gift in themselves. 'A great part of Christians, enchanted by unbridled freedom of thinking and judging, drink up greedily the poison of evil doctrines and destroy in themselves the wonderful gift of faith' (69).

The state in which separated Christians find themselves without any fault of their own is in contradiction to their share in the gifts of Christ. Through their objective situation they are heirs, to a lesser or greater degree, of the ungodly forces of dissention. Even if we make all allowances for their good faith, even if for the sake of the argument we assume that they are all reconciled to God in Christ, then it still remains true—and this must be said if we wish to give a faithful account of the papal teaching—that they bear within themselves the seed of destruction. They are unable to deny their origin; they remain heirs of schism or heresy. In the eyes of Catholics, separated Christians, even when they are in the friendship of God, are always menaced by forces which are inherent in their Churches and their creeds. We shall describe from our documents this seed of dissention, considering first its origin and then its present effects.

THE ORIGIN OF DISSENTION

The papal documents which we are considering repeatedly refer to the origin of separated Christian bodies, but we must clearly distinguish the passages which apply to the secession of the East from those which describe the cleavage of Western Christendom. The difference between schism and heresy is a fundamental one. While schism directly attacks ecclesiastical unity, the visible unity of obedience and love which Christ bestowed on his Church, heresy undermines the foundation of faith, the authority of God the Revealer, and does not differ from apostasy except in degree. The sin of schism is directed against a created good, the sin of heresy against uncreated good (70). Both the schismatic and the heretic exclude themselves from the Church of Christ and his saving grace because, directly or indirectly, they refuse obedience to him and his order of salvation. If it is true that schism and heresy attack the Church at very different levels, they are still related in as much as they both sin against the Church's unity. Hence a purely ecclesiastical schism easily leads to doctrinal divergences; and it is not rare that schismatic Churches even fall into heresy. Breaking one link which binds to the Church, the other bonds which unite men to her are weakened also (71).

In the East

It is remarkable to observe how, in referring to the genesis of the Eastern secession, the Roman documents of our period hesitate to place the blame (72). While in the case of heresy the authors and defenders of the new doctrine are accused without reluctance, the origin of the Eastern dissention is attributed to the forces of wickedness without specifying where exactly the guilt is to be found. The rift was brought about 'by the perverse wiles of him who instigated the first schism in heaven' (73). Though the East is accused of 'breaking the sweet yoke that bound them to the Apostolic See' (74), though Photius is said to have originally acknowledged the primacy of the See of Peter by sending envoys to Rome and receiving papal ambassadors (75), though the Oriental Church leaders who favoured the breach of ecclesiastical communion are repeatedly called evil and wicked men and compared to the 'enemy' of the gospel who came to sow tares among the good seed, there is nevertheless a realization that the actual separation was prepared by a long history of mutual distrust. 'As the ages rolled by, the waves of suspicion and hatred arose, and great and flourishing nations were drawn away from the Roman Church' (76). We read in a remarkable sentence that "Many evils in former times and even the sad dissention . . . came about by necessity from mutual ignorance, national contempt, and from prejudiced opinions followed by a lasting *estrangement* of minds' (77).

Recounting the history of the reconciliation of the Ruthenian Church with the Holy See, the encyclical *Orientales Omnes* (1946) speaks of the 'evil men' who sought to destroy ecclesiastical communion after the Union of Brest-Litovsk. What were their motives in this endeavour? Was it covetousness, was it political ambition, or was it prompted by the inadequate instruction of a people ill-prepared for the union? We do not know, says the encyclical (78).

There are no doubt questions which the study of history cannot resolve, and perhaps it is impossible to determine the person, or the party, which was responsible for the final rupture between two Churches which had long been growing apart. The schism had been prepared by the experiences of centuries. The remarkable reserve of the recent official documents in placing the blame could possibly be inspired by a desire not to offend; on the other hand, this sort of toning down is not characteristic of papal pronouncements. It is more likely that the popes are conscious of the political and cultural factors which favoured the cleavage, and of the Latin contribution to the widening of the rift. It is perhaps to these latter historical incidents that Pius XI is referring when he asks the Christians of the East 'not to blame the Church of Rome for the sins of individual members, for sins which she herself condemns and endeavours to repair' (79).

Is it theologically conceivable that due to a growth of misunderstanding and prejudice there is reached a point of estrangement where communion with the Apostolic See is severed—without a formal sin of schism? The objective situation of the severed Church is so abnormal and endangered that it is hard to believe that God, 'who does not desert unless he has first been deserted', would permit a fall into such a state, without a previous proportionate sin on the part of men. However this question may be resolved, however much or however little wilfulness is claimed for the Eastern Rift, one thing is certified in our documents, namely, that the state of separation of Orthodox Christians is contrary to the will of Christ and a negation of the government established by him. This negation, whatever our judgment on the culpability, remains and lives in the heart of the dissident Churches of the East.

In the West

In reference to the beginning of the Protestant Reformation the statements of the Roman documents are much clearer. They accuse the innovators of breaking away from the unity of faith, of having tampered with the divine deposit of faith handed down by the apostles. Certainly, the pronouncements of the popes admit that grave abuses in the Church and the decay of morality in the Catholic world had prepared the way for the Reformation. Here is an excerpt from a sermon of Pius XI:

'It was the fatal tendency of the human element to be infected and corrupted—the human element accompanies the divine here on earth—the negligence and the indolence of the friends of good, the faithless audacity of the promoters of evil, the bad example in high places and the ready yielding below, and finally the return to paganism of private and public morality that unleashed, in the Europe of the 16th century, the terrible anguish of the Reformation' (80).

There is a tendency in modern times to explain the disasters in history from the social and cultural background which made them possible, and to reduce the responsibility of the acting individuals by an analysis of their psychological situation. This tendency we notice also in the Roman documents. We read that 'the spread of error was made easy by the general decay of morality' (81) and that 'once the breach had occurred, there happened by necessity what the Reformers had perhaps not intended: the heart of Christianity was destroyed in their ranks, leaving little more than the outward appearances' (82). Yet this tendency to understand and to distribute the guilt among all the parties concerned is susceptible to exaggeration. The unity of faith and its crisis is not a subject which can be left to historical speculation alone. Christian faith is not a conviction from which one drifts away by adverse circumstances; it is a divine gift for which God has decreed a special providence. We are, in fact, warned in the instruction *Ecclesia Catholica* 'that in giving the history of the Reformation the faults of Catholics should not be so exaggerated, the guilt of the Reformers so obscured, and accidentals moved so much into the centre of attention that the defection from the Catholic faith is hardly noticed and not fully appreciated' (83). In spite of all mitigating circumstances, there stands at the root of all movements of heresy the heresiarch, the inventor and promoter of a new doctrine. Whether the popes speak of Nestorius or Eutychus or the Reformers of the 16th century, it is to them that they attribute the authorship of the cleavage of faith.

'It does not help however' writes Benedict XV 'to recall the sad history of the ancient discord (of the 16th century); better to wipe it out by our common tears and, if possible, to cast it into eternal oblivion' (84). But whether we want it or not, we are heirs of our past; and hence the seed of negation, which at one time produced the division of Christendom, lives on in the institutions to which it gave birth. Protestant Christians are forever exposed to the dormant forces of unbelief, which their good intentions cannot make ineffectual.

THE DYNAMISM OF DISSENTION
In the East

The denial of the divinely established government of the Church on the part of Eastern dissidents wounds the organic integrity of Revelation, and initiates a tendency towards decay. According to the views expressed in the documents of the Holy See, the separated Churches of the East have suffered a decrease of spiritual fecundity. In one place we read, 'As long as they remained in holy unity, these Churches flourished marvellously' (85), and in another, that by breaking the bond of obedience 'they forfeited the splendour of their former greatness, their renown in the arts and sciences, and the dignity of their office' (86). But the references to these destructive effects of the rupture are so rare that it is not easy to estimate in what exactly, in the eyes of the Roman pontiffs, this loss of glory consists.

A sentence of the famous letter *Mit Brennender Sorge* of Pius XI, addressed to the German people, may give us a hint. We read, 'The historical development of national Churches (the Pope is probably referring to the West), their spiritual stagnation and their subjugation by secular powers, demonstrates the hopeless unfruitfulness to which any branch severed from the living vine of the Church is condemned' (87). The two evils which are here mentioned as consequences of schism, torpidity of spirit and governmental oppression, appear again in the encyclical *Oriental Omnes*. Here we read, and this time with reference to the East, that in the period preceding the Union of Brest-Litovsk 'the sole hope of the Ruthenian Church to achieve the desired renewal and reform and to be freed from grave oppressions was the reconciliation with the Apostolic See' (88). We shall not be untrue to our documents when we say that the denial of the papal authority established by Christ will upset the divine equilibrium of the dissenting Church, and open the way for corruptions which are, by an interior logic, the consequence of this denial. When the legitimate authority which is the guardian of the Church's independence and the centre of its living tradition has been rejected, the dissenting Church lies a prey to the usurping power of the state and becomes vulnerable to the weight of its own stagnation. Thank God, this seed of dissention is not the only active principle in the dissident Christianity of the East; their unity of faith and sacrament, retaining its orientation towards the fullness of Christ, is still an inexhaustible source of grace.

In the West

Compared to the relative silence in our documents about the negative potential innate in the separated Eastern Churches, the ills which threaten Protestant Christianity as a result of the defection from the ancient faith are described at great length. Especially in the encyclicals of Leo XIII we find countless references to the state of religion within Protestantism and its effect on culture and society (89). Summarizing his remarks we may say that in the eyes of Leo XIII there lives in Protestant Christianity a restless seed, inherited from the Reformation, which bears fruit in a fourfold way: the formation of sects, instability of doctrine, a tendency towards rationalism, and—worst of all—a growing decay of the divine substance of faith. What is his reasoning?

The new principle, the *proprium*, which the Reformers introduced into Christianity was not this or that theological theory, but the principle of private judgment (90). This principle, as explained by Leo XIII, is in direct contradiction to the Catholic vision of Christianity. Christian faith is wholly from God; and it is God's judgment which saves and not man's. Interpreting the words of Christ according to one's own understanding, and not in total obedience to him and in accord with the authority he has established, introduces at the very root of faith a human element which must tend to invalidate the supernatural character of the Christian religion. Since the minds and characters of men are so varied, and more than that, since divine truth so much exceeds the grasp of human understanding, it is clear that with the concept of private judgment in matters of revealed religion the dividing principle is invented for an ever-growing number of denominations and sects. However wellmeant is the wish to follow the Scriptures alone, the fact remains that the teachings of Protestant Churches are at variance with one another, and have never been constant. This instability of doctrine makes the Protestant in his religion dependent on his own research to such a degree, that he usually refuses to accept as binding the creed even of his own Church. This exaggerated emphasis on personal choice will lead to a devaluation of the divine testimony and to a purely historical approach to the Bible. The result, in many cases, is a rationalistic criticism of Holy Scripture, the rejection of the divine authorship of these books, and what was originally the sole source and criterion of Revelation gradually becomes discredited in the eyes of great multitudes.

Still, this is not the gravest judgment which we read on the destructive dynamism of Protestantism. There is a law according to which the multiplication of creeds takes place: the progressive corruption of the divine substance of faith. Leo XIII laments: 'From the patrimony of truth which the authors of the Reformation took along with them into separation, there remains to them hardly an article of belief that is certain and supported by authority. Many have gone so far as to uproot the very foundation upon which alone rests all religion and the hope of mankind: the divinity of our Saviour Jesus Christ' (91).

These descriptions are taken from documents written at the turn of the century, and they reflect the unglorious past of Protestant theology at that period. (Be it remarked that we do not have to go very far in these same documents to discover that the thought of Catholics in many parts of Europe was passing through a desert of half-belief at the same time.) But even so, who can deny that for centuries Protestantism has been conspicuous for its tendency to multiply creeds and split up into smaller groups! That in our day we witness an opposite tendency—and this on a large scale—seeking the return to the fellowship established by Christ is due to the vivifying influence of grace. It is derived from the inspiration of the Spirit, and consequently for the Church 'it is a source of joy in the Lord' (92). It is the judgment of our documents that the Ecumenical Movement of to-day is not the product of the ungodly heritage of Protestantism; it is rather the fruit of the faith and the spirit of prayer which has survived among its followers. The seed of discord, which lives on and seeks to undermine the faith in the God-Man, is not without its counter-current; divine grace which continues to be accessible and present to the dissident Christians of the West has an indomitable resilience towards the fullness in Christ.

*   *   *

The destructive effects which we have described in following the observations of the papal letters create a definite spiritual setting peculiar to the various dissident Christian Churches and groups, a setting where error is alive and where even truth has an equivocal ring. While a dissident Christian can find Christ through the profession of his unfinished creed, a Catholic is no longer free to depart from the integral Christian dogma taught by the Church. Protestant doctrine with its belief in Christ may mediate, at least materially, salvation to its followers; to the Catholic however, it is simply dangerous. In the Roman documents dissident Christians are 'separated brethren' as long as they are considered in their own milieu; but if the occasion demands that they be looked upon as missionaries of their creed carrying their doctrines to those who possess the Catholic faith, they are no longer 'brethren', but the promoters of error. The seed of negetion which lives in them without being able to obstruct the flow of grace, would radically destroy supernatural life if it should leap over to Catholics. Hence we read in the letters of Leo XIII that he repeatedly protested against the activity of foreign 'heretics' in the city of Rome (93). Hence, also, we read that emigrated oriental Catholics who find no church of their own rite in their new home, in North America, may fall a prey to the offers of 'schismatics' and 'heretics' (94). This caution, or we may say, this fear in the face of those who bear the contagion of error does not easily please us to-day; we are wont to think that truth, defended by its own evidence, does not require hedging in to preserve its purity. The Church of our day encourages co-operation with other Christian groups on a social level, but she does not tolerate joint action in matters of revealed religion. She has retained a prophetic dread of all religious doctrines which do not stem from the fullness of revealed truth. This is not a modern sentiment; it is however a biblical one. 'Anyone who advances and does not abide in the doctrine of Christ, has not God . . . If anyone comes to you and does not bring this doctrine, do not receive him into the house or say to him "Welcome". For he who says to him "Welcome" is a sharer in his evil works' (2 John 9-11).

THE RESULTANT SITUATION

By enumerating separately the supernatural patrimony and the seed of dissention, we do not wish to give the impression that dissident Christians possess certain parts of Revelation wholly and completely in common with us, while the proper elements of discord, denying this or that point of doctrine, exist among them in a clearly definable isolation. We have chosen the division into divine patrimony and seed of error as a means of presenting the papal testimony in a convenient form, and to demonstrate that the Roman documents of our period do not support the view that dissident Christians, not even those of the West, are devoid of a living supernatural heritage. In our documents they are considered as Christians, as men who have access to Christ, as separated brethren. Yet the two conflicting legacies of which dissident Christians are heirs do not exist side by side among them in a clearly separable way. They affect one another and mingle. From the two opposing traditions proceed spiritual currents engaged in permanent strife with each other—a buoyant stream of grace towards fulfilment, and a downward rush of heresy towards death—so that there is never an element of one tradition which is not exposed to the influences of the other. Hence, distinct as they are, the two traditions are united inextricably in their historical situation.

The proportions between these two legacies in dissident Christianity will of course vary greatly according to the religious body and, within the same community, according to the individual Christian. Some Churches are closer to the plentitude of truth than others. Orthodox Christians sometimes exhibit such a vigorous life of grace, such perfection of spirituality, such a flowering of holiness that the weight of discord implied in their tradition does not achieve a noticeable effect. On the other extreme we may find a Protestant in whom the seed of grace, which he inherited from the Church of Christ, is always at the point of being drowned by a sea of contradiction. Between these two limiting positions is contained the whole of separated Christianity which sincerely seeks to obey Christ. Witnessing the conflict which goes on in the hearts of dissident Christians, the Catholic Church cannot remain unmoved and passive. In Chapter 4 we shall determine, beginning from the principles we have just established, what the function or task of the Church must be with respect to her dissident members.

The two traditions, moreover, which make up the historical setting of dissident Christians come together in something that must be called a psychological unity. In and through his milieu, the dissident Christian believes himself to be simply in the presence of the Christian religion. By one act of the mind, it seems, he accepts divine Revelation as well as the unorthodox interpretations of his teachers. He receives the Word of God not through the perfectly transparent medium of the Church but rather in the tainted light inherited from his community. A Protestant may believe in Jesus Christ, and believe in him as one who founded no visible Church. While theologically speaking there is a profound cleavage between the authentic and the spurious, psychologically speaking the religious belief of a dissident Church may hold together in an organic unity. Hence in studying the doctrines and practices of a dissident denomination it is not sufficient to enumerate the articles of belief and isolate them for closer examination; we must rather see them in relation to the whole, to the Christian vision from which they are taken (95). The whole body of beliefs of dissident groups (who differ from us in doctrine) is marked by the co-existence of two influences, and even their grasp of the central Christian mystery, received in faith, must be coloured in some way by the light and the atmosphere in which it is professed.

Speaking of the situation in certain sections of Protestant Christianity, Pius XII said: 'The tares of rationalism have entered in various ways the thoughts and sentiments of many Christians, weakening in them what has remained of the divine seed of truth, thus causing the spread of darkness, division, and loss of faith in the divinity of Jesus Christ' (96). Here a Protestant situation is visualized as a field where good grain and weeds grow together, compenetrate and compete with each other. According to another image which stresses more the psychological unity of a dissident spirituality, we could describe their situation as that of an organism injured or even diseased. But how can Christian faith be wounded and still live? This brings us to a question which we have met on a previous page.

The 'Faith' of Protestants

Christian faith being one and indivisible, how can it be possessed by those who differ from us in creed? That Protestants have access to Christian faith we have shown; but the question remains how this can be reconciled with the unique and indivisible character of faith. In other words, we must investigate the relationship of the faith accessible to Protestants with the faith of the Catholic Church.

Faith is uniquely determined by its formal motive (*id quo*), which is the authority of God revealing, and by its formal object (*id quod*), which is the divine message of salvation. Thus faith is one, and all justifying faith must be essentially undifferentiated from the faith of the Catholic Church. Accidentally however faith may vary from person to person. In our context we are interested only in the modifications of divine faith with respect to its formal object (*id quod*).

There are no doubt various ways of knowing what God has revealed. The young child beginning to learn his religion has a faith which is unaware of many revealed doctrines held by an adult Christian. Both, to be sure, have an identical object of faith, namely all that God has revealed; but the child will believe some mysteries only implicitly in the readiness to believe them all. Thus Catholic theology comes to the distinction between *undeveloped faith*, which believes some articles of faith explicitly and others only implicitly, and a fully *developed faith*, which accepts the divine message in the explicit form of the full Catholic creeds (97). Undeveloped faith is not a rare thing; it is the normal way for children to grow into believing, it is found in unlettered Catholics, and with respect to certain articles of the Catholic creed to-day, the faith of former generations was undeveloped. This distinction in no way compromises the indivisibility of faith, not even with respect to its object; for whether developed or undeveloped, faith formally believes all that God has revealed (98).

If a Protestant professing a creed different from ours has the faith which justifies, it must be substantially the Catholic faith. Adhering to Christ as the source of truth and salvation, he is ready to obey whatsoever Christ may ask him. If he only knew, he would gladly accept the gospel in its totality; as it is, his faith contains only implicitly the whole extent of revealed truth. His faith then is undeveloped with respect to the faith of the Catholic Church.

However, and this is a formidable difficulty, how can a creed which is made up of articles of faith and of erroneous opinions be accepted with divine faith however undeveloped? Being founded on God's Word faith cannot be subject to error. When an impure creed is the object of belief, only the revealed truth in it could possibly be embraced by faith, the error would always remain a human opinion. But is such a mixture of convictions possible in the human mind without uprooting the divine gift of faith?

It is a fact that such a situation may even arise within the Catholic Church. It may happen that an unenlightened pastor at a remote corner of the earth teaches an erroneous opinion to his parishioners, and the people, being used to receive the doctrine of the Church from the mouth of her ministers, assent faithfully to what is actually a grave error. This false opinion, living psychologically mixed in with infallible faith, will not destroy the virtue of faith. St Thomas knew of this problem; he spoke of human conjectures which are sometimes held to be of faith (99). It would seem then that undeveloped faith does not purify the mind of all errors, not even of those which are in contradiction to the fully developed profession of faith. In the minds of the faithful there may exist a mixture of believing and conjecturing in a manner unknown to them. There is of course no mixture possible *ex parte objecti*, for no error can be believed with divine faith. But under certain conditions a psychological unity can embrace what is as formally distinct as divine truth and human error. Would not St Thomas want us to apply exactly this sort of reasoning to his own 'denial' of the immaculate conception of our Lady? (100). He believed the doctrine implicitly (implicit in the readiness to accept the whole gospel), even if he rejected it explicitly (at a time when it had not yet been defined by the Church). We may say, then, without fear of self-contradiction, that the faith of a Protestant is implicitly Catholic, that he receives the Word of God in obedience in spite of the spurious opinions which he adds to it, that his is an undeveloped Catholic faith hidden in an obscuring formula.

We must however go one step further. As we have seen, the Protestant Christian does not possess the divine patrimony on neutral grounds but rather against the background of dissidence. Into his creed are mixed not only erroneous human conjectures but heretical opinions with all the weight they have received in the course of controversy. Unknown to him the heritage of discord will militate against the supernatural. Hence even with the firmest, divinely-given intention to adhere to Christ, the Protestant always remains threatened in his faith by the framework in which he holds the truth. The innate tendency of faith towards integrity may come to contradict uncompromisingly the inherited negation, or the corroding force of error may attack the foundation of the divine gift; in either case there may come a point when a choice is no longer avoidable—a choice which could end in heresy and the extinction of faith.

This contradiction between the living faith and the professed creed is an anomaly. Not only is there a full and integral truth which Christ asked men to accept, but he also called into existence a divine milieu in which this faith would unfold and grow. Outside the Church faith lives in an environment which is not normal, not connatural to it. The separation of faith from its divinely appointed teacher is an exception, and apart from the normal way foreseen in the economy of salvation.

Unenlightened faith within the Catholic Church, such as the faith of children at school or of uninstructed adults, implicitly believes all that the Church teaches as the Word of God. It does not differ from the explicit faith of the Church, save accidentally, *in regard to its development*. But this distinction does not suffice to characterize the faith accessible to a Protestant. We must conclude that, in addition to differing *in regard to development*, the faith accessible to Protestants differs from ours *in regard to its situation*. It is a very special kind of undeveloped faith; hidden in an unauthentic creed it is in contradiction to its environment. By its own tendency it seeks to escape from the ill-fitting frame in which it is cast. It is the kind of faith which is ever restless; it endeavours to burst the creed which contains it. At the same time it is exposed to forces of dissention which seek to destroy from within the God-given assent to divine revelation by successively removing the remnants of credibility. This is the situation, exposed and unprotected, of the 'faith' of Protestants, an anomalous situation for a divine gift.

The Relation of Dissident Christians to the Catholic Church

What is the relationship of separated Christians—we are now speaking again of Eastern and Western dissidents—to the Roman Catholic Church? It is obvious from what we have said about the unity of the Church in Christ, that there can be no supernatural union to the Head which remains unrelated to his Body. We cannot speak of a fellowship with Christ outside and apart from the Catholic Church. Wherever the Holy Spirit has been sent by Christ to dwell in the souls of men, there must be present in proportionate measure the Body vivified by the same Spirit. The sanctification effected by the Holy Ghost does not extend farther than the saving influence of Christ's Body. Pius XII writes, 'Those who are separated from one another by faith or ecclesiastical government cannot live in the one Body nor by the one Spirit' (101). Hence we must choose. Either we deny the possession of sanctifying and sacramental grace to dissident Christians, or we must assign them a real and definite relationship to the Catholic Church. After our description of the divine patrimony surviving in dissidence, we have no choice left.

According to the terminology laid down in *Mystici Corporis*, to which we have had occasion to refer, dissident Christians cannot be considered *reapse*, really and truly members of the Church; for even if they were united to us by faith and sacraments, they would still lack the bond of ecclesiastical communion. This point however should not be pressed, since, in denying membership to those who are visibly separated from the Church, the encyclical speaks only of two groups, of those who have chosen to cut themselves off and of those who were severed by way of punishment (102). The celebrated passage says nothing about those who were born outside. Moreover, it is quite certain that through baptism dissident Christians are radically and vitally initiated into the Body of Christ, even if their membership remains incomplete for other reasons. Judging then from the official documents which we are studying, the relationship of dissidents to the Catholic Church is complex; it cannot be reduced to a simple formula. Their state of separation gives them a note of inner contradiction, and puts them in a situation which recalls the exposed and unprotected character of faith among Protestants, as we have described it above. It is the judgment of our documents that all dissident Christians, even those of the Orient, are threatened by a fundamental insecurity.

That there should be believers in Christ outside the Church of Christ is not within the normal economy of salvation. The Lord has provided a social body for his believers, a community to protect and develop their faith, to receive and return their love. He appointed the apostles as the columns of the young Church which were to hold up the entire structure. In the New Testament we know of no Christians independent of an apostle, and of no Churches unattached to the mother Church at Jerusalem, the symbol of apostolic unity (103). The only separate Christians which we come upon are those who have left the doctrine or the discipline of the apostles and who unless they repent, are headed towards eternal loss. Our situation of a divided Christendom is unknown in New Testament times; it is obvious that in the first generation of Christianity we cannot find Christian groups that have guiltlessly inherited false doctrines or ecclesiastical divisions from their elders. According to the economy of salvation established by Christ and experienced in the apostolic age, Christian faith was found only in the Church, the household of God.

A certain analogy to dissident Christians, however, is found in the Jew Apollos and the disciples at Ephesus, of whom we read in the Acts of the Apostles (xviii. 24–xix. 7). On the one hand it seems certain that they were believers in Christ. Apollos had a profound knowledge of the Old Testament, and he had been instructed in the life and the teaching of the Lord. Urged by his spirit of faith he preached the doctrine of Jesus to the assembled congregation, and it was perhaps due to his witness that the twelve men of Ephesus called 'disciples' (the technical name for the Christian brethren) found their faith. 'Did you receive the Holy Ghost when you became believers?' Paul asked them. Believers they were, but they had not received the entire doctrine preached by the apostles.

We do not know where Apollos was taught the gospel, but at the time when he came to Ephesus he was still ignorant of Christian baptism. He was only acquainted with the baptism of John. Priscilla and Aquilla took him aside, and at their home 'they taught him the way of the Lord more precisely'. In a similar way, the disciples at Ephesus had learned to believe in Christ without being told about the baptism of the Church. They had not even heard that the Holy Ghost promised in the Scriptures had been poured out on the faithful. They had but received the baptism of John. We must suppose that Appollos and the disciples had received the gospel from men who knew nothing about the completion of Christ's work by his death and resurrection. Perhaps their information was related to certain disciples of the Baptist who, having learned to believe in Christ, had fallen away from him due to an excessive veneration of their master. We may indeed have a group of Christians at Ephesus who received an incomplete gospel as the result of a wilful deformation on the part of their teachers—a strict analogy to dissident Christians. But whether or not Apollos and the disciples derived their faith from the dissenting followers of John the Baptist, it is to the Baptist that St Paul points as his main witness; he tells them to be baptized in the name of Jesus whom John prophesied. Beginning with what is sound and holy in their faith he leads them to the integral doctrine of the Christian community; and just as Apollos listened to the instruction of Christian laymen, so the twelve disciples of Ephesus receive the testimony of Paul. They show an immediate willingness to accept from the Church the full gospel and the sacraments.

If our interpretation is correct, the group of disciples at Ephesus call to mind the situation of dissident Christians. Theirs was an undeveloped faith, born outside the apostolic community, perhaps even affected by an inherited distortion. Only their readiness to listen to the apostolic teaching distinguishes them from dissident Christians, and it is precisely the unwillingness of these latter to receive the integral doctrine from the Church which makes their situation so problematic, even without personal guilt. They certainly have a more developed faith than our twelve disciples, but their scruple gives them a note of elusiveness which cannot be attributed to the men of Ephesus.

It is to this problematic character of dissident Christians that a celebrated sentence alludes, a phrase coined by Pius IX and quoted by Pius XII in a conspicuous and important context of *Mystici Corporis*. Men separated from the Church 'are in a state where they cannot be secure as to their eternal salvation' (104). A Catholic, to be sure, is never certain of his salvation, but this insecurity is not due to his state as a member of the Catholic Church; it is rather the effect of the fickleness of the human heart which may or may not remain faithful. Because we do not know whether we shall persevere till the end, 'we must work out our salvation in fear and trembling' (Phil. ii. 12). The insecurity of dissident Christians however is of a different nature. Apart from the moral venture which they share with their Catholic brethren, they live in an insecurity which is the result of their state of separation, of not belonging to the unique ark of salvation, of not being true heirs of the promises of Christ. Their hope unto the Last Day is not equal to ours. Can they really be certain of their faith in the Word of God? Can they know without a doubt that they have never rejected the voice of the Spirit, or of the Church, leading them on to fullness? Can they estimate whether their divine patrimony is still undeformed and a source of new life to them? Their situation relates them insecurely to the divine pardon. Eschatologically their state is insecure: this seems to be the conviction of the popes.

On the other hand we must not minimize the union of dissident Christians with Christ, the Saviour and Head of the Church. They have his sacraments, they have his faith. Even a Protestant who has nothing left of the Church save the New Testament will not be prevented from having a living faith in the Word of God by his incomplete awareness of its content. Having found the newness of life, dissident Christians are vitally related to the Body of Christ. Certainly, they 'will lack many of the graces and gifts which can be found only in the Catholic Church' (105), but they cannot be denied sanctifying grace on any other grounds than a Catholic; sin alone separates them from Christ. The dissident Christian is an heir of two divergent traditions, but his essential relationship to God is determined by the divine patrimony. He is justified, although menaced by his environment. Two opposing currents cross in his soul, but it is the supernatural which holds the ground. Hence it would be wrong to characterize the situation of separated Christians as a state of spiritual death illumined by actual graces; it is rather a spiritual life threatened, in various degrees, by dissolution. Theirs is a Christianity alive but sick, a wounded source of spiritual life. Only in the Church can they find their health and their home.

What, then, is the relationship of dissident Christians to the Body of Christ? We have seen that in addition to a complete membership characterized by the triple bond of creed, sacrament, and ecclesiastical communion, there are also other ways, less complete but salutary, of belonging to the Catholic Church. After our analysis of the Christian situation of dissidents, it will not do to call them simply members of the Church *in voto*. We must be more precise. Dissident Christians are attached to the Church not in an invisible manner, like the so-called holy pagans who are justified in a hidden and almost miraculous fashion; dissidents are incorporated into the Body of Christ through the visible rite of baptism, even if their membership afterwards does not grow in the normal manner established by Christ. If the intention to belong to the Church (which is included in baptism) is not revoked by a contrary decision, there is no reason to suppose that the visible root which they have taken in the Church has been eradicated. Through their baptism then, dissident Christians are visibly related to the Catholic Church. Orthodox Christians, on the same principle, are in visible union with the Church through the whole of their sacramental life.

But even apart from the sacramental order, dissident Christians are visibly related to the Church, or at least partially so, through the public profession of their faith in Jesus Christ. By their (incomplete) testimony to the Lord, they are recognizable as believers. They have, moreover, received their divine gifts through the visible mediation of the Catholic Church: they were reborn through her baptism and justified by her gospel. If we say that they belong *in voto* to the Church, we must specify that this *votum* is concretely embodied in various visible bonds, in elements of the Church which they possess *in re*. Dissident Christians remain children of the Catholic Church, visibly born even though visibly separated.

From the description of separated Christians in the official documents of the Holy See, we have tried to determine their relationship to the Body of Christ. Coming to a conclusion we realize that whatever theological language be employed, it must contain a good number of variables since it has to account for a wide range of different situations. Statements which would be too severe, and therefore untrue with respect to Orthodox Christians may still be undiscerning with respect to some groups of Western dissidents. For all dissident Christians, however, it is true to say that they are in union with the Church of Christ by diverse visible and invisible links, and that at the same time they are withheld from her in various degrees by an inherited contradiction. Attached to the Church, they must remain outside her unity. We conclude that dissident Christians —and we recall that we defined 'dissidents' as guiltlessly separated Christians—belong to the Body of Christ, the Catholic Church, with a membership which is *initial* (as against non-Christians), *incomplete* (to distinguish them from Catholics), *partially visible* (in contradistinction to the 'holy pagans'), and finally *threatened* (which refers to the great variable introduced by the seed of dissention).

CHAPTER THREE

DISSIDENT CHURCHES

IF we determine the religious situation of divided Christendom only in terms of the individual's relationship to the Catholic Church, we make the task too easy for ourselves. In the last chapter, it is true, we did not treat dissident Christians simply as individuals. We considered them rather as bearers of a partial Christian tradition, that is to say, as men who received the gifts of Christ not merely from the unpredictable stirring of the Spirit, but from the wounded sources available to them in their own religious communities. Yet in order to acquire a theological view of divided Christianity we must also investigate the nature of these separated Christian bodies.

THE NATURE OF SEPARATED CHURCHES

In the official documents which we are studying we find few explicit statements about the nature of separated Churches; we must nevertheless attempt a theological justification of the attitude taken by the Holy See towards these Churches. With absolute clarity our documents only tell us what separated Churches are not: *Separated Churches are not members or branches of the Catholic Church*. In our first chapter we have expounded the doctrine that the Church of Christ, founded on the apostles under the supreme leadership of Peter, is visibly one with a unity of faith and government: consequently only those Churches are parts of the universal Church which are in communion with the See of Peter. This conclusion, we would say, is *de fide* (1).

While denying perfect membership to individual dissident Christians, we admitted that they belong to the Catholic Church in an incipient way by baptism and the implicit desire of faith. Can a similar argument be devised for separated Churches? We believe it cannot. Since social bodies are not persons and lack individual consciousness, the missing factors of integrity and unity cannot be replaced by a proportionate *votum*. Even if all the members of a separated Church belong to the Catholic Church by baptism and supernatural desire, the social body itself contains elements which are in contradiction to the divine constitution of the Church; and for this reason it can in no way be a part of her. 'No congregation whatsoever separated from the external visible communion and obedience to the Roman Pontiff can be the Church of Christ, or in any way whatever belong to the Church of Christ' (2).

We must clearly distinguish, however, between the patrimony of grace surviving in dissidence and the separated Church in which this partial patrimony is alive. The isolated patrimony is easily definable in terms of theology (it is the totality of the means of grace and their effects, in dissidence), but only with difficulty is it circumscribed in the concrete order of history. For separated Churches, however, the very opposite is true. Their historical identity is obvious; what is extremely difficult to grasp and evaluate is their nature in the light of theology (3). Theologically speaking, a separated Church is not one thing; it is an accidental union of elements which are contradictory in character. It is the confluence of two traditions, the one of divine descent, the other of schismatic or heretical origin, which have coalesced in a definite historical society. There is an abysmal difference between an Orthodox Church which has retained an almost uninjured Catholic life and a separated Christian body of Protestant denomination which has preserved only the sacrament of baptism. Every dissident Church has its own peculiar character; thus we cannot speak of a common logical species of dissident Churches, nor make many statements which are applicable to all of them.

Nevertheless we venture to say that all separated Churches are in a certain sense *mysterious*. A separated Church is not a social body that can be judged simply in the light of human wisdom, nor is it merely a mass or multitude of dissident Christians. In what sense, then, does it hide a theological mystery? A separated Church not only distorts divine Revelation by its erroneous articles, it also makes Revelation present in the world. Certain gifts of Christ are accessible to men as the result of the social structure of a dissident Church. Christian sacraments are administered in some countries because a dissident Church order demands it. (Thus the children born in Iceland would not be reborn in Christ, were it not for the legislation of the local Protestant Church demanding infant baptism.) In certain areas the faith in Christ is made possible to men because a dissident Church proclaims, in sermons and by recommending the sacred texts, the (partial) message of salvation and the life of Christ (which demonstrates the credibility of this message). Thus the dissident Church cannot be considered as an anti-Church, as a body simply spreading corruption; it is rather a social structure responsible both for the *impediments* to and the *presence* of a divine tradition. Through his separated Church, the dissident Christian learns about Christ and comes to have faith in him, even if this faith be threatened by an ill-fitting formula. In the last analysis these means of grace belong the Catholic Church, but historically speaking in certain areas of the earth these means are not avaliable to men, except for a dissident Church.

What is the reason for this double character of separated Christian communities? The divine patrimonies torn from the Church not only contain elements which concern and effect individual souls; they also include society-building elements, that is, practices and institutions tending to transform a collection of men into a social body. In most separated Churches, to give an example, Christian baptism is not only made available to those who desire it, but having inherited the tradition of infant baptism these Churches, in as much as they are societies, draw into the newness of life all children born into their community. Needless to say, the amount of society-building elements of authentic Christian origin varies enormously from Church to Church; but even for the separated Church which has retained very few of the social gifts of Christ, we must acknowledge that it is not simply a body perpetuating error, nor simply a mass of dissident Christians, but that it is, as a society, historically responsible for the continuity of a partial Christian tradition in the world.

This mysterious nature of the separated Church initiates among its members a process of spiritual recovery. If we assume for the sake of argument that at the time when the Church seceded from the See of Rome all its members committed the sin of schism, then the schismatic Church ceased to be an instrument of grace for all those who belonged to it. As time goes on, however, the children of the schismatics are baptized and instructed in Christian doctrine. Since they are quite unable to endorse the schism of their parents unless they are given an adequate understanding of the conflict, it is very likely that many of them receive the gifts of Christ in a spirit of perfect obedience. Many Christians of the new generation will be *dissidents*, not schismatics. As further generations pass, only the educated members will have access to the sources of the conflict, and hence be in a position to ratify the schism of their elders. Thus the schismatic Church, by reason of its divine heritage, is drawn into a process of recovery; while its external structure, including the errors on things divine, remains unaltered (or even suffers further harm!), its salvific function with regard to its members will be transformed. The isolated Church will continue to proclaim certain untruths, but it will cease to spread an atmosphere of resistance to Christ and his decrees, an atmosphere which extinguishes the Spirit; its spiritual climate will, in spite of the errors, be largely determined by a readiness to receive all of Christ. Because of their guiltless ignorance, dissident Christians who are members of such a body will have access to Christ through the sacraments and the preaching offered by their separated society. In a separated Church, we conclude, the sacramental and objective Christian elements outlast the schismatic intention of the wangling party and begin to produce a living, though wounded, Christanity among the succeeding generations.

This process of recovery within a separated Church does not contradict what we have said about the dynamism of error. The principle of dissention living at the heart of a separated Church will attack and often reduce the Christian legacy, and thus indirectly affect its members. But as long as a Christian means of grace does belong to the structure of a separated Church, it will have a direct influence on the new generation, on the children born into the community and, in the course of time, multiply those who find Christ by means of a partial tradition.

Christian communities severed centuries ago from the Catholic Church by movements of schism or heresy may be called 'schismatic' or 'heretical' if we derive the name from their evil origins. Such a connotation however would be misleading. It could be taken as a judgment on the present members of such a community, or at least as an indication that the process of recovery, active in the pale of a separated Church, is not really appreciated. The Roman documents of our period never speak of 'schismatic' or 'heretical' communities when they refer to Christian bodies separated centuries ago from the Catholic Church. They call them *dissident* Churches or communities (5). We shall remain faithful to this terminology which, we believe, is not without theological significance. It is true, the process of recovery does not affect the structure of such separated bodies, but it does create a new theological situation where great multitudes not knowing the genesis of their partiality have access to Christ through what appears to them as ecclesiastical traditions.

Can we draw a clearer picture of dissident Churches from the official Roman documents? Unfortunately our sources do not give us many references. One thing however is obvious; there is an enormous difference between Eastern and Western separated Christian communities. The Roman documents give the impression that the dissident communities of the East differ from those of the

West not only quantitatively (by having retained a greatere number of Christian elements) but even qualitatively (by being theological realities of a different order). This difference is symbolized by the names which our documents apply to these communities.

The Dissident Churches of the East

The documents of the Holy See normally refer to the separated Christian bodies of the East as 'Churches' (6). They are addressed as Churches, and as Churches they are asked to be reconciled to the Holy See. The dissident bodies of the West, on the other hand, are never thus called; they are designated by a variety of other names purposely chosen to avoid calling them Churches. They are spoken of as institutions, congregations, communities. In the body of papal literature we never find the term 'Church' used in the empirical or descriptive sense which we have so often employed in these pages; whenever the word 'Church' is used, it is done so advisedly with the full acknowledgment of its theological implications. Hence we must investigate why and in what sense the dissident Christian societies of the East are still 'Churches' in the eyes of the Apostolic See.

The Church of Christ being one, what do we mean by Churches in the plural? The one Church of Christ, the Church universal with its visible centre at Rome, is made up of local apostolic communities, of Churches, which are organically united under the supreme jurisdiction of the Roman bishop; we have explained this family character of the Catholic Church in our first chapter (7). Denoting both the universal and the local community by the same term 'Church' we are not introducing an equivocation, for the local apostolic Churches have the same essential structure as the universal Church. Now, when parts reproduce the nature of the whole, the name for the whole can be applied in strict analogy to these parts. Thus the term 'Church' in its proper and universal sense refers to the whole Body of Christ on earth, and in its proper and particular sense to the local apostolic communities which make up this Body. Hence there is no ambiguity when we say that the unique Church of Christ is made up of Churches.

Orthodox communities are not part of the Catholic Church; hence they are not Churches in the true sense. It is clear, moreover, that when the Roman documents ascribe to them a similarity to a Church, the comparison is made not with respect to the Church universal— which is numerically one and has no sisters—but with respect to a particular Church (such as the Church of Lyons) or to a group of Churches (such as the Church of France). In the eyes of Rome—if we understand our documents correctly—the dissident Churches of the East have retained enough of the Christ-given social and sacramental structure that they could be integrated into the Catholic Church as soon as they acknowledged papal primacy. Such a reconciliation would not add new ecclesiastical elements to the Eastern Churches, as would necessarily be added to a Protestant body returning to unity; their return to unity would merely heal and purify elements which they already possess (8). It is as Churches that they shall enter the Church universal. In this sense we understand the oft-repeated guarantee of the popes that by the restoration of unity the hierarchical orders of the Eastern Churches, their liturgies and their authentic traditions will not be touched (9). The dissident communities of the East have the structural perfection to become local apostolic Churches by a reconciliation with the See of Rome.

But we must go further in characterizing the separated bodies of the East. What we have said in the last paragraph is true of all schismatic bodies the very minute they leave the unity of the Church: they are severed, but reconcilable communities. We have not sufficiently taken into account that in our context we are speaking of Churches that have for many centuries undergone a 'process of recovery', of Churches to whose members Pius XI attributed collectively a sincere obedience to Christ and whose sacramental life he approved (10). We must investigate therefore more closely the similarity of dissident Eastern Churches to authentic ecclesiastical bodies.

The mission which Jesus Christ committed into the hands of the apostles, and through them to the whole Church can be divided into three offices, distinct though interrelated—the perpetuation of his own role as Prophet, Priest, and Lord. The Church perpetuates his prophetic office in her infallible magisterium, his priestly role in her sacramental life, and his pastoral power in her own spiritual government. Wherever these three offices are truly found, we have the presence of the Church of Christ. Thus they are fully embodied in every Catholic bishop and his Church in communion with the pope. We may add that in the order of application (and in this order only) pastoral power or jurisdiction is the primary element, since the Church teaches and sanctifies through her rightly appointed ministers.

As soon as a Church withdraws from the Roman communion, the schismatic bishops lose ecclesiastical jurisdiction. 'Bishops who deliberately secede from Peter and his successor, are deprived of the right and the power to rule' (11). Due to the interdependence of the three offices of the Church, the rupture of ecclesiastical communion throws the dissenting Church into complete disorder, authentic jurisdiction disappears, the teaching office of bishops loses its authority and the sacramental life becomes illicit and constrained, even when it is valid.

This however is not the present situation of Orthodox Churches. We have already emphasized the validity of their sacraments and the approval of their sacramental practices on the part of the popes. Certainly, dissident bishops have no ordinary jurisdiction. But for the sake of the sanctification of the multitudes, the Roman Church could grant a leased jurisdiction to dissident bishops for their flocks, a conditional jurisdiction producing its salutary effect as long as there is good faith. Has the Church such an intention with respect to the Eastern Churches? The question has been the object of many studies in recent years (12). No explicit statement can be found in the law books of the Church; but from her practical decisions in certain concrete cases (13) and from the nature of her mission in the world (14), most authors conclude that she tacitly concedes a certain jurisdiction to dissident bishops. There is, however, no perfect agreement on the extent of this leased jurisdiction. The majority of theologians who have studied the problem—and we include, as the most reliable witness, the Roman canonist A. Coussa (15)—are at one that for the internal *forum* the Church means dissident bishops to have a share in authentic jurisdiction: all sacraments are judged to be validly and licitly administered in the dissident Churches of the East, even those which require jurisdiction for validity. Serious doubts arise only as to whether a limited jurisdiction has been granted for the external *forum*, for that area precisely which concerns the dissident Church as a society. It seems to us that if the Church wishes to grant a certain jurisdiction for the sake of a healthier sacramental life, she will also concede the jurisdiction necessary to legislate for the protection and the right use of these sacraments. But whatever the judgment on a jurisdiction for the external forum, it is certain that the Church tacitly concedes *some* limited jurisdiction to dissident bishops, a jurisdiction which is derived and borrowed but, at the same time, real and of a certain permanence.

This leased jurisdiction, however limited, imparts to the separated Churches a new quality: it gives lawfulness and health to their sacramental life, and it grants a certain authority to their ecclesiastical magisterium (at least in regard to its sacramental doctrine). Dissident bishops, to be sure, are far from being ordinary pastors set over a Christian flock (16); on the other hand, they exercise certain offices, especially those related to the sacraments, equipped with authentic episcopal power. Thus considering the age-old 'process of recovery' and the tacit approval of the Roman Church, it seems that *the dissident bodies of the East are reconcilable communities enjoying a certain ecclesiastical life*. It is not unreasonable, then, when M. J. Le Guillou writes that Rome regards the Orthodox communities as *wounded Churches*, but as Churches none the less (17).

Attempting to characterize more precisely the nature of Orthodox Churches, Yves Congar suggests that they are Christian communities verifying imperfectly the quality of a local Church, imperfectly because they exclude the principles established by Christ to build up a universal Church which are the ultimate criteria of faith and ecclesiastical communion (18).

* * *

The dissident Churches of the West are never called 'Churches' in the Roman documents. Protestant communities, it is true, differ greatly among themselves; some of them have preserved so many elements of ancient Christianity that to all appearances they are true ecclesiastical bodies. If even to these latter the Roman documents will not concede the name of 'Churches', it is because their sacramental life is judged to be too incomplete, because they are not sacramentally linked to the apostolic succession of bishops; they have not retained enough of the Christ-given social structure to be reconciled to the Catholic Church by the sole submission to the bishop of Rome. Theologically speaking, the dissident Christian bodies of the West are not Churches.

On the other hand, what we have said about the mysterious nature of dissident Churches applies also to Protestant bodies: they too are responsible not only for the impediments to Revelation but also for its presence among men. Their Christian patrimony, incomplete as it is, also contains certain society-building elements (such as, for instance, Christian baptism) which render the social body capable of transmitting instruments of grace and of initiating a process of recovery in succeeding generations. On account of these society-building elements inherited from the Church, the Protestant community is more than a multitude of dissident Christians; it is a society which, in spite of its erroneous articles, is historically responsible for the regeneration of its members (in good faith). That this mediation of grace is historical and not formal, that is, not as such appointed by Christ, we shall see in the next chapter.

THE SUPERNATURAL GOOD IN DISSIDENT CHURCHES

The partial Christian patrimony, surviving in dissidence and perpetuated in a separated Church, embraces not only the means of grace borrowed from the Catholic Church, but also the fruits of grace among dissident Christians, their prayers, their spirituality, their holiness. That such gifts of Christ exist in separated Churches we have shown to be the judgment of our documents, but we must further investigate the attitude of the Roman Church towards the supernatural good found outside her canonical borders. Is the supernatural good in dissident communities a rival of the Catholic Church? Is the eucharistic liturgy celebrated in an Orthodox Church or the Christian fervour of the Ecumenical Movement a good which is lacking in the Church, and which consequently reduces her claim to uniqueness? The answer we find in our documents. The Church does not and cannot regard the manifestations of grace in dissident bodies as movements of competition; on the contrary, she rejoices at Christian vitality wherever it may be found.

The Church's attitude towards dissident Churches is double-valued: she approves and fosters what is born of grace and in a sense belongs to her, and she deplores and rejects the principles of error in which she can have no part. This attitude, we wish to stress, is not merely a theoretical judgment which remains on the level of theory; it is a practical conviction of which we find countless proofs in the documents of the Holy See. In our living attitudes to theological realities it becomes apparent whether our professed opinions correspond to our inner convictions, and it is in unguarded moments when the popes do not treat expressly of the Church's catholicity that they reveal their catholic heart which welcomes the advance of revealed religion wherever the Holy Spirit is pleased to blow, and which suffers at the decay of Christian elements, even if—humanly speaking—the Catholic community could profit by it.

In his letter to the English, Leo XIII praises them for their virtues, for their attention to social problems, for their educational system based on religious teachings (19). He rejoices that 'reflecting men have become disturbed at the influence of rationalism which weakens and paralyses religion', and that they 'fearlessly and unceasingly proclaim the rights of God and of Jesus Christ' (20). Moreover he is grateful for their observance of the Lord's Day and their reverence for Holy Scripture. What he deplores is the decay of religion, the waning of faith, and the widespread rejection of the Bible as the Word of God. The same note is struck in all the pronouncements of Leo XIII which touch upon Protestant Christianity: they lament the growing rationalism which attacks the written source of Revelation and seeks to destroy faith in Jesus Christ (21). When, on the other hand, in a new generation, the fidelity to the Holy Ghost in Protestant Christianity is waxing and producing fruits such as the Ecumenical Movement, the Roman letters do not hesitate to acknowledge the Church's joy (22).

Sometimes uninstructed Catholics are tempted to derive a certain satisfaction from the ruin of Christian elements in dissident communities; they love their Church, but they fail to realize that the supernatural values found in dissidence, far from militating against the Church, are really doing her work. We shall look in vain for any overtones of satisfaction in the Apostolic Letter *Apostolicae Curae* (1896) announcing the invalidity of Anglican Orders. If Leo XIII must reject their authenticity, it is only after a long investigation, 'showing the greatest consideration and charity to men of good will' (23), on the basis of the historical records. It would indeed be an un-Christian sentiment to derive joy from the disappearance of any sacrament; for reducing the presence of Christ among men must strengthen the power of darkness in the world. On the contrary, the Church is glad when dissident communities return to Catholic elements which they have long neglected. From the viewpoint of human calculation it might be argued that a great resemblance of dissident bodies to the Catholic Church could instill in dissidents a false satisfaction and retard their return to the Mother Church; from the viewpoint of faith, however, we know that a greater possession of Christian truth binds men more closely to Christ, and consequently to his Body. The Catholic Church gains by the recovery (if it is sincere) of true Christian elements in dissident Churches. The manifest love of Mary, the mother of Jesus, which we witness in many Protestant quarters (24) is sometimes not welcomed by unthinking Catholics; they consider it as an imitation of Catholicism to which Protestants have no right. The very opposite attitude is expressed by Pius XI: 'It is a cause of great consolation for us that in our day certain Protestant groups appreciate more deeply the dignity of the virgin motherhood of Mary, and feel drawn toward venerating and loving her' (25).

Even more effectively can we illustrate our principle with respect to the dissident Churches of the East. Far from considering their supernatural heritage as a rival of the sanctity of the Catholic Church, the popes rejoice at the manifestation of grace among the Orthodox and are worried about its decay. We shall single out two remarkable instances. Speaking about the sacred liturgies of the dissident Oriental Churches, Leo XIII designates them as 'a precious ornament of the whole Church' (26). The ancient divine liturgies, even if they existed only in dissident Churches, are considered not only as belonging in some sense to the Catholic Church, but even as accruing to her honour. Perhaps more conspicuous still is Pius XII's attribution of martyrdom to the persecution suffered by Orthodox Christians for the profession of their faith. It is accepted doctrine that there can be no martyrdom apart from the true Church, but so convinced is the Pope that all gifts of grace ultimately belong to the Church that he sees no contradiction in calling Orthodox Christians dying for their Lord martyrs of the Catholic Church (27).

The Church's attitude to dissident Churches, we have said, is not univocal but complex: she rejoices at the increase of authentic Christian values and deplores the falsification and corruption of the divine gifts. When the popes desire the return of dissident Christians to Catholic unity, they do not envisage a human victory over another party, but the unfolding of the gifts of Christ. Sometimes Catholic authors give the impression, at least by the tone and tenor of their writing, that the Church is a party against other parties, that the Catholic Church and other Christian bodies are societies with the sole difference that the Catholic Church is right and the others are wrong, and that consequently the stakes of the Church rise as the luck of the others falls. This dishonourable attitude is based on inadequate theological suppositions. The Church is not one religious society among others. Already in connection with her social framework, we remarked that the Church is a society *sui generis*, which is *in* this world without being *of* it. She is mother and universal mediatrix of salvation so that neither as society nor as teacher is she on a par with, or even comparable to other Christian bodies. Her attitude to dissident Churches is wholly based on faith. Being gifted with the universality of the cross, she can rejoice at the spiritual success of other Christians because it is her own success too.

From the practical attitudes of the popes we conclude: the Catholic Church does not lack the supernatural good found in dissident Churches. In the instruction *Ecclesia Catholica* we are told that dissident Christians returning to the communion of Peter 'do not contribute anything essential to the Church which had hitherto been lacking in her' (28). How can this be true? *While the supernatural values (the divine patrimony) dispersed in dissident Christianity await their re-entry into the Church, they already belong to her even in separation.* These values are not lacking in the Church; hence returning to their proper place in the visible community they do not add an essential perfection. Something, no doubt, is lacking to the Church with respect to the supernatural good living in separation; yet what is lacking to her is not the good existing among dissidents, but precisely that which is lacking to this good, namely its health.

Because the Church is the Body of the Lord, no supernatural perfection is lacking *in* her; yet something is lacking *to* her, namely all that is still unredeemed, still held by the powers of darkness (29). In our context this means that the perfection lacking to the Church is not the good in dissident Churches but exactly the measure to which this good is contaminated by error. It is not the liturgy of a dissident community which is lacking to the Church (it already belongs to her) but that which is wanting to this liturgy, namely, the taint of deception which prevents its complete integration into the Body of Christ. Hence on returning to their supernatural home, dissident Christians do not add or bring along to the Church an essential perfection. The wounded supernatural heritage which they bring with them will be purified in the unity of the mystical Body: this purification is the good which the dissident patrimony receives, and this is also the good which the Church receives.

If the Catholic Church has a function in separated Christianity, this task can never lead her to disregard authentic Christian elements; it can only intend the healing and completing of these elements in the unity of Christ's Body.

CHAPTER FOUR

CATHOLIC ECUMENISM: ITS FOUNDATION

'IN order to render perpetual the work of redemption, the eternal Pastor and Bishop of our souls decided to build a Holy Church in which . . . all the faithful would be united by the bonds of one faith and charity' (1). This introductory sentence of the dogmatic constitution *Pastor Aeternus* of the Vatican Council expresses simply and profoundly the function, the role, the *munus* of the Church in the salvation of mankind. Its purpose is to render perpetual the work of the Saviour. Jesus Christ, who accomplished universal redemption through his triumphant death on the cross, decided to reconcile the faithful to God by incorporating them into his Body; since according to divine providence not all men were to be contemporaries of the Saviour, he founded a Church so that, in it, he and his atonement might be present to all generations. Because of the intimate ties of grace and charity which unite the faithful to Christ their Head, the Church does not remain a passive instrument in the diffusion of divine redemption; it is rather a living organism of grace, reconciling the world to its Creator by an activity which is at once that of Christ and that of the Church. This function of the Church, this law of her being is, as we have seen, the continuation of the mission of the divine Son himself. 'As the Father has sent me, I also send you'. It is the mission of the Church—mission here is taken in a wide sense—to mediate the redeeming Christ, the one Mediator between God and man, to preach him so that he may be believed and to impart him so that he may be loved, in other words, to render him present in the world.

By her nature the Church is dynamic. 'The Church was born for no other reason than to extend the reign of Christ over the whole earth and to make all men participate in his redemption' (2). Her nature tends by its first motion, not to preserve and protect what has been gained for Christ, but to carry Christ ever farther into the world and to illuminate with his grace the regions where there is still darkness (3). By her very nature the Church is never at rest. She is in motion, not only with respect to the Last Day but also as regards Christ's kingdom on earth. She is the voice announcing Christ from

Jerusalem to the ends of the earth, and the hallower preparing an abode for him wherever he is not yet at home. This salvific mission of the Church manifests itself in different ways, that is, gives rise to various activities according to the different surroundings in which God calls her to work. When living in a Catholic community, her holy function will find expression in the *pastoral ministry* among the people; with respect to unbelievers it will give rise to her *missions;* and when considering her divine role with regard to severed Christians, it will produce an activity which we shall call—*ecumenical.*

In a study of the history and the use of the word 'ecumenical' W. A. Visser't Hooft gives, as the last one of seven meanings, the sense in which the word has been used in modern times: Ecumenical is 'the quality or attitude which expresses the consciousness of and desire for Christian unity' (4). This usage of ecumenical is certainly not of Catholic origin; it is never employed in the papal documents in this sense, except when they refer to the Ecumenical Movement. In recent years, however, the term has found favour with Catholic writers, and at present it seems to be in common use (5). Ecumenical being equivalent to favouring-Christian-unity, we call ecumenical the role of the Church with respect to divided Christianity. In this chapter we shall determine on what grounds the Church is called to an ecumenical action, and having derived its proper principle, we hope to come to a precise definition.

MISSIONS OR ECUMENISM

By ecumenism we understand the divine office of reconciliation entrusted to the Church as it manifests itself with respect to severed Christians. Does this ecumenism belong in the proper sense to the missions of the Church? Is it part of the Church's effort to redeem with the gospel of truth those who as yet live in darkness, or is it rather an activity *sui generis* seeking to bring to completion elements of divine Revelation which suffer from an unprovided and isolated existence? Is the aim of Catholic ecumenism simply the growth of the Church, its extension over new territory where Christ's gifts have not been received, or is it to purify and integrate into the unity of the Church all the gifts which Christ has cast into the world?

The question is an important one. On the answer will depend our attitudes, theoretical and practical, towards separated Christians. It will determine whether in our contact with dissident Christians we deliver our message of grace against a background of supernatural ignorance, as we do in missionary work among non-believers even

CATHOLIC ECUMENISM: ITS FOUNDATION 79

when we appreciate their natural wisdom; or whether ecumenical work consists in something quite different, in the delicate task of discovering what the Spirit of Christ has wrought in dissident Christian groups and of pointing to the perfection of these gifts in the Catholic Church. Sometimes non-Catholic Christians have the impression that the attitude which sees no essential difference between missions and ecumenism is the official position of the Catholic Church, that the Church seeks to 'absorb' all Christians into its fold without considering and valuing the spiritual gifts of which they may be heirs.

It cannot be denied that there are Catholic writers who consider the Church's task with respect to dissidents as part of her missions. These are the authors already mentioned in the last chapter who do not wish to acknowledge a supernatural patrimony among separated Christians; for them ecumenism equals proselytism. There are, however, other theologians for whom the ecumenism of the Church properly belongs to her missionary activity. Some of them believe that in the legislation of the Roman Church non-Catholic Christians are included among the people who are the object of her missionary work (6). Others conclude, in an attempt to define the theological concept of 'missions', that the 'material object of missionary activity is every region where a native Church has not yet been established in all stability' (7), and that consequently dissident Christian territory is also a mission field of the Church.

On the other hand, judging from the official Roman documents of our period, it is quite certain that the popes do not regard the ecumenism of the Church as a part of her missionary activity. In the extensive literature on missions published in the Acts of the Holy See, including papal writings as well as other official documents, there is not a single reference to separated Christians (8). Seeing that non-Roman Christians constitute a large section of the world population, it is unthinkable that the popes would be silent about them if they really considered them as belonging to the Church's mission field. On the contrary, it is always taken for granted and sometimes explicitly defined that the missionary task of the Church is 'to preach the truth of the gospel to pagan peoples', that it is 'the extension of the rule of Christ and his salvation to men who have not the faith' (9). The encyclical *Evangelii Praecones* teaches clearly that 'the proximate end of mission work is to bring the light of the gospel to new peoples and to gain new believers for Christ' (10). Certainly, the ultimate end of the missions is the firm establishment of the Church in a certain area, that is, the cessation of the mission with the beginning of the normal pastoral ministry (11). In this ultimate end missions and ecumenism concur; for both envisage, as the final end of their own proper activity, the fully established presence of the One Church.

In the official Roman documents of our period dealing with dissident Christianity—and they constitute a considerable bulk—there is never a suggestion that the concern for Christian unity belongs to the missionary activity of the Church (12). The documents employ a terminology which brings out the distinct character of ecumenical work; the work of reunion aims at a 'reconciliation', a 'restoration', a 're-integration', a 'return' of dissident Christian communities to the one fold of Christ. It envisages not a conversion to something new, but a return to a fullness once possessed, not an initiation into the Christian life, but the re-integration of wounded Christian traditions into the perfection of the Body of Christ. It is not a mere question of individuals; the severed Christian traditions themselves are to be healed and reunited to the Church of Rome. Hence ecumenism is not exclusively concerned with dissident Christians; even the Christians who are outside the Church in bad faith (schismatics and heretics) belong to the field of ecumenical action, since they also, in spite of themselves, are heirs and carriers of true elements of the Church.

We admit that our division of the Church's task into pastoral, missionary and ecumenical activity cannot be supported from present ecclesiastical legislation. The Codex of Canon Law divides the 'sacred missions' of the Church into two sections (can. 1349–51): home missions in countries where the Church is fully established, and foreign missions in non-Catholic territory. These latter are subject to the direct administration of the Holy See through the Congregation for the Propagation of the Faith (*Propaganda Fide*). This division, however, does not intend to teach theology. This is apparent when we consider that, according to the present *Codex*, non-Catholics living in Catholic areas are to be considered as under the care of the local ordinaries, while Catholics living in mission territory are subject to the *Propaganda* (13). That the legislation of the Church in this matter cannot be taken as a mirror of her diverse functions will be clear when we consider that until the year 1917, Roman Catholic Christians of Eastern rites—and the Church has never in her history been without non-Latin members—were subject to the administration of the *Propaganda Fide!* (14). If we want to understand how the Church regards her divine task in the world into which Christ has sent her, we must turn to other sources.

CATHOLIC ECUMENISM: ITS FOUNDATION

The Roman documents of our period keep in complete separation the Church's role among separated Christians and her missions properly so-called. They consider the world for which Christ died as divided into three areas: the Catholic Church, dissident Christianity, and finally the regions where Christ is not yet known. The twofold division which we saw suggested in the *Codex* is extremely rare in our documents. Usually the popes speak of three spheres: 'the children of the Catholic Church, those who differ from us in faith, and those who have no faith at all' (15). A famous sentence of Leo XIII, quoted verbally by Pius XI in his encyclical *Quas Primas* on the Kingship of Christ, gives us the formal doctrine. The Pontiff shows that according to biblical teaching Jesus Christ is King not only over the Church in which his rule is fully recognized and through which it becomes effective on earth, but that his kingship extends over the whole world. He writes: 'His kingdom extends not only over Catholic peoples (the Church), nor only over those who by holy baptism belong by right to the Church, though erroneous opinions keep them apart or disagreement severs them from fellowship (dissident Christianity), but it embraces also those who are devoid of the Christian faith (heathendom). Thus the whole of the human race is in all truth in the power of Jesus Christ' (16).

The kingdom of Christ then, which covers the whole earth, is conceived in three concentric circles: the innermost circle containing the Catholic Church in which the reign of Christ is joyfully acknowledged, the second circle marking off the separated Christians who follow Christ without recognizing his full kingship in the Church, and finally the outer circle spanning the world of unbelievers who are subject to Christ against their will or at least without their conscious consent.

This threefold division is not biblical. The New Testament knows only a bi-partition: Christ's sovereign rule over a willing Church and over an unwilling 'world' (17). As we have noted above, the phenomenon of dissident Christians is unknown to the New Testament writers; it does not enter into the normal economy of salvation which means to dispense the divine gifts in the fullness and security of the Church. The circular segment on our diagram which designates dissident Christianity is not a part of the established order of redemption; it is an anomaly which by right should not be there. Hence we believe that the threefold division which we have drawn does not contradict the essential partition, laid down in the New Testament, between the Church and 'the world'. In the thought of the popes dissident Christians are in union with the Church, by right belong to her, and have received an initial membership; thus, considering the human family as purchased and destined to enter the Body of Christ, there are only *two* cities of men, those who have not yet entered and who militate against it, and those who have entered either completely or initially.

In our day however the threefold division of mankind (18) which we find in the papal encyclicals remains necessary; without it, we cannot account for the present divided state of Christianity. In each of the three areas the Church has a proper and well-defined task: pastoral, ecumenical, or missionary. These activities are essentially one, when we consider their first principle (the mandate of Christ) and their ultimate end (the peace of Christ); they are however formally distinguished by their proximate principles and their proximate ends. These we must investigate further with reference to the Church's ecumenism.

THE CATHOLICITY OF THE CHURCH

'The Church is said to be "Catholic" because, extending over all peoples and through all times, she retains with greatest stability the unity of faith and communion' (19). The catholicity of the Church is the way of her unity; it is the unconfined and unconfinable character of the unity which is destined to embrace all peoples. Conversely, the unity of the Church is the mode of her universal vocation; it is the structure and social harmony of her catholicity which, for all its diversity, is built up as a body 'closely joined and knit together'. These two properties of the Church, her unity and her catholicity, qualify each other and neither of them can be defined adequately without the other. The unity of the Church is not that of any social body, nor is her catholicity the universality of an ideal. But both conjoined, as the catholic unity of the Church, represent the double quality by which the Christian community is fitted to embrace all men in the singleness of the gifts of Christ.

CATHOLIC ECUMENISM: ITS FOUNDATION

When delineating the Church's catholicity as found in the papal writings of our period, we shall have to repeat some of the remarks we made in reference to the Church's unity. This is not surprising. For the principle of both, the catholicity and the unity of the Church, is identical: it is the Saviour Jesus Christ who came to redeem the fallen children of Adam (catholicity) through his victorious death on the cross (unity). Since we have presented the unity of the Church by following two separate approaches, the unity of God's People and the unity of Christ's Body, we wish to adhere to the same method in depicting the Church's catholic nature. For just as the unity of the Church takes shape through the intention of Christ when founding his holy Church and proceeds from his unique and irrevocable sacrifice on the cross, so also is the catholicity of the Church the result of Christ's command to teach all nations and the fruit of his cross lifted up from the earth attracting all things. Lest we repeat ourselves beyond need, we ask the reader's permission to be brief.

The Catholicity of God's People

In a letter to the Chinese hierarchy Pius XI writes: 'The very name of "Catholic" or "universal" whereby we signify the Church shows that she belongs to all nations, that she must embrace all peoples, and that according to the divine will of her Founder Jesus Christ no distinction of race or class can be found in her' (20). The sovereign will of Jesus Christ, here as always, is the sole criterion of ecclesiology.

'When about to ascend into heaven, he sent his apostles in the power in which he had been sent by the Father, and he charged them to preach and spread his teaching. "All power is given to me in heaven and on earth. Go therefore and make disciples of all nations . . . teaching them to observe all that I have commanded you" (Matt. xxviii. 18–20) . . . Christ commanded his apostles "to preach the gospel to every creature" (Mark xvi. 15), "to carry his name before nations and kings" (Acts ix. 15), and "to be witnesses of him to the ends of the earth" ' (Acts i. 8) (21).

Materially the catholicity of the Church is based on the common situation of fallen man, the universal need of reconciliation. 'The mission of Christ is "to save what was lost", not some nations or peoples only but the whole human race without distinction of time or place' (22). Formally the catholicity of the Church is due to the universality of God's love, his unbounded will to save man. 'It is true that Christ has only one Bride, the Church; yet the love of the divine Bridegroom is so universal that in his Bride he embraces every member of the human race without exception' (23). It was this love which prompted the Lord to give command and power to the apostles so that, preaching the gospel from Jerusalem to the ends of the earth, they might found a holy People recruited from all parts of the world. The Church is catholic by reason of its vocation: it was called into being by a universal will to redeem a universal situation. It has received a structure, both social and interior, which by the superior form of its unity provides a home for every human being without vagueness and without violence. There can be no frontier where the Church has no access and no land where she is a stranger.

It is perhaps not necessary to point out that the catholic unity of the Church does not make her a totalitarian advocate of uniformity. The command and power of Christ from which she derives her universal character does not set out to subject men, to crush their liberty and dominate their thinking. On the contrary, the Church's catholicity preserves the diversity of gifts among nations, and guarantees the free scope of authentic traditions and values. Since her mission is to mediate grace, that is, to give a new and supernatural orientation to the totality of human life, she does not come to destroy but to fulfil. There is at the heart of the Church a very positive outlook on the world which is destined to be saved by Jesus Christ, and which he prepares for this grace by countless gifts. What else are the goodness, the virtues, and the talents of heathens if not the fruit of divine initiative? 'From the very beginning the Church has always followed the rule of wisdom that whatever is good, noble and beautiful in the character and mental gifts of various peoples shall not suffer loss or hindrance when they submit to the gospel of Christ' (24). 'Everything in the customs and usages of nations which is not inseparably linked to religious error must be considered with sympathy and if possible, protected and encouraged' (25).

The People of God is called to embrace all peoples in the freedom of its catholicity. 'Under the enormous vault of the Church there is room for the development of the special qualities, talents, tasks, and vocations which God the Creator and Redeemer has bestowed on individuals and on whole nations. The maternal heart of the Church is great and wide enough to see in the development, according to God's plan, of such proper qualities and special talents the richness of variety rather than the danger of isolation' (26).

CATHOLIC ECUMENISM: ITS FOUNDATION

The Catholicity of Christ's Body

Considering the Church as the Body of Christ, her catholicity will appear not so much the result of his command as the effect of his atonement on the cross. 'Through the outpouring of his blood given in ransom Jesus Christ freed all men without exception from the yoke of their sin. There is not a single individual who is to be excluded from the gifts of redemption' (27). On the cross the reconciliation of humanity to God the Father is achieved once and for all. On the cross the Church is in a sense fully established with all her members. 'It was on the tree of the cross that he purchased his Church, that is, all the members of his mystical Body; for they would not become united to that Body by baptism, were it not for the saving power of the cross on which they had already become in the fullest sense the property of Christ' (28).

In our first chapter we emphasized the completeness of redemption on the cross of Christ. The Church, we said, is *one* on the cross. But by the very principle by which she is one, she is also universal. If Christ's victorious death on the cross assures the unity of his followers—because they live from the same event—it also justifies the unbounded claims of the Church on the men of all ages. Jesus Christ crucified is the name by which all men are to be saved; there is no other source of salvation. In the Body of Christ wrought on the cross, fallen humanity is destined to find the healing of its wounds and the friendship of God.

We have spoken of the Church's call to catholicity. In the light of Christ's complete atonement on the cross this view is made more profound. The fullness of grace which Christ at that moment bestowed on his Body not only indicates that no man, no nation is to remain outside the Church but also demonstrates that there can be no area of human life, no depth of soul, no gift of character which fails to find purification and fulfilment in the Church. In the Church men are grafted onto Christ; they live from his life, and every expression of their supernatural vitality is fed from this divine-human source. The Church is in a sense the extension of Christ's humanity, and she is catholic precisely because the divine Word has espoused human nature without reserve, without reserve save sin. 'As the Son of God has assumed a true human nature, the Church likewise embraces all that is authentically human wherever and in whatever form she may find it, in order to lift it up to the source of supernatural power' (29). Raised up on the cross Jesus Christ draws all men towards himself. Through his Body, which he left on earth for this very purpose, the Lord radiates his saving influence into the humanity which he wants to sanctify. From the Church Christ's grace goes out into the world; and wherever it is received, it retains its ordination towards the Church. Christian grace is given on every occasion for the sake of drawing men more deeply into the Body of Christ, and even when it is bestowed outside the Church (30), it is a gift which is destined to achieve its fulfilment within her.

'Through this profound root (the invisible union of Christ and his Body) the Church is firmly fixed at the centre of human history as in a field moved and agitated by divergent forces, exposed to attacks which threaten her unity. Far from being shaken however, she unceasingly radiates her own proper life of integrity and unity by sending new forces into a torn and divided humanity, forces meant to heal and to reconcile, unifying forces of divine grace, forces of the Spirit, Unifier of men' (31).

God, the sole author of salvation, has made the Church the harbour of grace, its divine milieu. She is the *pleroma*, the fullness of him who fills all with all. The Church is catholic with the breadth and length and height and depth of the supereminent charity of Christ.

Two Aspects of Catholicity

We have promised to be brief, and hence this must suffice as an outline of the Church's catholic nature. It is usually said, and justly so, that the Church's missionary impulse is based on her catholicity (32). Being universal both by vocation and redemptive power, the Church is alive with a missionary zeal urging her not only to love all men with Christian charity, but to preach to them the Word of God and reconcile them in the grace of Christ. The catholic unity of the Church is said to be the *ratio formalis*, the essential foundation, principle, and justification of her missionary activity. On account of her divinely established universality the Church is not an intruder in new cultures and nations. On the contrary, it is her appointed task to redeem with her Christ-bearing voice all peoples, even the most remote human societies. The Church is missionary because she is catholic.

If her catholicity is the proper foundation of the Church's missions, what proper formal principle shall we assign to the Church's ecumenism? From the first section of this chapter we have concluded that in the documents of the Holy See missions and ecumenism are distinct movements; they concur in their ultimate aim of consolidating the One Church, but they differ in their proximate ends.

CATHOLIC ECUMENISM: ITS FOUNDATION

Missions and ecumenism then must have formal principles which are at least relatively distinct. Moreover we saw in Chapter 2 that separated Christianity, which is the milieu, the material object of the Church's ecumenism, is formally distinct from heathendom, the Church's mission field. Now a formal difference in material objects demands a proportionate difference in formal principles. We are thus obliged, if we wish to be consistent, to investigate carefully the catholicity of the Church, the generating motive of her whole expansive drive, in order to find in it the proper principles, at least relatively distinct, of her missionary and ecumenical activities.

The catholicity of the Church may be considered in two distinct ways. Since Christ has come into the world to save what was lost, the Church has a claim to universality with regard to the whole human family fallen in Adam. In her all sins are repaired and all virtues sanctified. Just as the veil of the temple was rent at the death of the Lord, so the barriers which separate nations and cultures must fall in the Church. We may speak of the catholicity of the Church *with regard to nature*, with regard to the whole of creation estranged from God. This catholicity is perhaps more evident when we think of the Church as God's People called and destined to embrace all human families. The Church's catholicity with regard to nature is the proper principle of her missionary activity; it justifies her claim to extend the kingdom of grace over the whole earth by preaching and mediating Christ to the unredeemed.

However there is another way of considering the Church's universality, an aspect which is more clearly revealed when we envisage the Church as the Body of Christ: it is her catholicity *with regard to grace*. What do we mean by this unusual terminology? Since Christ wishes to save mankind by grafting the redeemed into his living Body, the Church has a claim on all that is truly supernatural. Even if Christian grace is bestowed outside the community of Peter, it remains true that whatever is supernatural is in some definite way due to the Body of Christ and points in some definite way to fullness in that Body. Just as Christ is the anchorage of grace, so the Church is its harbour. Every gift of Christ is given with a view to the Church. Ultimately there can be no private Christians; they are all in the Church or on the way to her. The Church's catholicity with respect to grace motivates her claim on all that is of the order of grace, on all Christians, on their faith and their sacraments. Because she is catholic with the universality of the cross, she is not an intruder when she calls her separated sons to return to their origin. She is not a tyrant when she claims that by right they belong to her. She does not deck herself with stolen finery when she considers her own the ardent prayers and holy virtues of all Christians. Rather is she the ground in which all works of grace have their roots —and their harvest. If she is the new Eve cut from the side of the second Adam asleep on the cross, then she has a universality not only with respect to the whole of creation 'groaning and travailing in pain' (Rom. viii. 22)—catholicity with regard to nature—but also with respect to the whole of the supernatural order, 'the new creation in Christ' (Gal. vi. 15)—catholicity with regard to grace. This latter, we claim, is the proper foundation of the Church's ecumenism. Because the Church is the proper milieu of all the effects of grace, she is ecumenical (33).

We have noted that the word 'ecumenical' does not occur in the documents of the Holy See in the modern sense in which we apply it in these pages. Our sources use 'ecumenical' almost as a synonym of catholic. However it is not without significance that whenever Pius XI speaks of the 'ecumenical unity' of the Church, he refers to her universal character with respect to Oriental Christianity (34). Particularly in the encyclical *Ecclesiam Dei* he frequently appeals to the ecumenical unity of the Church, seemingly singling out that aspect of her catholicity by which she embraces all authentic Christian traditions and values in the freedom of a diversified unity. This we have called catholicity with regard to grace.

THE MOTHERHOOD OF THE CHURCH

The Church is catholic because Christ has entrusted her with a unique task towards the whole human family. By mediating the grace of salvation to men the Church extends the boundaries of God's People, engrafts new members into the mystical Body or, in another terminology, bears new children for Christ. The Church is mother. 'The Church of God, loving mother of the human family, embraces with perfect charity all men of whatsoever race or rank, and by prayer and effort provides for their salvation and happiness' (35).

The Church claims a universal motherhood. 'The Church is a mother, a real mother, a mother of all nations and individuals. Because she is a mother . . . she belongs equally to all, she can in no place be a stranger; she lives in all nations or at least should do so according to her vocation' (36). The Church is mother, we conclude, on exactly the same theological footing that she is catholic.

However, this universal sense of the Church's motherhood is comparatively rare in the papal documents: for with respect to unbelievers the Church is mother only potentially, not in actual fact. They are as yet children unborn, nay, unconceived; the Church has not given them of her own new life (37). Hence with much greater frequency does the Church call herself mother in the strict sense, with respect to Christians, that is, with respect to those men to whom she has actually given life through the gospel and the sacraments of Christ. In countless passages we find references and even eloquent descriptions of the Church's maternal role in bringing forth and protecting the life which Christ brought in abundance; we read of the new birth in her baptism, of the life of faith engendered by her infallible testimony, and of the increase of life at her sacramental fountains (38). Since all the means of grace were entrusted to her, she must be called the mediatrix of all grace.

Lest we be misunderstood, we repeat what we have emphasized in the first chapter: the Church is mediatrix not by interposing herself between the Christian and his Lord, by acting as it were as a go-between; rather does she mediate Christ by rendering him present. He is the sole source of supernatural life, but it is by her divine 'signs', the message and the sacraments, that he becomes our contemporary as Lord and Saviour. Hence Pius XII can write, 'Under God, we owe everything to the Church, our mother' (39).

THE CHURCH, MOTHER OF DISSIDENTS

When the popes call the Church mother of Christians, 'mother and mistress of all the faithful' (40), they do not exclude the dissidents; on the contrary, in many contexts they specifically include them. They are her sons, albeit wayward sons. As such they are recalled 'to the common mother of all' (41), 'to their afflicted mother, the sole mediatrix of grace' (42). The Church 'awaits them not as strangers but as sons who return to their own paternal home' (43). To dissident Christians this is, perhaps, not an appealing thought; they do not enjoy being taken under the wing of the Catholic Church. However, the universal mediation which we attribute to the Church does not produce a patronizing attitude towards dissident Christians. It gives rise to an *ecumenical attitude* which we shall describe on a later page.

What exactly is meant by calling the Church the mother of dissidents? Is this merely a figure of speech referring to the historical derivation of dissident Churches from the Catholic Church, in the way in which England may be called the mother of the United States? Or does it signify a real relationship in the present? Do the popes wish to imply that dissident Christians have received their gifts of grace through the Catholic Church? When speaking of the Church's catholicity with respect to grace, we said that every supernatural gift is bestowed by God because of, and for the Church. This is the order established by Christ on the cross: to draw all men into his Body. Now our question goes further. We must investigate whether even in the concrete historical order the supernatural life of dissident Christians is derived from, or visibly mediated by, the Catholic Church.

According to the teaching of our Roman documents, Jesus Christ committed into the hands of the Church *all* the means of grace. 'If he had wanted, he could have bestowed the abundance of his graces directly on the human race; but actually he willed to do so by means of a visible Church' (44). 'To the Church he entrusted *all the means* to lead men to their eternal salvation' (45). The Body of Christ holds the life-giving sacraments and the redeeming message. It is through this Body that men receive Christ.

The Sacraments

The unique mediation of the Church is obvious for the sacraments. According to the biblical account, the apostles were commissioned to baptize those who believed on their word, and to break the bread which was to unite them into one Body. From the beginning these Christian rites belonged to the Church. The sacraments were given, not to individuals or Christian groups, but to the whole mystical Body in order to increase its life in God and its likeness to Christ the Head. 'By endowing it with sacraments, the Saviour of the human race wonderfully equipped his mystical Body with the means of fostering the life, growth and health of the members' (46).

The sacraments belong to the Church and her life, even when they are administered outside of her fold. It is she who regenerates to the life of grace when a Protestant minister validly baptizes; for the command 'to baptize in the name of the Father and the Son and the Holy Ghost' was given to her. It is she who is present at the Eucharistic mysteries celebrated by an Orthodox congregation; for the words 'Do this in commemoration of me' were said to her alone. It is the voice of the Church which is heard at the absolution given by a dissident priest; for to her it was said 'Whose sins you shall forgive, they shall be forgiven'. So much is the Church in possession of the sacraments that she can legislate and at times does legislate about their use in dissident Christianity (47).

It is a magnificent thought that the Church saves even where she is not acknowledged. She is invisibly present at every baptismal font, and it is her membership which is conferred on the baptized. As the sign which Christ gave to the Church is re-enacted, he himself produces the gift; he initiates into the life of grace and impresses an indelible mark, the mark of the Church, through which the Christian is qualified to participate in her worship and her sacramental life. In the strictest sense, the Church is the mother of all the baptized.

Holy Scripture

Of equal, if not of greater importance, however, is the question whether the Church can be called the mother or mediatrix of the living faith accessible to dissident Christians. On the one hand, it seems that through the faith which comes from hearing, dissident Christians have a life-giving relationship to Christ which is not communicated by the Church; on the other hand, our documents teach us that *all* the means of faith belong to the Church. How are we to understand this?

'The Holy Ghost communicated to the Church the fullness of truth. His ever-present assistance guards her from falling into error, and enables her to develop and make fruitful unto salvation the seeds of divine doctrine . . . Therefore no further and fuller manifestation or revelation of the divine Spirit can be thought of or expected' (48). The Church has been given to preach the whole of Revelation with a divinely protected voice. First Christ introduced her into the truth which he heard from the Father (cf. John xv. 15), and then he sent his Holy Spirit to teach her all truth (cf. John xvi. 13). Because the Lord remains with his Church until the consummation of the world, her testimony cannot fail. She is the appointed prophet of Christ's gospel. In her we encounter divine Revelation together with the arguments pointing to faith (*motiva credibilitatis*) and the authentic interpretation of the message. Since faith comes from hearing, no man can come to a saving knowledge of Jesus Christ except through the witness of the Church to the Word spoken by God.

That the faith of Orthodox Christians is born from the preaching of the Church is easy to see, when we consider that they receive as authentic the testimonies which fully expressed the Catholic faith for many centuries: Holy Scripture interpreted by the faith of the Christian community, the early Councils and the ancient liturgies. But we must investigate how the faith accessible to Protestants who accept from the Church only the Bible is mediated by the prophetic witness of the apostolic community.

Divine Revelation is an act of God, or, from the human point of view, a series of acts in which God sovereignly intervenes in history for the salvation of men. It is the Word of God, spoken fully in Jesus Christ, which lives on in the Church and is faithfully echoed in the prophetic transmission of God's People. This 'supernatural revelation is, according to the belief of the universal Church, contained both in unwritten traditions and in written books. These books are called sacred and canonical because "being written under the inspiration of the Holy Ghost they have God for their author and as such have been delivered to the Church" ' (49). Thus the Bible divinely inspired is posterior to the Church and her testimony. The books of the Bible were written for the Church, for the community of Christians who had already found faith through the preaching of the apostles. The books of the New Testament then were not written into empty space, or to groups of unbelievers, but rather to Christian congregations with a creed and a liturgy. Hence the Bible's inspired and consequently inerrant teaching must be understood against the background of the living faith of the Church. In her alone can Scripture be understood according to the mind of its Author. 'Writers without the true faith only know the bark of Scripture and never attain to its pith' (50). Only in the Church is the Bible in the full sense the Word of God.

However, the Bible is not simply a supplement to the Church's preaching. 'This treasure handed down from heaven', writes Pius XII in reference to Scripture, 'is the precious source and divine norm of the Church's doctrine on faith and morals' (51). Catholic tradition centres about the holy books as its source and norm, elucidating their teaching as held in the consciousness of the believing community, and safeguarding the true interpretation which alone conveys the mind of the Author. The Bible is the record of the Church's preaching; but the Church has not produced it. With respect to Scripture the Church is not mistress but guardian (52). She cannot touch it; she can only hand it down and explain its meaning. In the Bible the Church has an instrument of grace resembling in a certain sense her sacraments. The Bible is a sign announcing salvation, a sign handed by God to the Church, a sign communicating the Word of God unto salvation, not through the faith and witness of a human author but through the inspiration of the Holy Spirit. The Church passes on the Bible as the sacrament of her doctrine. 'Dissident Christians should not forget that they have received both Testaments from the

Church, and from nowhere else. It must be ascribed to her vigilance and perpetual care that the holy books have come down to us intact through the vicissitudes of times and events' (53). Protestant Christians, then, are dependent in their faith on the Church's witness to Holy Scripture, and on her guardianship of the holy books.

'The Church has always retained and exercised the guardianship conferred upon her by God for the protection and the glory of his holy Scriptures' (54). In our period, the interventions of the Roman magisterium abound, aiming to protect the integrity, inerrancy, and divine authorship of Scripture. In a wider sense, however, the Church acts as guardian of Scripture in every doctrinal decision, for it is with the infallible help of Catholic doctrine that we understand what God has revealed in his Scriptures. The Bible is not a book that can be understood by itself; it can be understood only through the testimony of the Holy Ghost which the Lord has communicated to the apostles, and through them to the whole Church. Christian doctrine is not contained in Scripture like a theorem in its premises; it cannot be extracted by human intelligence alone. If a doctrine is made known in the sacred text, a spiritual insight is very often necessary—an insight supplied by God through the prophetic organ (magisterium) of his Church—in order to elucidate the divinely-intended meaning among several possible interpretations. Hence the Church's guardianship over Scripture cannot be confined to the material protection of the single books; it includes practically the whole of her infallible magisterium which guards the true meaning of the biblical Revelation by supplying a divine commentary (Catholic dogma).

Protestant Christians, therefore, receive from the Church much more than a canonical collection of sacred books. They are dependent in their faith on the Church's guardianship, in the wide sense, over the Scriptures; to a large, though incomplete extent they receive the Bible in the light of Christian tradition. Even if the Reformers pretended to judge Christian doctrine by Scripture alone, in actual fact they interpreted the biblical testimony on the central Christian mysteries (the Trinity and the Incarnation) in accordance with ecclesiastical tradition. With a happy inconsistency they accepted the clarification of the scriptural texts given by the early Councils, and this not only in regard to doctrine but even as to the terminology employed (55). Protestant Christians receive the Bible in a Christian setting inconsistently abridged; they receive the Bible somewhat as they receive baptism, as an instrument of faith established by God, the full significance of which only becomes apparent in the authentic life of God's holy People. If they separate themselves from this tradition and interpret the books of Scripture on a rationalistic basis, the Bible becomes a closed book to them, in which they do not find him to whom every page gives testimony.

* * *

We conclude that the Church, with reference both to the living faith and the sacraments of grace, is the mother of dissident Christians. Not only has she a claim on all the effects of grace, as we have pointed out in connection with her catholicity, but she herself has been God's instrument in producing them. The supernatural exists in the world through her mediation. Hers are all Catholic Christians, and hers is all that is of grace in separated Christianity.

It is clear however that the Church's motherhood with respect to her dissident sons is only partial. It was not she who generated the seed of dissention which continues to live in their hearts. If it did not sound so theatrical in English, we could speak of the Church's 'forsaken motherhood' with respect to dissident Christians. '*Mater derelicta*' (56) she is neither to pagans nor to Catholics; it defines her specific role in separated Christianity, in that anomalous region which is attached to the Church but which does not belong to her. It is this motherhood of the Church which, specifying and developing what we have called her catholicity with regard to grace, must be called the proper principle or foundation of her ecumenical activity.

A remarkable confirmation of our conclusion we find in the role which is assigned to Mary, the mother of Jesus, in the documents of the Holy See.

A NOTE ON OUR LADY

According to Catholic faith, Mary is the mother of Christ, mother of the whole Christ, of the Head and the members (57). While she gave birth physically to Jesus, the Son of God, she is spiritually the mother of all Christians, by reason of her first consent—'be it done unto me according to thy word'—and of the part she was called upon to play in the atonement of her Son—'and even thy soul a sword shall pierce, that the thoughts of many may be revealed'. Mary is mother—'Son, behold thy mother'—in a way that recalls the motherhood of the Church. Christ lived in Mary, his mother, just as he lives in the Church: in order to be given to the world as Saviour. Mary is a type, an image of the Church; she embodies and anticipates the Church's task with respect to a world awaiting redemption. Now just as the motherhood of the Church extends to separated Christians,

CATHOLIC ECUMENISM: ITS FOUNDATION

at least to the extent that they belong to Christ, so we also find Mary in our documents as the mother of all Christians in dissidence. This is a point which deserves our attention as an unexpected confirmation of our argument.

While the popes set great store on the Marian piety of the Orthodox Churches as a link which binds them to the Church of Rome, they are equally aware that the veneration of the mother of Jesus is a stumbling block for the majority of Protestant Christians (58). It is true that in recent years a more positive outlook on Mary has developed in many Protestant quarters, and that there are not only Anglicans but also Lutherans and Calvinists who do not want to withhold their praise from her who prophesied, 'All generations shall call me blessed'. Nevertheless to some Catholics it may seem more prudent to observe a comparative silence about Mary in order not to confuse Protestants and thus delay the hope for a *rapprochement*. There are certainly more central aspects of the Christian faith which deserve our attention. Such a silence need not necessarily imply a reprehensible dogmatic compromise; it could be prompted by the recognition that some forms of Marian piety are largely determined by a popular inclination proper to a particular culture, and in no way oblige the universal Church. To gauge the true mind of the Church in matters of devotion and piety we have her official prayer, the liturgy (59).

Before our Lady's Assumption was defined in 1950 as being contained in the revealed Word of God, there were many Catholic writers who were opposed to the definition; they feared that speaking about Mary with so much precision would widen the breach between Christians. Humanly speaking they were undoubtedly right; to this the consequent literature bears ample witness (60). And yet in the dogmatic letter which defined and announced Mary's Assumption into heaven we read—with surprise perhaps—that one of the reasons for the solemn definition was an ecumenical concern of the Pope. 'The definition gives rise to the hope that all who glory in the name of Christ will experience an increase of desire to participate in the mystical Body of Christ, and a growth of love towards her who has a maternal heart for all members of this exalted Body' (61). What are the reasons which would justify such an expectation? The passage we have just quoted, we may add, is no isolated example. There is hardly a papal document dealing with the reunion of Christendom which does not express the confidence that Mary will bring healing to the divided followers of her Son (62). This constant emphasis on Mary's prayer for Christian unity is theologically significant.

The encyclical *Adjutricem Populi* (1895) of Leo XIII explains in detail Mary's relationship to dissident Christians: Mary is the mother of all Christians, and she remains the mother of those who have left the unity of the Church. Since it was her vocation to bear Christ to the world, it continues to be her mission to generate by her intercession 'other Christs' in the world, brethren of her first-born Son. More than that, wherever Mary sees the traits of her Son obscured in the face of a Christian, she intercedes that he may be drawn again into greater likeness to Christ. According to the letter *Adjutricem Populi*, Mary's concern is not merely the holiness of individual Christians; her main intercession is for the unity and perfection of the whole mystical Body. Unity among Christians is the great cause of prayer for which Christ has appointed his mother. She intercedes, we are told, 'that the good of unity which is the wonderful fruit of her maternity may be led to perfection in the Christian family' (63).

We shall cite a passage which summarizes the whole encyclical.

'To intercede for the cause of our separated brethren belongs in the most proper sense to the function of Mary's spiritual maternity. Mary has given birth to all those who belong to Christ, and she was able to bear them only in the unity of faith and love. "Christ is not divided!" (1 Cor. i. 13) In this fellowship therefore we all must live the life of Christ in order to "bring forth fruit for God" (Rom. vii. 4) in one and the same Body. As a mother blessed by God with the perpetual fruitfulness of a holy posterity, Mary has the task of bearing as it were again for Christ all those whom hapless circumstances have torn from the unity of the Church' (64).

In this passage we could replace 'Mary' by 'the Church', the representative by the reality she embodies, without detriment to the meaning. From Mary's part in the kingdom of God we can discern the maternal function of the Church.

This is the doctrine which causes the popes to speak of Mary in connection with Christian unity, even if humanly speaking a cautious silence might be more effective. They realize that in the last resort Christian unity is the gift of God and not the product of human diligence; it belongs to the order established by Christ on the cross. To further the triumph of the Lord born of the Virgin Mary, they judge, we must venture to proclaim the uncurtailed folly of the cross and not be silent about the human roots of divine salvation.

The role of Mary as mother of separated Christians, concerned about their return to unity, is a confirmation of our thesis that the Church has a function *sui generis* with respect to separated Christianity, which is formally distinct from her missionary activity. The motherhood of Mary, as we have described it from our documents, demonstrates in a new way the initial membership of dissident Christians in the Catholic Church, and the Church's maternal task of bringing to fulfilment the supernatural gifts which they have already received from her.

CATHOLIC ECUMENISM

So far we have defined Catholic ecumenism only with reference to its milieu. We have said that it was the office of reconciliation entrusted to the Church with regard to dissident Christianity. Having in this chapter determined the proper principle of ecumenism, we are now in a position to define more precisely in what Catholic ecumenical action formally consists. After two remarks on the final and efficient causes of ecumenism, we shall attempt a strict definition of ecumenical action in the language of the schools. Must we apologize for this rigour? It is true, such a formal language reducing reality to the bare essentials does not tell us a great deal about the *exercise* of Catholic ecumenism—to this we shall come in the next chapter—but we must have recourse to a strict definition in order to place the ecumenical role of the Church in its ecclesiological context.

The Catholic Church recognizes the conflict going on in the heart of dissident Christianity between the divine patrimony of grace tending towards Catholic fullness and the principles of error seeking to corrupt the good seed. Confronted by this situation the Church cannot remain silent. She must offer her assistance in the effort to bring to perfection the divine heritage and to dispel the aberrations. With respect to the Christian situation in England, Leo XIII gives the following principle: 'Nothing should be left untried that may tend to avert injury to souls (the elimination of error) or favour their advance (the fostering of the good seed)' (65). If the wounded heritage of grace surviving among dissident Christians can be brought to its authentic perfection, it will impel them towards the Catholic Church; and conversely, if the influence of error existing among them can be abated, the infected traditions will return by their own tendency to full health in the Catholic Church. *We define therefore Catholic ecumenism as the Church's appointed function in severed Christianity which consists in fostering towards perfection the wounded Christian patrimonies in dissidence and in reducing towards elimination the human falsifications associated with them.* Catholic ecumenism aims to help in the victory of grace among separated Christians (66). It seeks to foster the healing of all Christian elements in isolation; and because the perfect health of partial Christian traditions can only be found in the unity of Christ's Body, ecumenical action is a work of reunion.

The last end of ecumenism is the return of separated Christians to the Church of Christ, that is, to the Roman Catholic Church; about this there can be neither doubt nor difficulty in the mind of a Catholic. It is part of his faith; it is part of his faith that the Church is the unique home of all Christians. This does not mean however that the ecumenical effort of Catholics aims at converting dissident Christians as a missionary intends to convert his listeners. Ecumenism is not missionary action; we have established at length the formal difference between the two. Missionary work is exercised in a milieu of supernatural ignorance (even when grace has been bestowed prior to Christian preaching), and since there is no middle ground between unbelief and Christian faith, the progress made by a missionary prior to conversion is of no supernatural value: if he fails to convert, his preaching does not communicate the life which the Lord has brought. The ecumenical witness of the Church, on the other hand, is delivered in a milieu which is spiritually alive, and every step leading to perfect reconciliation implies a greater abundance of supernatural life. Hence if by her effort (be it no other than her prayer), the Church can help separated Christians to take a single step towards Christ or to throw off a single fallacy, she is fulfilling her ecumenical role in a fruitful way. Ecumenical work does not aim at drawing dissident Christians into the Church irrespective of their spiritual situation; it aims rather at curing their wounded life towards full integration into the Church. If the *ultimate* end of ecumenism is the return of all Christians to the Catholic Church, this must be reached through the *proximate* end, the gradual healing of the isolated gifts of Christ.

We wish to be very clear on this point, which is an issue of primary importance. The proper final end of ecumenism is the return of separated Christians to the Catholic Church. But this return is not a conversion from death to life (as is the aim of missionary work), but the purification and unfolding of the divine gifts surviving in separation. If we wish to be faithful to our principles, we are not free to regard dissident Christians simply as individuals outside the unity of the Church; we must look upon them in the light of theology, and thus consider them as heirs of a partial Christian tradition. Ecumenical action aims to contribute to the healing growth of these severed Christian patrimonies. It is far removed from proselytism or 'convert-making'. Certainly, the popes frequently invite dissident Christians to return to the Church from which they have sprung; certainly, also, the Church receives with great joy any Christian who finds his way back to her; certainly, in fine, it is a Christian duty to become a member of the Catholic Church as soon as one recognizes the will of Christ concerning his Body—nevertheless ecumenical action *formally* aims at the healing of the isolated gifts of Christ in the hearts of dissidents. This does not exclude conversions to the Catholic Church; on the contrary, it looks forward, ultimately, to the return of whole traditions to the Church of Christ. But formally and in the proper sense, the immediate aim of ecumenism is the assistance offered to dissident Christians (even if it be only by prayer) in leading to perfection the heritage of grace and in eliminating the seed of error. *Ultimately* it aims at reconciliation; *immediately* it aims at healing in whatever degree is possible.

The final end of ecumenism, the perfect reconciliation of Christians, is the ideal for a distant future; 'God alone knows the hour of his gift', writes Leo XIII (67). A long and arduous way must be traversed before such a reunion becomes a real possibility. The proximate end of ecumenism concerns precisely this *way*. The last end is hidden in the inscrutable providence of God, but the proximate end is within our reach: to help towards the healing of displaced Christian patrimonies. In the terminology of our documents this proximate end of ecumenism is *munire viam*, to pave the way or prepare the road for an eventual reconciliation (68). Ecumenical progress is 'a journey' (69), a 'gradual process' (70); it is to produce among dissident Christians 'an adherence to the Church of increasing closeness' (71), 'a growing desire to participate in the Body of Christ' (72). The ecumenical task is to 'foster' and 'make easier' the ultimate return of Christians to the Catholic Church (73). Pius XII prays that 'the way which divine Providence maps out for the Western world may lead *more and more* towards the lost unity' (74).

This is the perspective in which most Catholic ecumenical writers see the Church's effort for Christian unity. Lambert Beauduin writes: 'We must regard the question of reunion as the Jews regarded the coming of the promised Messias. Their religion consisted in expecting and preparing his coming, not in seeing or experiencing it' (75). The proper ecumenical task is to increase the adherence of dissident Christianity to the Church—to foster full integration (76).

The right understanding, therefore, of ecumenism lies between two errors. On the one hand, there is an eagerness to convert dissident Christians to the Catholic Church without respecting what is holy and of divine origin in their midst—Pius XI warned us of 'an immoderate zeal which will increase rather than diminish the resentment of dissidents with its harmful effect on souls' (77)—and on the other hand, there is indifference about the salvation and sanctification of dissident Christians—'We must run to meet them', wrote Leo XIII (78). This middle position does not make ecumenism a calculating thing; it knows a tremendous zeal born of the universality of Christ's gift. The Church is not free to look upon ecumenical action as a work of supererogation: it is an essential part of her divine mission. The work for the reunion of Christians, we read, 'is divinely committed to the Church' (79).

The whole task of reconciliation committed to the Church rests on her apostolic hierarchy. Jesus Christ wanted to link his gospel and his saving action to an apostolic body, infallible and indefectible, so that through its succession in time his own redemptive work might be perpetuated throughout history. All work in the Church for the salvation of souls is an extension of her apostolic mission; either it is in some way the radiation of her hierarchy, or it is not authentically derived from Christ. This principle must also be applied to Catholic ecumenism: it is an action proceeding in some way from the hierarchy. 'The work of reunion belongs above all to the office and the charge of the Church. Hence it behoves bishops, whom "the Holy Ghost has placed to rule the Church of God", to bestow upon it their special attention' (80). But even if the charge is necessarily exercised by bishops, it is not confined to them; together with them and under their direction, it is the work of all Christians, in proportion to their role and vocation in the Church.

In the Church of to-day the apostolic hierarchy is ordinarily no longer in direct contact with the groups to whom the Church brings Jesus Christ. In areas where the Church is fully established, the immediate ministry is exercised by pastors and their assistant priests, in mission territory the task of evangelizing is entrusted to special missionaries. The same custom prevails in the ecumenical action of the Church. The immediate contact with dissident Christians is rarely established by bishops; usually the work is assigned to priests who have a specialized theological training. In fact, the instruction *Ecclesia Catholica* encourages bishops to appoint priests in their dioceses to study the whole movement for

CATHOLIC ECUMENISM: ITS FOUNDATION 101

Christian unity carefully and to acquire the scholarship which will qualify them to take part in ecumenical discussions with other Christians (81). These theologians we shall call 'ecumenists'; it is they who exercise in a special way the ecumenical role of the Church. Through them, we may add, the Catholic Church participates in the Ecumenical Movement, even if she does not take part in it officially through her hierarchy.

We are now in a position to give a precise definition of Catholic ecumenism as we have derived it from the principles set down in the documents of the Holy See. Ecumenism is part of the essential mission of the Church to reconcile the world in Christ. It is addressed to dissident Christians in as much as they are heirs of partial Christian traditions. Catholic ecumenism is the Church's function in dissident Christianity (material cause), proceeding from her catholicity or more specifically from her spiritual maternity (formal cause) and directed at least remotely by the apostolic hierarchy (in the line of efficient casuality), which aims at healing the wounded patrimonies of grace (proximate final cause) with a view to integrating them ultimately into the One Church (ultimate final cause).

The effect which ecumenical action has on the Church herself we shall discuss in the next chapter.

CHAPTER FIVE

CATHOLIC ECUMENISM: ITS EXERCISE

IT is the purpose of our study to extract from the recent documents of the Holy See a theological view of the unity and disunity of Christians. We have tried to remain close to the papal writings; and whenever we went beyond their explicit teaching we have done no more than give an interpretation of their attitudes or draw conclusions from their principles. In this way we have derived our concept of the Church's ecumenical role. Many pertinent things in connection with Christian unity which are current in Catholic ecumenical literature we have left unsaid, not because we believe them to be at variance with papal doctrine, but simply because they would lead us beyond the restricted purpose of this study, which is a theological interpretation of the Roman documents. To this method we shall be faithful in our last chapter, on the exercise of Catholic ecumenism. It is not our intention therefore to give an historical account of the Roman attitude towards the various reunion movements of the past, nor to list the official approbations and condemnations of the methods employed by Catholics in furthering the cause of Christian unity. Our purpose is to present a theological characterization of ecumenical action. Unfortunately—and this is a difficulty for which there is no solution—our sources do not supply us with enough material to develop a complete doctrine. Since we do not want to fill in the silence of the papal letters by independent developments, save the immediate conclusions from principles established so far, we must confine ourselves to a few remarks on ecumenical action, on its means and their theological quality.

THE ECUMENICAL WITNESS

The principal exercise of Catholic ecumenism is the *ecumenical witness* of the Church, supported and paralleled by the *ecumenical charity* of all Christians. We shall show that this ecumenical witness, given as it must be outside the World Council of Churches, is inspired and determined by a characteristic attitude which, in spite of its faith in the unique and visible Church of Christ, resembles

CATHOLIC ECUMENISM: ITS EXERCISE

from many points of view the ecumenical intention of other Christians. But it is only on the level of charity that the ecumenical efforts of all Christians, Catholic and non-Catholic alike, move along identically the same lines.

THE WORLD COUNCIL OF CHURCHES

Since by her witness the Catholic Church intends to assist all Christians in the discovery of the given unity of God's people, we may ask why she does not officially participate in the Ecumenical Movement as it is embodied in the World Council of Churches. Is there a dogmatic obstacle, or is the refusal merely a question of pastoral prudence? (1)

Catholic participation in non-Roman ecumenical movements has been condemned by the Church several times. On two occasions we are given a detailed account of the reasons which prompted the ecclesiastical decision. There is first of all the set of letters of the Holy Office, composed in the years 1864 and 1865 and published again in the *Acta Apostolicae Sedis* of 1919, forbidding Catholics to join the 'Association for the Promotion of the Unity of Christendom' (2). The reasons given are dogmatic: the Association is based on an ecclesiology which is incompatible with Catholic faith. According to the Roman letters, the underlying theory of the Association recognizes the Church of Christ as existing in three Catholic bodies, Anglican, Roman and Greek, which are united in charity, the essentials of faith and an ecclesiastical tradition, while they remain structurally distinct. The second indictment is the encyclical *Mortalium Animos* (1928) forbidding Catholic participation in the Ecumenical Movement of the late twenties. Again the reasons put forward are dogmatic. According to the encyclical, the basis and underlying conviction of the movement was an ecclesiology which denied that the Church of Christ is a unique and visible society in history. 'The Church, they say, is by her nature divided into sections, that is, she is composed of several Churches and distinct communities which remain separate and apart from certain agreements teach different doctrines' (3). Both movements then, according to the judgment of our documents, stood for principles which are in contradiction to the divine constitution of the Catholic Church.

These condemnatory judgments as they stand do not apply to the Ecumenical Movement of to-day as it is represented in the World Council of Churches. The Council denies that it holds a particular doctrine on the nature of the Church. Its sole basis is the common faith in Christ, God and Saviour (4). On the witness of the New

Testament, the Council believes that Christ has called into existence a Christian Church, and it intends to be an instrument for advancing the reunion of separated Churches in the One Church of Christ. The Council recognizes that unity has been given once and for all in Jesus Christ, and by enabling the Churches to meet and give common witness, it seeks to further the realization, not of a man-made unity, but of the unity which the Lord gave to his people. Yet the Council does not presuppose or imply a particular ecclesiology. The *Statement of Toronto* (1950) is so clear and definite on this point that we shall quote the pertinent sentences.

'The World Council of Churches cannot and should not be based on any particular conception of the Church. It does not prejudge the ecclesiological problem. Membership in the World Council does not imply that a Church treats its own conception of the Church as merely relative. Membership in the Council does not imply the acceptance of a specific doctrine concerning the nature of Church unity . . . and it does not imply that each Church must regard the other member Churches as Churches in the true and full sense of the word' (5).

At the time of the Toronto Statement it seems to have been the intention of the Council to word its office and function in a way that would enable Catholic participation. The statement mentions specifically that belonging to the Council does not imply a spiritualized conception of the Church such as was condemned by Pius XII in the encyclical *Mystici Corporis* (6). It can safely be said, moreover, that the Council as it is described in the official texts, is not apt to mislead dissident Christians into a false satisfaction with the relative unity within their divided state. The Council does not seek to replace the One Church by assuming the role of some sort of Super-Church (7). While the Council is called a witness to the unity among Christians in as much as it expresses the common intention of obeying Christ, it is at the same time an equally convincing witness of their disunity. Because the Churches are divided, they need the Council as an instrument of reunion. The Council of Churches is a prophetic voice which condemns as much as it pacifies; its tragic confessions of division and guilt are meant to stir a holy restlessness and dispel an easy and illusory hope. To such a voice, it would seem, the Catholic Church could add her own ecumenical witness.

However, in spite of the intention to leave open the ecclesiological problem, the messages and approved reports of the Council occasionally betray convictions about the nature of the Church which reach deeply into theology, into a theology which is difficult to reconcile with Catholic faith. When the documents of the Council declare the common guilt of Christians in bringing about divisions and strife, they sometimes go so far as to attribute a failure to the Church itself. 'The Church is called to deep shame and penitence for its failure to manifest Jesus Christ to men as He really is' (8). But if the Church could become unfaithful to her Lord, then Christ's gospel to which she is the only witness on earth, and Christ's life of which she is the sole mediatrix, could be obscured and suffer harm in a world hating God. If the Church could sin, then the gates of hell could come to prevail against her.

The documents of the World Council, it is true, also contain many passages expressing the holiness of the Church. The quotation given above is followed by the assurance that 'in spite of the Church's failure, she remains the Church of God in which, and in which alone God is pleased to reveal himself and his redemptive purpose in Jesus Christ, in Whom and in Whom alone the renewal of man's life is possible' (9). At another place we read: 'In spite of our unholiness, we know that the Church of God is holy, for it is God's action and not our penitence which sanctifies and renews it' (10). But when viewing together the texts on the holiness and unholiness of the Church, we get the impression that in the eyes of the World Council God's dispensation for the Church does not differ essentially from his dispensation for the individual Christian. The uncertainty which marks the individual Christian in as much as he is at once transformed by grace and vulnerable to sin is also applied to the Church (11). In this age the Christian, and the Church, remain on trial. It is true, she is holy (and one and indefectible) by the gift of God; at the same time she remains susceptible to a radical deformation. In the eyes of the World Council, the Church is the continuation of Christ's redemptive mission in the world, but she holds this office in the same frail hands in which an individual believer bears his own Christian loyalty. The Church anticipates the glory of the kingdom, but this anticipation is not structurally determined to be an unfailing instrument in God's design. It is difficult to see how in such a theology the Church can be called the *body* of the Lord.

According to Catholic doctrine, the Church cannot fail in manifesting Jesus Christ. We do not deny, of course, that we are sinners. We must daily confess our sins and ask forgiveness, as we forgive those who trespass against us. We must equally acknowledge that Catholic leaders and Catholic groups may at times be responsible for the increase of hate and injustice in the world, and that on account of their selfishness the witness of the Church does not find ready acceptance. But to speak of the Church of Christ as a sinner is unbiblical language. The Church on earth is not simply the community of redeemed sinners; she is the community of redeemed sinners transformed into the Body of Christ, and this so irrevocably that her holiness on earth is no longer vulnerable to the infidelity of her members. Her course through history is a pilgrimage in which the sanctity and (by inflicting wounds on her) the malice of her members conform her more closely to the crucified Son in Whom the Father is well pleased. Waiting in exile for the Day of Judgment, the Church herself is no longer under the divine sentence to which her members must remain subject.

The passages in the official declarations of the World Council dealing with the guilt of the Church are difficult to reconcile with Catholic doctrine. On the other hand, we must not make the mistake of interpreting the statements of the Council as we would the declarations of an ecclesiastical magisterium. The Council does not intend to teach authoritatively. It gives a common witness to the Christian faith of the member Churches, a witness which does not demand to be received as binding by all participating Christians, but only offers them a prophetic light in which to examine their own positions. Hence it can still be said in all justice that, while the member Churches may have definite ecclesiological beliefs, the World Council itself does not stand for a particular theology of the Church.

The World Council of Churches does not pretend to teach a unified doctrine with a necessary interior continuity. With the exception of its faith in Christ, God and Saviour, the doctrinal statements of the Council are totally dependent on the beliefs of the member Churches, or even on those of the appointed theologians. The Council is not obliged to consistency; its positions can change. It is not unreasonable therefore to ask whether there are leading groups or influential circles in the Council, and if so, where their theological sympathies are situated. Even if the official basis of the Council does not present dogmatic obstacles to Catholic participation, it could still happen that the theological atmosphere of the Council as it is created by the majority of its theologians, is in contradiction to the principles of the Catholic Church.

In the Toronto Statement we read that the Council 'includes Churches which believe that the Church is essentially invisible as well as those which hold that visible unity is essential' (12). But what are the respective proportions of these groups in the Council? There are no doubt member Churches which hold exactly the views of the Church which were described and denounced in *Mortalium Animos*, namely the belief which denies that Christ founded his Church to persist as a single community throughout history. It is the opinion of some authors that this group is not only the stronger one, but even growing in influence (13). If we compare, for instance, the Toronto Statement (1950) with the Faith-and-Order Report of New Zealand (1955), we notice a definite development of thought. While the former document left open the possibility that the Church of Christ now exists on earth as an historical society, the latter seems to deny this possibility. We read: 'No denomination has within itself the fullness of catholicity. Catholicity implies universality and the fullness and the wholeness of the gospel. No one denomination has yet realized all the gifts that Christ would make to his Church' (14). If we understand this sentence correctly, the Catholic Church could not, without compromising her faith, combine her witness with the present voice of the World Council of Churches. It is not unthinkable, however, that a greater Catholic participation in the ecumenical quest at the time of the Toronto Statement might have prevented the development which we believe to have observed.

The spiritual climate of a movement is an elusive thing which is difficult to understand and to evaluate, particularly for outsiders. We do have, however, an evaluation according to the norms of Christian tradition coming from within the Council: the Orthodox Churches, which joined the Ecumenical Movement for the sole reason of rendering witness to the truth, hear with our ears and speak as it were with our tongue. Their two public declarations at the Evanston Assembly (1954) teach Christian doctrine with a clarity and dignity that profoundly impresses the Catholic reader (15). Studying the documents of the Council's commissions and interpreting them from within, that is, with the full knowledge of what is really meant and intended by the statements, the Orthodox delegates at Evanston came to the conclusion that 'the whole approach to the problem of reunion is entirely unacceptable from the standpoint of the Orthodox Church' (16). This is a severe judgment. It is not directed against the basis of the Council, nor against the approved statements as such, but it objects to additional theological presuppositions implied in the general method of approach. The leading majority of the Council seem to have adopted a definite ecclesiology.

Not the official basis, but the actual situation of the World Council precludes the participation of the Catholic Church, unless indeed she were to assume a protesting partnership, as do the Orthodox Churches in order to make her witness more audible. But even if, according to the present decision of the hierarchy, Catholic ecumencial action must be exercised outside the Council of Churches, it is regrettable that there are Catholics who have little respect and no sympathy for the work of this Council. The Ecumenical Movement is a fruit of the Spirit and to Catholics a cause of holy joy (17); and even if the Church does not officially take part in it through her hierarchy, she participates in it formally through her ecumenical theologians. Very few Catholics who read the Report of the Evanston Assembly will have overlooked the fact (and failed to be grateful for the gesture) that, in spite of the Church's *non possumus*, General Secretary Visser't Hooft mentions in his introductory speech the contribution of Catholic theologians to the main theme of the Assembly, Christ the Hope of the World (18).

THE ECUMENICAL ATTITUDE

Ecumenical action of Roman Catholics must be exercised outside of the World Council of Churches. In the last chapter we have discussed the essential character of this ecumenism: it is the task of the Church to encourage the Christian elements in separation and to discourage their spurious additions. In actual fact this action implies a great variety of diverse activities exercised by the hierarchy, by ecumenical theologians, and by the faithful in general. In our present context we are mainly interested in the work of the theologians. To be sure, not all Catholic writing on Christian unity is ecumenical. According to our definition of ecumenism a speech, a dialogue, a study, an essay, a book cannot be called ecumenical if it is not inspired by the intention to foster the healing growth of separated Christian patrimonies. This is the common light in which ecumenists consider their subject matter. This is the formal principle which gives a single direction to theological endeavours apparently quite unrelated, and which unites all Catholic ecumenical action and thought to constitute a single act, the ecumenical witness of the Church.

The ecumenical witness of the Catholic Church has its own proper character, distinguishing it from the witness demanded of her in other tasks and other circumstances. This character is determined by the religious situation of separated Christianity and the maternal role to which the Church has been appointed. The Catholic ecumenist will give testimony to the faith of the Church—but he will do so with an attitude which is conscious of her ecumenical obligation.

CATHOLIC ECUMENISM: ITS EXERCISE

This attitude we wish to describe. It resembles in many ways the attitude of non-Catholic Christians concerned about Christian unity. The Catholic ecumenical attitude is characterized by the ready acknowledgment of the Christian values in other Churches, by an unwillingness to proselytize, by the search for truth in all sincerity, and by the certain hope that not only the others, but also the Catholic Church will benefit from a return to unity. At the same time and without contradicting the above notes, the Catholic ecumenist believes with the certainty of faith that the Catholic Church is the home of all Christians. We shall discuss these points one by one, to the extent warranted by our official documents.

The ready acknowledgment of the Christian elements in other communities

It cannot be denied that for many centuries Catholic theological literature on Christian disunity was highly contentious: it defended or it attacked. The apologetics of those days put its main effort on the demonstration of Catholic dogma and the refutation of heterodox claims. It was a literature designed for schismatics and heretics who were considered as being only one step away from the Church; if they could be convinced of this or that point of Christian doctrine, they would return to the Church from which they were still aware of having sprung. The disputatious tracts addressed to heretics could not admit the presence of supernatural elements in separated Christian bodies because, as we have pointed out, the ill-will of the dissenters radically kills all the effects of grace. But even when after some generations the ill-will of great multitudes could no longer be taken for granted, Christian controversial literature remained unchanged, not concerned about fostering the holy and eliminating error in whatever degree possible, but aiming at converting heretics from death to life. In the ears of many writers it would have sounded daring to speak of a patrimony of grace surviving among dissident Christians.

This period has come to an end. Catholic writers have learned to acknowledge Christian patrimonies in separated Churches, and we have shown at length that the recent documents of the Holy See do not betray the slightest hesitation on this point. More than that, we have pointed out that the Church rejoices at Christian vitality wherever it may be found: all the gifts of holiness which the Spirit produces among men are meant for the Church and belong to her, even when they remain visibly separated.

It was Pius XI above all who advanced a regular movement of good will and sympathetic understanding with respect to Orthodox Christianity (19). In his letters and speeches, particularly during the first half of his pontificate, we find repeated and forceful demands for a spirit of mutual *benevolence* (20) with the purpose of creating an atmosphere in which the truth may be more readily apprehended. The language of Pius XI is indicative of a new age in the history of Christian disunity. Here is an excerpt from one of his speeches which has become famous:

'For a reunion it is above all necessary to know and to love one another. To know one another, because if the efforts of reunion have failed so many times, this is in large measure due to mutual ignorance. If there are prejudices on both sides, these prejudices must fall. Incredible are the errors and equivocations which persist and are handed down among the separated brethren against the Catholic Church; on the other hand, Catholics also have sometimes failed in justly evaluating the truth or, on account of insufficient knowledge, in showing a fraternal spirit. Do we know all that is valuable, good, and Christian in the fragments of ancient Catholic truth? Detached fragments of a gold-bearing rock also contain the precious ore. The ancient Churches of the East have retained so true a holiness that they deserve not only our respect but also our sympathy' (21).

The Catholic attitude towards Protestants differing from us in faith is a great deal more complex. While the Roman documents acknowledge their partial Christian patrimony, they do not insist in the same way on a spirit of sympathetic appreciation. There should, of course, be no difference in charity, but we know that we must love *in veritate* (John xvii. 17), and that we cannot show unreserved sympathy for a spiritual heritage which is not in harmony with divine Revelation. Nevertheless there must be the same spirit of fairness, of honest research, of true appreciation of their authentic Christian values. This attitude, however, may be coupled with the fear of seeing uninstructed Catholics misled into error (22). The two opposing traditions of Protestants, which we have described in a previous chapter, set the limits to our sympathy and to our brotherly relations, and if it is true that we can enjoy spiritual fellowship with them, we can never do so without a profound grief. The greater the charity that holds us together, the greater will also be our pain at the barriers which separate us—against the will of Christ. To this grief the papal writings give ample witness, even while they acknowledge that 'there are millions of men in East and West who have preserved more or less vividly the vestiges of Christ' (23).

Acknowledging the Christian patrimonies in dissidence, the ecumenist does not overlook the errors by which these may be affected. On the contrary, since he intends to contribute to the healing of severed traditions, he must clearly understand the wounds from which they suffer. It is thus in the interest of the Church's ecumenism when Pius XII reprimands certain Catholic writers who 'set aside the problems which divide' (24) and 'who pay attention to the things that unite rather than to those that separate' (25). Our recognition of Christian elements in dissidence does not imply a compromise; it is wholly grounded on the search for truth, seeking to distinguish the authentic from the false.

The refusal to proselytize

Acknowledging that dissident Christians may have access to Christ through the partial message of their communities, the ecumenical witness of Catholics cannot reasonably aim at converting them from darkness to light. We have explained at length the difference between ecumenical action and missionary work. Only when this difference is forgotten, only when the Christian elements in dissidence are disregarded, can the work for Christian unity deteriorate into a proselytism which seeks to draw dissidents into the Church by neglecting, instead of perfecting, their divine patrimony. Catholic ecumenism, however, regards dissident Christians precisely in as much as they are heirs of a wounded tradition of grace; its formal object is the healing of these traditions in view of their perfect health in the unity of the Church (26).

Ecumenism is the assistance in the struggle going on between the two opposing principles in dissident Christianity. The ecumenical witness of Catholics aims at contributing to the victory of the authentic tendency in the minds of dissident Christians at a point where they are open to two opposing possibilities. Thus, in order to protect their faith in the mystery of the Church, the popes warn the separated Eastern Churches of the unorthodox theories on Christian unity which come to them through Protestant influence (27). Or, in order to increase the Christian patrimony of Protestants, the popes frequently remind them to renew their veneration of the Virgin Mary whose task it is, then as now, to bring forthChrist (28). Quite generally we may say that, if Catholics assist dissident Christians better to appreciate and more fully to live the sacrament of baptism, for instance, or the communal worship of the Eucharist, or the spiritual value of the liturgy, or the evangelical character of monastic life, or the love of patristics, or the nearness of the saints—

then the Church is properly exercising her ecumenical function. By means of her witness, the orientation of dissident Christianity to the Body of Christ is increased and activated.

The official documents of the Holy See, we have pointed out, are not the place where the ecumenism of the Church is normally exercised; this is properly speaking the work of theologians. Usually the popes confine themselves in recalling the final end of all reunion movements, the return of dissident Christians to perfect reconciliation with the Catholic Church. We do not want to omit, however, an interesting document of Leo XIII, the encyclical *Tametsi Futura* (1900), which illustrates in a remarkable way (if our interpretation is correct) the nature of the Church's ecumenical witness.

Tametsi Futura is an eloquent sermon on Jesus Christ in the form of a letter, addressed 'not so much to those who willingly hear Christian doctrine, but rather to the unhappy men who call themselves Christians while living without faith or love of Jesus Christ' (29) Pope Leo proclaims the gospel message: Jesus Christ has come to save man from sin and eternal perdition; he alone is our life, on this earth and in the world to come. But what is remarkable about the letter is that Pope Leo seems to encourage orthodox Protestants who believe in the God-Man to be his allies in the fight against unbelief. How does he do this? The letter expounds the Catholic doctrine on Jesus Christ, the one Mediator, in a way that will be understood by Protestants. While not failing to mention the Church and her divine appointment, the almost exclusive emphasis of the letter is on the return to Jesus Christ. So much has the Pope this return to Christ at heart that he is willing to present Catholic doctrine by emphasizing what we hold in common with Protestants and leaving unaccentuated what separates us. He does not enter upon a defense that human nature remains essentially good after the fall; on the contrary, describing the helplessness of fallen man he uses a language which is closer to the terminology of the Council of Orange than to that of Trent. He does not explain at length that in fallen man human reason is not deprived of its connatural light; rather does he stress that 'without Jesus human reason is left to its own weakness, and deprived of its strongest support and purest light' (30). He does not defend the possibility of a purely natural goodness but rather writes, 'Even if man were able to discover the whole of natural law by his own reason—which he cannot—and even if he should observe all of it throughout his whole life—which he cannot do without grace—he would hope in vain for his eternal salvation, if he had no faith' (31). Certainly, this is common Catholic doctrine; but the emphasis in *Tametsi Futura* is unusual. We have the impression that Leo XIII wants to call all liberal Christians back to Christ, to Christ as he is immediately accessible to them through the sources of their own milieu. He exhorts 'all Christians wherever they may be'—we understand this to mean Catholics and Protestants—'to make every effort to come to know their Redeemer' (32).

The encyclical *Tametsi Futura* exhibits the characteristic notes of the ecumenical attitude. If our interpretation is correct, Pope Leo implicitly acknowledges the virtue of faith among Protestants, and he speaks to them in order to bring an alloyed tradition to greater purity. He desires to heal in whatever degree possible—in view of perfect health in the Catholic Church.

The sincere search for truth

There is one point on which Catholic and non-Catholic ecumenists are perfectly agreed: the unity of Christians which the Lord has promised is a unity in truth, and an advance towards this goal will come about only through a greater apprehension of the truth, divine and human, of our religion. Ecumenism demands patient research and the progress of thought. There are two aspects to this search for truth: we must understand more correctly the beliefs and practices of the various Churches (an historical inquiry), and we must strive for a greater penetration of the Word of God (a theological inquiry).

There can be no advance towards unity unless we know one another, unless we are willing to abandon our prejudices and acquire a critical knowledge of the facts. In the eyes of the popes the removal of bias and preconceived notions constitutes an important part of the common work for Christian unity. In his letter to the Scottish hierarchy (1898) Leo XIII describes the advance that has been made in their country: 'We see Catholics being considered more fairly and more amicably every day. Catholic teaching is no longer openly held up to contempt, but rather receives the sympathy of many and the obedience of some. The sophistry of opinions so frequently preventing the appreciation of truth gradually falls into disuse' (33). It must be confessed however that, as far as Western Christianity is concerned, the frequent papal pleas against prejudice and for a fair examination of the facts are usually made in favour of Catholic claims. With regard to Eastern Christians, the situation is different. Recent popes, especially Pius XI, have stressed the obligation of Catholics to rid themselves of preconceived notions about the Orthodox Churches. We read: 'The remedy for the great ills of separation cannot be applied unless the impediments of mutual ignorance, contempt, and prejudice be first removed' (34). Or again 'There is no hope of progress unless the absurd opinions be dropped which in the course of centuries the ordinary people have acquired about the doctrines and institutions of the Eastern Churches, and unless the agreement of their Fathers with the Latin Fathers be more thoroughly studied' (35).

We must study the doctrine and the practices of separated Christians. If it is the task of the Catholic ecumenist to distinguish between an isolated Christian tradition and its spurious additions and if, beyond that, he wishes to contribute to the healing growth of these traditions, then he cannot be satisfied with a superficial knowledge of the dissident Churches to which, or of which, he is writing. He must acquire a real insight into the heart of their doctrine; he must listen before he can speak. Because Protestants often remain indifferent to Catholic thought (36), the opinion is voiced occasionally that Catholic theologians need not go out of their way to study dissident doctrines and seek ecumenical contacts. However, as Catholics they are obliged. Whether their efforts succeed or fail, they are called to the ecumenical task by the very mission of the Church.

Do we find this need for study and penetration of dissident theologies expressed in the documents of the Holy See? Most certainly in regard to Orthodox Christianity! Among the recent popes it was particularly Pius XI who emphasized the obligation of Catholics to study and understand the theology, liturgy, and piety of the separated Eastern Churches. He repeatedly returned to the subject (37). Perhaps the most important document in this connection is the encyclical *Rerum Orientalium* (1928), where the Pope shows at length the necessity of Oriental studies, and records the progress that has been made in the years preceding the encyclical. In order to advance this movement he suggests that diocesan bishops send some of their priests to study at the Oriental Institute at Rome, and demands that Catholic Universities create a special chair for Oriental Studies (38). We must study the doctrines of dissidents and give them access to our sources, Pius XI tells us, 'in order to further charity and a mutual esteem' (39). These studies will even produce an enrichment of our own theology (40). Finally, 'from the right understanding of things there may emerge human fairness and sincere benevolence which, conjoined with the charity of Christ, will favour the advance of religious unity—if God grants it so' (41).

Such a stress has never been made in favour of Protestant studies.

We do read however in the instruction *Ecclesia Catholica* that bishops are urged to appoint priests in their dioceses to study the problems of Christian unit (42) and consequently also, we infer, the doctrines and theories of Protestants. There is, moreover, an important passage in *Humani Generis* where in a general way Catholic scholars are summoned to study systems of thought which are not native in the Catholic Church. 'It is the duty of Catholic philosophers and theologians to know thoroughly even the more or less false doctrines of men: firstly because we can heal an illness only after having recognized its true character, secondly because even in false systems there often is hidden a grain of truth, and finally because it stimulates the mind to search and study more carefully certain truths of philosophy and theology' (43). Even if this exhortation was not written with specific reference to Protestant thought, there is no reason why we cannot *mutatis mutandis* apply it there also. The Catholic theologian must study Protestant doctrine in order to understand the origin of its hidden wounds, to discover the extent of supernatural survival, and to return to his own theology with new and fruitful questions.

At this point we must add an important remark. The same fidelity to truth which prompts the Catholic ecumenist to abandon his inherited prejudices and to study dissident theologies from their sources, also obliges him to be honest in his presentation of Catholic doctrine. Wishing to increase the common ground between the Church and dissident Christians, some Catholic writers, it seems, have given in to the temptation to obscure the clarity and precision of Catholic dogma by formulations which, although perfectly orthodox, also admit an heterodox interpretation. In recent years we have two long paragraphs in the Roman documents reprimanding all attempts to extenuate the doctrine of the Church, and to strive for a gradual assimilation of Catholic doctrine and dissident beliefs (44). Thus we read:

'Care must be taken that from a spirit which is known to-day as irenic it does not happen that, through comparative study and the vain desire for the progressive assimilation of various creeds, Catholic doctrine—whether dogma or connected with dogma—is conformed and accommodated to the doctrines of dissidents to such a degree that the purity of Catholic doctrine is compromised and its authentic and certain meaning obscured. Bishops shall not allow the dangerous way of speaking which gives rise to false ideas and to deceiving hopes which can never be fulfilled . . . The whole and integral body of Catholic doctrine must be proposed and explained.

... All must really be said, clearly and openly, for the double reason that dissident Christians seek the truth and that apart from the truth a true union can never be attained' (45).

It would however be misunderstanding these warnings, were we to conclude that the popes wish to impede the further development of Catholic theology. The ecumenical witness of the Church is dependent on the particular milieu, or the situation, in which it is delivered, and if this situation is of a new and untried quality, the witness itself demands new thought and the unfolding of theology. Writers who over-simplify Catholic doctrine, who use credal formulas without hearing through it the Word of God, who pretend a uniformity on matters where the Church does not demand or even wish uniformity—fail against the truth entrusted to the Church, and do harm to her ecumenical witness. This tendency to reduce theology to a stationary minimum is criticized by Pius XII in his encyclical *Mystici Corporis*. He writes, 'Some people, disturbed by a groundless fear, regard the doctrine (of the Mystical Body) as a dangerous thing, and shrink from it as though it were the apple of Paradise, beautiful but forbidden. This is not reasonable; the mysteries which God has revealed cannot be harmful to men, nor are they intended to remain barren like a treasure hidden in a field' (46).

This brings us to the second aspect of the ecumenical search for truth: to understand more profoundly the meaning of Revelation concerning the problems of Christian unity. It can truly be said that the Catholic theologian continues to seek the truth, though he does so in a sense far different from his non-Catholic colleagues; his quest is entirely within the supernatural wisdom entrusted to the the Church. His progress is not an evolution from error to truth, but rather from truth to greater insight; it implies a real increase of knowledge, a passing from an unanswered question to the reply in the light of Christian Revelation. Is such a progress possible in the Church? According to Catholic belief, the Church holds the truth of the gospel infallibly. 'It would be an error to assert that in matters of doctrine not even the Catholic Church possesses the fullness of Christ, but must receive something towards its perfection from others' (47). The Church indeed holds the fullness of truth. But what does this mean? It does not mean that the entire message which God has revealed to men has found complete and final expression in the Church of to-day. She possesses the fullness of truth in the sense that, having received the revealed Word into her keeping, she is, with a divinely-assisted hierarchy guarding her from error, the source and the home of all saving truth. But she does not exhaust the meaning of Revelation. 'Scripture and tradition', writes Pius XII, 'contain such an immense treasure of truth that they can never be exhausted' (48). In this sense the Catholic theologian continues to search for truth.

Contact with dissident Christian thought often raises new questions which demand a deepened understanding and sometimes a development of Catholic doctrine. Pius XI believed that the study of Oriental Christianity will contribute to 'a richer knowledge of Catholic theology' (49). There is a vast area, untravelled in part, which is open to an ecumenical theology, that is to say, to a theology which deals with the problems raised by Christian disunity in the light of the Church's ecumenical function (50).

At one time Pius XI expressed a conviction in regard to the Church's missions which is of significance also for her ecumenical action. Since the great directives for action proceed from the realm of ideas, the Pope said, good intentions and sacrifices alone no longer suffice in missionary activity; these efforts must be accompanied by a knowledge which sheds light and points the way (51). To an even greater degree this rule holds the work for Christian unity. There must be scholarship and discernment; there must be insight. In this attitude we are at one with the intentions of the World Council of Churches.

The anticipation of the benefits of reunion also for the Catholic Church

According to Roger Aubert (52), it is only in recent times that the official documents of the Holy See have been ready to admit that the divisions of Christendom actually do harm to the Catholic Church, and that the whole mystical Body will benefit from the perfect reconciliation of Christians. In former times the benefits of a reunion were foreseen only for the separated Churches. However, Pius XI and Pius XII are quite outspoken; they look forward also to the wholesome effects of Christian unity on the Catholic Church. 'From the full and perfect unity of all Christians the mystical Body of Christ and all its members, one by one, are bound to obtain a great increment' (53).

The essential constitution of the Catholic Church, we recall, is indefectible and remains untouched by Christian factions. Since the Church is perfect with the fullness of Christ's gifts, it is by no means obvious what can be meant by the benefits for the whole Church proceeding from the reunion of Christians. We must investigate this problem with care; but faithful to our method, we shall confine ourselves to statements, or conclusions, from our Roman documents—even if this leaves us with an incomplete picture.

A house divided against itself cannot stand. A Christian world divided into competing religious bodies is so much weakened that even the Catholic Church, situated at its centre, will not remain unaffected by the attacks against Christianity. Although the Church will not be overcome by the gates of hell, she may nevertheless lose a multitude of members from her own fold and observe the decay of Christian elements outside her own borders. Since in our day we witness organized attacks against the Christian faith on a new and terrible scale, it is not surprising that the official letters coming from Rome encourage and even urge the ecumenical efforts of all Christians. 'Particularly in our days' writes Pius XII 'when war and strife alienate men from one another all over the world, all Christians should be urged again and again to work for a union in and through Christ with every effort inspired by Christian charity' (54). A few years later we read, 'Against the confederate forces (of anti-Christians) there cannot remain disjoined and separated those who by the sacred character of baptism have been appointed to fight the good fight of the Saviour' (55). The unity of Christians will strengthen the Church in her fight against ungodliness; it will increase her power to resist and her hope of victory.

But we read of another effect of Christian reunion on the Catholic Church. Jesus Christ gave to his Church a visible *note* of unity to certify before the world that his people is one, and that he had been sent by the Father (cf. John xvii. 21). This note of the Church can never be lost or even be changed; it is rooted in the solid unity of faith and government which the Lord has guaranteed to his apostles. But it is the task of the Church to make the note of her unity ever more radiant—by mutual charity and social harmony among Catholics—in order that the world may recognize with ease and security the credentials of divine salvation. This note of unity, we read in the papal writings, will be given more convincing visibility through the perfect unity of all Christians. In the words of Benedict XV, 'Since the truth of the Catholic Church shines forth above all in her unity, nothing is more to be hoped for than that all men who have been torn from the one fold will change their minds and eventually make their return' (56). Approving and recommending the January octave of prayer for Christian unity, the same Pontiff writes: 'The unity of faith is the principal note vouching for the truth of the Catholic Church. . . . Hence we are happy to learn that special prayers have been composed in order that men may plead for this end of unity' (57). This end of unity (unity taken here as a note) is to certify the divine mission of the Church and to lead men to find faith in the Christ of God. Hence from the return of all Christians to the unity which they have left, Benedict XV foresees that the missionary force of the Christian faith will be greatly increased. When all Christians again profess the identical creed, the total witness to Christ will receive a new quality, which can be expected to produce new life in mission lands and in the so-called Christian countries. Such considerations naturally abound in the Ecumenical Movement, which has inherited the concern of the Protestant International Missionary Council. Neither are they missing, from a different point of view, in the Roman documents. The popes of our period do not fail to acknowledge, then, that the missionary witness (and not only the missionary success) of the Catholic Church suffers from the divided state of Christendom.

The reunion of all Christians, we conclude, will be of benefit even to the Catholic Church: it will reinforce her resistance to God's enemies and expand her missionary influence in the world. In other words, through the return to Christian unity the redemptive work of the Church will achieve a greater unfolding. While the Body of Christ is fully equipped to reconcile all humanity with God, this saving mission is prevented from its most perfect and complete manifestation by the persistence of Christian factions.

Is this all that can be found in the papal letters on the gain of the Catholic Church as a result of Christian unity? We read no direct reference to the problem, occasionally discussed in Catholic ecumenical literature, of how the Church will benefit from the return of separated Christian traditions which have produced spiritualities and values not found to the same extent within the borders of the Catholic Church (58). A somewhat obscure sentence however, related to this subject, demands our interpretation. In the encyclical *Ecclesiam Dei* Pius XI writes in connection with Oriental Christianity: 'When individual men and whole peoples are thus perfectly reconciled, the conjunction of the Church (*conjunctio Ecclesiae*) will at once be perfected through the return of all who for whatever reasons have been separated from her' (59). Though the exact significance of this 'conjunction' is not explained in the text, it seems to us that its meaning can easily be surmised. We recall what we have said about the supernatural good in dissident Churches (60): the divine patrimonies (the means of grace and their effects) surviving in dissidence continue to belong to the Church, albeit not in the most perfect manner. Only their wounds prevent full integration into the Catholic community. The conjunction of the Church, then, which in a divided Christendom must remain incomplete, is the visible continuity of the means of grace (the sacraments and the gospel) and the visible union of their effects (spirituality and holiness). The Church still awaits the perfect synthesis of her supernatural gifts in dispersion. With sacraments outside her visible borders the Church cannot reach her most perfect equilibrium. Something, also, is wanting to her as long as the endangered holiness of Orthodox Christians, of Anglicans, of Lutherans, . . . is not rendered secure and universal in the fold of the Lord.

What happens when these partial traditions are fully and visibly conjoined to the Catholic Church? The Church, we have said, does not thereby obtain a new essential perfection which has been lacking in her; she obtains but the perfections which these traditions receive, that is, their perfect health. 'From the re-establishment of this conjunction there will arise the richest fruits both for Universal Christianity and in special way for the Orientals themselves' (61). We may conclude therefore that the perfect reconciliation of all Christians will not only expand the redemptive mission of the Church, but also enrich her by the perfect healing which her isolated gifts will experience in the continuity of her body.

The disunity of Christians crucifies the Body of Christ (62). While it is true that the divisions do not affect the divinely given unity of the Church, they do put the Church in a situation where this unity cannot achieve its full and normal effect. Ecumenical action, then, adds something to the Church in the line of her unity. The movement for Christian unity is a movement *for the unity of the Church* (63).

The faith that the Catholic Church is the home of all Christians

The ecumenical attitude of Catholics as we have described it so far resembles the ecumenical attitude of non-Catholic Christians. But this resemblance is not an identity. Every trait of the Catholic attitude is profoundly modified by the certain conviction, a conviction of faith, that the Church is the home of all Christians. In the last chapter we have outlined the universal mediation of the Catholic Church: she is the field in which all trees of grace have their roots and their final harvest. But the preceding paragraphs have demonstrated that the spiritual maternity which Christ has assigned to his Church does not prompt her to regard dissident Christians in an overbearing or belittling manner: knowing that they, and therefore also she, will benefit from a return to unity, she offers them her own witness towards the recovery of their partial Christian traditions. The Church is gifted with the all-embracing catholicity of the cross, but this does not mean that she intends to 'absorb' dissident Christians into her fold (64). She has a high regard for all that is authentically Christian among them, and looks forward to the perfect unfolding of these gifts in her own life. 'Dissident Christians may certainly be told that in returning to the Church they do not lose the good which God's grace has hitherto imparted to them but rather that by their return this good will find perfect consummation' (65). Having derived the Christian life from the incomplete patrimonies of their own communities, dissident Christians returning to the Church will have access to the sources of grace in greater purity without the hazard of deformation.

It is easy to see what this purification will mean for dissident Christians who return to the Church from the Protestant climate of the West. Quite apart from the sacramental recovery, there will be in most cases a real enlightening in the doctrines of faith. It is not so immediately obvious however what the Church can offer to Orthodox Christians; yet even they have been wounded by a principle of dissention which continues to be active among them; even they are in need of healing. The Catholic Church offers them the holiness of her own life, of that life which Christ has brought in abundance (66). It was the will of the Lord that the whole Body be so connected to a visible centre that 'the hidden life with Christ in God' should not be independent of the historical communion with the bishop of Rome. Following our documents, the Apostolic See must be called the centre of unity, of life, of charity (67), not because a canonical relationship can by itself communicate holiness but because the Lord has attached his promises to a visible society. 'This we announce to you that you may have fellowship with us (the visible community), and that this fellowship with us be also with the Father and his Son Jesus Christ (the invisible life)' (1 John i. 3). We cannot enter the society of the Church, or move closer to it, without at the same time and in proportion to our disposition being drawn into the holiness which she proclaims.

This is the doctrine. It remains the task of an ecumenical theology to demonstrate for the single denominations that the supernatural elements which dissident Christians possess cannot attain their complete and proper unfolding save in the Catholic Church (68). If Orthodox Christians, to give an example, conceive of the Church above all as the community of love, we must—assuming that this corresponds to a traditional Christian intention—return to our own sources to know and experience the Church as the community of love in such a way that its Christ-given hierarchical and legal framework is seen not as a hindrance to charity, but as a guarantee of its greater unfolding on earth (69). If a Protestant conception sees the Christian life above all as a total obedience to the Word of God, we must—assuming that this corresponds to an evangelical intention—return to our sources and discover how the Church is the place where we encounter the Word of God, where we must respond in obedience to the call of God, where every man stands alone before his God, Judge and Saviour—alone, although a member of Christ's body; for we remain in the darkness of faith while this age lasts, and darkness isolates. So great is the freedom in the Church that a Christian may discover in it the community of divine love or, according to a different spirituality, experience the loneliness of exile while the crucified Church awaits the return of her Lord. The Church is the home of all authentic Christian visions.

Ecumenical theology must continue its inquiry into truth. It must uncover the fullness of revealed doctrine with all its nuances in order to show that every truly Christian aspiration—the *Anliegen*, as the Germans call it—finds its perfect answer only in the interior life of the Catholic Church.

The demand for the development of an ecumenical theology we find in our Roman documents explicitly with reference to Eastern Christianity. Pius XI demands that Catholic ecumenists try to set forth how the traditional doctrine of Oriental Christians is also contained, at least substantially, in the teaching of the Western Church. In this sense he writes in a letter on the 4th Congress of Oriental Studies at Welehrad: 'We urge not only Catholics . . . but also dissident ecclesiastics to be present at the Congress so that they can investigate the body of Catholic doctrine in all thoroughness, and discover its substantial conformity with the teaching of the Eastern and Western Fathers' (70). In *Rerum Orientalium* the same Pontiff urges Catholic theologians 'to study the doctrines of dissident Christians on the sacraments and the Church in order to compare and bring them together (*conferunt et componunt*) with Catholic truth' (71). Of course Pius XI does not envisage a dogmatic compromise; but realizing that the principal part of our divergence is due to a difference of mentality, he considers it the work of ecumenical theology to bridge the estrangement by removing the non-religious factors and showing the objective conformity between Eastern and Western doctrines.

We find no explicit statement in our documents demanding an

ecumenical theology which would set forth how the authentic Christian intentions of Protestants are contained in the principles of the Catholic faith.

* * *

The exercise of Catholic ecumenism resembles from many points of view the efforts of the non-Roman Ecumenical Movement. Even Maurice Gordillo in his somewhat severe article in the Vatican encyclopedia, writes that 'although in various ways and degrees, we all without exception (Catholics and dissidents) move towards unity by integrating what is lacking in the single Churches' (72). We have seen that these ways are not so very different. We all acknowledge Christian elements beyond our own visible boundaries, we all decline to treat other communities as mission fields, we all seek the truth with perfect sincerity, and we all expect from the reunion a good also for our own Church. The great difference in the Catholic approach to ecumenical action, a difference which profoundly qualifies the above-mentioned attitudes, is the faith of the Church that she alone is the Body of Christ, the holy People of God. In the darkness of the Church's pilgrimage the Catholic does not know all the answers to the problems of Christian unity and consequently shares with his separated brethren the honest search for truth, but he believes none the less on the authority of Christ that the Church is the home of all Christians.

ECUMENICAL CHARITY

Catholic action for Christian unity is not confined to the ecumenical witness of the Church; it is exercised on a much wider basis in an activity shared by all Christians, Catholic and non-Catholic, through the gift of supernatural charity. It is a fundamental principle of the gospels that there is no visible progress in the Christian community which is not prepared and in some measure effected by the interior life of its members, that is, by the holiness of their lives and their prayers for the divine gift. 'Seek ye first the kingdom of God and his justice, and all these things shall be added unto you' (Matthew vi. 33). This evangelical counsel has left its mark on every page of the papal documents on Christian unity: there can be no success unless 'we show forth the special note of Christians, which is charity' (73). If we investigate more closely the ecumenical charity of the Church (the unifying power of holiness and the role of common prayer), it is to understand how on this elevated level the ecumenical endeavours of all Christians move along identically the same lines.

The Holiness that Unites

The papal writings always connect the Church's effort for religious unity with the holiness of individual Christians. In ecumenical action, writes Leo XIII, 'the first place belongs to bishops and their clergy, but the second belongs to the laity who can aid the apostolic activity of their clergy by the goodness and integrity of their lives' (74). Holiness being a note of the Church of Christ, the visible imitation of Christ on the part of Catholics increases the credibility of the Church's witness; more than that, it will extend the contagious influence of Christian charity among men. 'That your fellow-citizens', wrote Leo XIII to Armenian Catholics, 'seeing your example of concord and charity, may recognize that in your midst is alive the spirit of Christ, the spirit of Him who alone can identify himself so closely with his own that they become a single body' (75). All Christian charity is apostolic.

If holiness in Catholic Christians gives greater vitality to the unifying forces of the Church, what will be the effect of holiness among dissident Christians? We have said above that moving towards the Catholic Church dissident Christians will experience an increase of new life; now we must ask whether the converse of this proposition is true. Has Christian charity a gravitation towards the mystical Body? In other words: Will the increase of holiness in dissident Christians generate of itself a tendency towards full membership in the Church? Our answer will be in the affirmative.

All holiness in this world is derived from Jesus Christ. The fullness of grace, which is in Christ as in its own proper and natural anchorage, God has made communicable to all men through the death and resurrection of his only-begotten Son. 'From him we have all received, grace after grace.' If we say with the 2nd Epistle of St Peter that grace is a participation in the divine nature (i. 4), we must not imagine this as a share in an abstract divine life removed from the course of history, as if it were the realization of some neo-platonic dream; rather must we think of it as a similitude to Jesus Christ in whom the fullness of the Godhead dwells corporeally. 'In him . . . you have received of that fullness' (Col. ii. 10). We are reconciled to God in the man Jesus Christ; through his gospel and our receiving it in faith, through his priesthood and our sharing in it in the sacraments, through his holiness and our imitation in charity we are united to God by a grace which is marked by the character of the man Jesus Christ. God alone produces grace, but as *instrumentum coniunctum* the crucified and risen humanity of our

Lord impresses its own likeness on the divine gift. Christian grace transforms man into the image of the Saviour.

However Christ is not satisfied with having his brethren, one by one, made similar to himself; he wants them to be so united in a body that together they reflect his own image. In other words, Christ communicated the abundance of his grace to the Church so that, in it, men may find their own likeness to Christ and at the same time be conformed to his image in holy community. Fully constituted on the cross with all her members, the Church is the harbour of grace just as Christ is its anchorage. 'As Christ is the way for all men, so is the Church' (76), writes Leo XIII. But the Church does not mediate salvation like a mechanical instrument; she is called upon to participate in the labours of Christ by an activity divinely supported (which we have called her co-operation), making her a living instrument of God's redeeming designs. As Christ, on account of his divine personality, is called *instrumentum coniunctum* in the dispensation of grace, so the Church may be called *instrumentum adiunctum* on account of her bodily union with the Lord. The Church continues the action of Christ. 'As the eternal Word of God wanted to use a human nature to redeem men by his own passion, in a somewhat similar manner he makes use of the Church to perpetuate his work throughout time' (77). The Church therefore belongs to Christ: as Bride she obeys her Lord, and as Vine she transfuses his life. Only through his Son and through his Son's Body does the invisible God bestow grace on this earth, so that grace must be called—with the help of two untranslatable French adjectives—*christique* and *ecclésiale* (78). Grace is not only marked with the character of Jesus Christ, but within these traits, bears the marks of the Church.

The same doctrine is expressed by saying that the Church is necessary for salvation *necessitate medii* (79). We have not only Christ's command to join the Church in order to find grace, but he himself established an economy of salvation such that grace can be found only through his Body. By its own quality grace belongs to the Church.

Christian holiness is altogether from Jesus Christ. He generates it, enlightens it, rules it, and nourishes it unto the abundance of life. Yet such is the order of salvation that Christ's generation of grace in man is unfinished without baptism, his enlightenment incomplete without the Church's magisterium, his rule over holiness imperfect without ecclesiastical jurisdiction, and his multiplication of charity insufficient without the sacraments. Thus the grace of Christ—and its proper effect of holiness—is so profoundly *ecclésiale* that it cannot grow in a man without at the same time increasing his union to the Church. Wherever men receive from the Holy Ghost and advance in the holiness of the gospels, they are drawn more closely into the Body of Christ by the gravitational force of charity itself.

For Catholics, we have suggested, the increase in holiness will mean a greater participation in the divine mission of the Church to mediate Christ. Living more faithfully from the Church, they will render her more visible and increase her effective power to save and unify. For dissident Christians growth in holiness will augment their orientation towards the Church. Living more profoundly from her sources, they shall belong to her in growing measure. We must conclude therefore that all authentic spiritual life among dissident Christians generates an invisible motion towards the Catholic Church, and that consequently holiness is an ecumenical concern in the strict sense.

With reference to Eastern Christians, Pius XI writes with a touch of holy annoyance: 'Catholics should at last understand that unity can be furthered not by disputes and wrangels but by the example of a holy life, above all by charity towards all Eastern brethren' (80). It is by the contagion of true Christian charity that we must attract separated Christians to seek, together with us, the fountains of holiness, so that by greater conformity to Christ we become more united in his Body. Charles Journet writes: 'The authentic sanctification of all groups bearing the Christian name is what we have to demand as the most immediate step. Their union to the Church will follow by way of corrolary. "Father, sanctify them in truth . . . so that all may be one . . . and the love with which thou hast loved me, be in them and I in them" ' (John xvii. 17, 21, 26) (81).

It should not be necessary to point out that the gravitation towards the Church which we ascribe to supernatural charity does not imply that Catholics are necessarily more holy than dissident Christians. Catholics have access to the total objective holiness of the Church of Christ, to the promised abundance of life in Christ; but if they fail to live from the pure sources and seek their nourishment elsewhere, they may experience a greater want of charity than dissident Christians who draw the waters of life only from troubled fountains.

On the other hand, the principle which we have discussed is not so withdrawn into the objective order as to leave us without visible witnesses. It would, in fact, be a worthwhile investigation to study the effect of holiness on the variations in religious belief. S. Tyszkiewicz has claimed that whenever the enmity towards the

Roman Church became stronger in Oriental Christianity, there were also forces at work lowering the supernatural life, and conversely that the dissident communities showing the greater holiness were those who were returning to Catholic principles, if not to the Catholic fact (82). But even in the West we do not lack examples where an imitation of Christ has led to an evolution of theological thought. In his study of Gerhard Tersteegen, the saintly Protestant hermit and preacher of the 18th century, Walter Nigg draws the figure of a man whose principles of life were almost completely Catholic (83). A remarkable example is found in the contemporary revival of monastic life in European Protestantism. By their search for the holiness of the gospels these courageous Christians are moved to dogmatic positions which are difficult to reconcile with the official doctrine of their Churches; at least, they must continually defend themselves against the accusation of introducing Catholic practices and opinions. It is indeed remarkable (and a great joy) to see a Calvinist religious community rediscover the value of liturgy and sacrament, and return to the Christian ideal of contemplation. Will such a life have an effect on theology? Here is a simple example: Explaining the life of the brethren, the Prior of the (Protestant) friary of Taizé, Roger Schutz, finds in the gospel the doctrine of our transformation in Christ, often repudiated by Protestants; he writes, 'The course of a Christian is a way of light. "I am", but also "you are the light of the world" ' (84).

The sermon on the Mount is an ecumenical programme, not only because humility solicits the reward of God, but also because the very weight of holiness draws towards the mystical Body of Christ. In the words of the Message of the Amsterdam Assembly of the World Council of Churches: 'In seeking Him we find one another' (85).

Prayer for Unity

Perfect Christian unity is the gift of God. 'The ultimate union will not be brought about by human counsel; it will be due to the goodness of God alone' (86). While it is true that all good things come to us from the Father of lights, the return to Christian unity is a good which is in a singular way the gift of God. It affects not only the spiritual life of individuals but, as we have seen, increases the perfection of the whole mystical Body. Even if the reunion of Christians demands the greatest possible effort on our part, it can never be the outcome of human industry. Only the Spirit of Christ, who completes what he has begun, can bring all the fruits of grace to perfect ripening in the Catholic Church. Prayer for unity, therefore, is a demand of Christian charity in all those in whom the Spirit has awakened the longing for his gift; and like the charity from which it proceeds, this prayer unites Catholic and non-Catholic Christians in an identical ecumenical effort: the continuation of Christ's prayer 'That all may be one'.

While the inspiration of the Spirit is absolutely necessary for the advance of unity among Christians, the Catholic reader feels a little uncomfortable at some of the formulations in the documents of the World Council which emphasize the intervention of the Spirit in a special way. They seem to speak of Christian unity as if it demanded a new act of God in addition to the order established a long time ago by Jesus Christ. 'The Church is being led to a belief that a mutually acceptable order, agreeable to the Word of God (the Scriptures), will be revealed by the Holy Spirit. The Word of God comes again to the Church in our day: "The Comforter even the Holy Spirit whom the Father will send in my name, he shall teach you all things"' (87). Such statements seem to imply much more than an unorthodox ecclesiology; it would be difficult to reconcile them with the unique character of God's revelation made known to us once-for-all in Jesus Christ, to which the same Council of Churches has frequently given very clear testimony. The Spirit intervenes, and may he do so often, to make us hear the Word of God with greater fidelity. But nothing new can be added. The unity of Christians, which is the object of our prayers and the longed-for gift of the Spirit, is none other than the one which he brought at Pentecost.

On the other hand, the loss of unity cuts so deeply into the Christian community that even the Church, praying that all may be one, strains her received terminology and asks God for her own unity. Thus we pray that 'the gift of unity be perfected in the Christian family' (88) or, more strikingly, that 'God may grant unity to the Church' (89). In the Roman liturgy we ask God to *adunare Ecclesiam* and to bestow the *donum unitatis* upon the Christian people (90). We pray *pro unitate Ecclesiae* (91).

The Church repeats Christ's prayer 'That all may be one' and 'That there may be one fold and shepherd', although she believes that this prayer has been fulfilled in her own community. Writing against the non-Catholic movements for unity of his day, Pius XI complains that these men 'constantly quote the words of Christ "That all may be one . . . and that there may be one fold and one shepherd" in the sense that Christ merely expressed a desire, or a prayer, which as yet has not been granted. They hold that the unity of faith and government which is a mark of the true Church of Christ has up to the present time hardly ever existed and does not exist to-day' (92). Christ's prayer for unity has been fulfilled in the Catholic Church. But it has not been fulfilled completely, it still remains a petition. Thus in another letter the same Pius XI pleads for the reconciliation of Churches so that Christ's promise for unity may at last be fulfilled (93). In the same sense writes Pius XII, that 'a pile of inveterate prejudices prevents the happy fulfilment of Christ's prayer "That all may be one" ' (94). Our Lord's petition for unity has been heard, but it has not been heard completely; the ultimate unity of Christians will be the continuation and fulfilment of the unity given to the Catholic Church. Or, as we have said above, *ecumenical action perfects the Church in the line of her unity* (95).

All Christians must pray for the grace of unity. Even if every advance in this direction is the gift of God alone, it is also his will that the gift comes to us as an answer to prayer. This prayer, we are told, is nowhere said with greater fervour than in the Catholic Church (96); and this must be so. While dissident Christians pray for reunion as they are inspired by the Holy Ghost to understand the unity of Christ's gift, the Catholic Church must intercede for this end by the very mission she has received from Christ, the Giver of his Spirit.

In her official worship the Church intercedes for unity every day (97). Her whole liturgy, according to Pius XII, is a prayer for unity; it is the perpetual prayer of the Church 'that she may daily grow in extension and be drawn together in unity' (98). But to the special emphasis on prayer which we notice in the papal documents of our period—there is hardly a letter touching upon Christian unity which is silent about prayer—there correspond certain complementary movements of prayer instituted or recommended by the Holy See. Of these we must mention the principal ones, since they are not without theological significance.

The first period of prayer for the cause of Christian unity introduced into the calendar of the Church was the Novena (nine consecutive days of intercession) preceding the feast of Pentecost. In the apostolic letter *Provida Matris* (1895) Leo XIII recommended that during Whitsuntide special prayers be said for the advance of Christian unity, and in his encyclical on the Holy Ghost (1897) he decreed that such intercession be made in all Churches on the nine days preceding Whit Sunday (99). Ever since, the Novena has been observed in the Catholic Church; yet although Leo XIII frequently referred to the origin and purpose of his institution (100), there are many Catholics who faithfully keep this period of prayer without being aware that it was established for Christian unity.

Secondly there is the January Octave of prayer for the unity of Christians. It had its origin outside the Catholic Church. It was initiated by Fr Paul Watson, the founder of the Friars of the Atonement, a religious community in the Episcopalian Church of America, and observed for the first time by this community in 1908 (101). After the reconciliation of the Friars with the See of Peter, the Octave was approved by Pius X, and has since been endorsed by the Holy See on several occasions and recommended to the Universal Church (102). In many countries bishops have made the observance of the Octave obligatory in all churches of their dioceses, and in the principal churches the eight days are often celebrated with solemn religious services and sermons to educate the faithful towards prayer for unity.

As a third great movement of prayer for the return to the unity of faith must be mentioned the rosary devotion during the month of October. In 1883 Leo XIII prescribed the daily recitation of the rosary in all parish churches during October as a special intercession for the welfare and growth of the Catholic Church (103). That this intention included the unity of the Church was expressly and emphatically stated by Pope Leo in the encyclicals *Adjutricem Populi* (1894) and *Fidentem Piumque* (1896) (104). On account of her close union to Jesus Christ, writes the Pope, Mary is the guardian of unity, and she will be in the midst of the faithful—as she was once in their midst in the Upper Room—when they pray 'that all who have received the gift of baptism may be united to Christ and among themselves by the bonds of one faith and perfect charity' (105). These October intercessions for the mystical Body of Christ have obtained great popularity in the Church.

Prayer is not only a way of asking for unity, it is itself a way of achieving it. Christian prayer does not stand alone; it is 'in Christ'. It is taken up by Christ into his own intercession, into the stream of perfect worship and love which proceeds from the man Jesus Christ in the wake of the Son's eternal return to the Father. In Christ, individual prayer becomes universal. Prayer accelerates the motion with which the chosen People follow their Lord into the glory which he has with the Father, and the greater the momentum of the Body, the more will it be drawn together and united by the bonds of the same divine orientation. Prayer not only pleads for unity, it unites.

This stream of reconciliation which Christ has initiated in the world is rendered present, in its entirety, in the eucharistic celebration of Christ's death. There the whole Church attends Christ's sacrifice on the cross mystically represented on the altar, and participating in it, it becomes her sacrifice also. Christ is not alone in giving himself to the Father; together with him his chosen Body surrenders itself, and this in such a perfect (because sacramental) way that in the eucharistic celebration the total life of Church (her co-operation) is focused on a single event which symbolizes and advances it. The eucharistic liturgy unites because in it, as in no other visible action, the whole Church acts as a single mystical person in Christ.

This communal aspect and unifying power of the eucharistic liturgy has not always been equally alive in the minds of Catholic Christians. It was central in the early Church. St Thomas knew the doctrine; he summarizes it, as is his wont, in a brief sentence of extraordinary weight: *res sacramenti est unitas corporis mystici* (106). The reason why we mention this doctrine here is the renewed emphasis given by recent popes to the social aspect of holy mass and its effect on unity (107). Pius XI declares that the sacrament of the altar is *effectrix unitatis* (108). To the Christians of the East he writes that 'we celebrate the eucharistic mysteries as pledge and foremost cause of unity' (109), and that the preservation of this sacrament in their Churches gives rise to the hope that God may grant the gift of unity which we pray for together, they and we, during the holy mysteries (110).

Common prayer is one of the most important aspects of ecumenical action. United prayer solicits the gift of unity. In prayer, moreover, the weight of that grace is increased which by its own inclination draws into the Body of Christ. Lastly, prayer makes us sensitive to the guidance of the Holy Spirit. For these three reasons then—impetration, sanctification, and illumination—common prayer unites; it is the gift preceding the gift, the divine preparation for the divine fulfilment. Christian prayer has an ecumenical orientation which is identical for Catholics and dissidents alike. Hence it must be the ecumenical concern of Catholics to accompany separated Christians into a more vigorous spiritual life; and in this they find themselves at one with the intentions of the World Council: 'We pray for the Churches' renewal as we pray for their unity. As Christ purifies us by his Spirit, we shall find that we are drawn together and that there is no gain in unity unless it is the unity in truth and holiness' (111).

'To pray together means to be drawn together', we read in the

Report of the Evanston Assembly (112); a Christianity which prays together disposes itself for the divine gift. Do we find this call to *common* prayer in the documents of the Holy See? The question is a delicate one. Since according to the *Codex Juris Canonici* Catholics are forbidden to take an active part in the religious services of dissident Christians (can. 1258), there can be no union of prayer between Catholics and non-Catholics in the fullest sense of the term. It is not surprising, therefore, that we find no explicit invitation in the Roman documents for a common and united prayer. We do find, however, that the popes who urge Catholics towards a more steadfast prayer for unity also ask dissident Christians to join in it.

All prayer born of a living supernatural faith is united in Christ. Even if prayer is not yet fully united in the same visible community, it is nevertheless common in Christ, and hence in an invisible manner it is already common in the Church. In this restricted but very real sense our documents certainly encourage common prayer for unity. We can unite our prayers in Christ, even while we must remain separated in distinct communities. Leo XIII writes to the English people: 'Since we place our confidence . . . in the wonderful power of God's grace, we have with full deliberation made up our mind to invite all Christians in England to take part in this endeavour (for Christian unity), and we urge them likewise to lift up their hearts to God, to fix their trust in him, and to pray to him for the help needed for this great cause' (113). Pope Leo asks all Christians in England for their co-operation in and their prayer for the movement of unity; and thus when he comes to speak of the end of ecumenical action, he words it in such a way that, for all its theological precision, it defines the object of prayer for us as well as for dissident Christians. Our aim is to further 'the great good of Christian unity' (114), or 'the unity of faith and wills' (115); we desire that 'an increasing number of men . . . will labour in all sincerity for the reunion with the Catholic Church' (116), and that eventually 'we all may attain to the unity of faith and the acknowledgment of the Son of God' (cf. Eph. iv. 13) (117). The final sentence of the letter reads, 'We pray that those who seek the kingdom of Christ and salvation in the unity of faith may enter on the full realization of their desires' (118).

There are several ways, all theologically correct, of denoting the unity of Christians, the object of our prayers. We may characterize it either by its *formal* element which is the holy will of Christ for his people, or by one of its *material* elements, such as obedience to papal jurisdiction, which is a consequence of Christ's will. If we designate the ultimate unity of faith by one of its material elements (such as the recognition of the pope), we exclude dissident Christians from praying with us; for no man may pray that an event may come to pass which he does not believe to be in harmony with the will of God. If on the other hand we define the reunion of Christendom by its formal element, we can invite dissident Christians to pray together with us, that the intention of Christ may triumph in the unity of his people.

In the Roman documents of our period, particularly in those of Leo XIII, we find the attempt to promote common prayer for unity by describing the ultimate end of ecumenism in terms acceptable to all Christians. The whole movement for reconciliation is summed up in a universal phrase coined by Leo XIII: *ad maturandum christianae unitatis bonum* (119).

There is perhaps one major exception to this rule; it is in connection with the January Octave of Unity—which significantly is not of Roman origin (120). From the very beginning, when it was observed in the Episcopalian Church of America, the Octave was directed towards the ecclesiastical structure of the Church, the recognition of the supreme jurisdiction of the Roman pontiff. Extending from January 18 (St Peter's Chair at Rome) to January 25 (Conversion of St Paul), its very dates point to the hierarchical centre of the Roman Church, thus establishing a curious contrast to the Pentecostal Novena of Leo XIII which prays for unity under the most spiritual and interior aspect of the Church, the Holy Ghost (121). In some countries the days of the January Octave have been given specific intentions in such an external way that dissident Christians cannot take part in it. That many separated Christians do, in fact, join us in this week of intercession is a gesture of great generosity (122); they realize that we pray with them for the final fulfilment of Christ's promise that all may be one, in the way in which the Lord wants us to be united in his Body. The official Roman approval of the Octave and the prescribed prayer emphasize the formal element of unity and render our common prayer possible (123).

The identical ordination of charity towards the unity of Christ's Body makes common prayer, 'common' in the limited sense we have explained, an ecumenical concern. So deep are the wounds inflicted upon Christendom that this community of prayer must for the greater part remain invisible. We must pray together in separate liturgies and distinct congregations. Only occasionally can our solidarity become manifest in a prayer visibly united. Thus the

Church has recently permitted that at the opening and closing of joint meetings of Catholic and dissident theologians the 'Our Father' or other approved prayers be recited in common (124). But even when the Lord's Prayer is said in disunited fellowships, the petitions of Christ transcend the barriers marring the divine gift and come together in the invisible community of an identical hope. 'Thy kingdom come!'

* * *

'All men in holy orders, and all those who . . . in various associations offer their help to the hierarchy, are called upon to foster the reconciliation of Oriental Christians with the common father of the Church—be it by prayer, or be it by publications' (125). Ecumenical action then, on the unofficial level of contact, is exercised by what we have called *ecumenical charity* and *ecumenical witness*. The former, being less specific, obliges all Christians whatsoever, while the latter having a precise and more technical function is above all the work of theologians. This ecumenism is a slow progress. 'We do not hide the great difficulties in this undertaking and our impotence in overcoming them, but with an invincible confidence we place our hope for success in God' (126). If one considers ecumenical action successful only at the final stage when dissident Christians return to the Church of Christ, one may well, seeing no results in the present, regard it as a fruitless and hence useless undertaking. But we have shown that an increased orientation of dissident Christians to the Body of Christ is already an ecumenical success, and that even if our generation never witnesses an actual reunion, we are obliged by the very mission of the Church to prepare the way for the ultimate gift of unity. Let no Catholic theologian call this an empty dream! 'Our eyes may not see the union of Churches which we are striving for', said Leo XIII, 'but let us not rashly regard this unceasing effort—by a sentiment unworthy of a Christian—as a vain utopia' (127). So fully has the message of Christ been established among us, that we lack no gift while waiting for the appearance of the Lord. God is faithful, and he has called us all into fellowship with his Son Jesus Christ (cf. 1 Cor. i. 6-9).

NOTES

Chapter 1: The Unity of the Church

1 The coincidence of mystical Body and Catholic Church is expressed in passing in many ecclesiastical documents; explicitly it is taught in *Mystici Corporis* (1943). Some years later in *Humani Generis*, AAS 42 (1950) 571, Pius XII definitely states that the doctrine is proposed by the *magisterium ordinarium* of the Church and to be received as such.
2 *Negli Ultimi*, AAS 38 (1946) 18: 'La Chiesa è un tutto indivisibile, perchè Cristo, con la sua Chiesa, è indiviso e indivisibile'.
3 For the New Testament doctrine on the Church as the People of God, see C. SPICQ, 'L'Eglise du Christ' in *La Sainte Eglise Universelle*, Cahiers théologiques de l'actualité protestante, Neuchatel 1948, pp. 175-219.
4 *Mortalium Animos*, AAS 20 (1928) 8.
5 *Satis Cognitum*, LA 16 (1896) 163.
6 Report of Section I at the Amsterdam Assembly: *The Official Report*, London 1949, p. 53. In the preparatory studies for Amsterdam (*The Universal Church in God's Design*, London 1948), we discover what may be called a consent among theologians that the New Testament only knows of a Church which is visible and in history. In the Report of the Faith-and-Order Conference at Lund we read: 'We are agreed that there are no two Churches, one visible and the other invisible, but one Church which must find visible expression on earth' (*The Report*, London 1952, p. 21).
7 Report of the Advisory Commission on the Main Theme of the Second Assembly, *Ecum. Rev.*, 6 (1953-4) 445.
8 *Denz.* no. 1821: 'Pastor aeternus et episcopus animarum nostrarum, ut salutiferum redemptionis opus perenne redderet, sanctam aedificare Ecclesiam decrevit, in qua veluti in domo Dei viventis fideles omnes unius fidei et caritatis vinculo continerentur'.
9 *Satis Cognitum*, LA 16 (1896) 164-5.
10 *Mystici Corporis*, AAS 35 (1943) 204: 'Divinus enim Redemptor mystici Ecclesiae templi aedificationem tum inchoavit, cum concionando sua tradidit praecepta; tum consummavit, cum clarificatus e Cruce pependit; ac tum denique manifestavit promulgavitque, cum adspectabili modo Paraclitum Spiritum in discipulos misit'.

11 *ibid.*, p. 238: 'Christus est enim, qui in Ecclesia sua vivit, qui per eam docet, regit, sanctitatemque impertit'.
12 *Mediator Dei*, AAS 39 (1947) 528: 'Quapropter in omni actione liturgica una cum Ecclesia praesens adest divinus eius Conditor'.
13 *Mystici Corporis*, AAS 35 (1943) 217: 'Quando Ecclesiae Sacramenta externo ritu administrantur, ipsemet effectum in animis operatur'.
14 *ibid.*, p. 238: 'Assuescamus necesse est in Ecclesia ipsum Christum videre'.
15 *The Report*, London 1952, p. 8.
16 *Satis Cognitum*, LA 16 (1896) 184: 'Imo Deus perfecit, ut Ecclesia esset omnium societatum longe praestantissima: nam quod petit ipsa tamquam finem, tanto nobilius est quam quod ceterae petunt societates, quanto naturà gratia divina, rebusque caducis immortalia sunt praestabiliora bona.— Ergo Ecclesia societas est ortu divina: fine, rebusque fini proxime admoventibus, supernaturalis: quod vero coalescit hominibus, humana communitas est'.
17 The context in which the Church is called a 'perfect society' is best explained by citing one of the errors condemned in the *Syllabus* of Pius IX: 'Ecclesia non est vera perfectaque societas plane libera, nec pollet suis propriis et constantibus iuribus sibi a divino suo fundatore collatis, sed civilis potestatis est definire, quae sint Ecclesiae iura ac limites, intra quos eadem iura exercere queat' (*Denz.* no. 1719). The independence of the Church as a perfect society is vindicated by Leo XIII in innumerable documents. In *Immortale Dei*, the most important encyclical on the relationship between Church and State, we read (LA 5 [1885] 140): 'Similiter intelligi debet, Ecclesiam societatem esse, non minus quam ipsam civitatem, genere et iure perfectam'. Therefore, Leo XIII continues, no ruler has the right to reduce the liberty of the Church or impede the free exercise of her functions. Torn from its context, this quotation and, indeed, the whole concept of the Church as 'perfect society' would be completely misleading.
18 *Sapientiae Christianae*, LA 10 (1890) 28: 'Ab omni politico genere imperii distat christiana res publica plurimum. Quodsi similitudinem habet conformationemque regni, profecto originem, caussam, naturam mortalibus regnis habet longe disparem'.
19 S. Tyszkiewicz, *La sainteté de l'Eglise christoconforme*, Rome 1943, chapter 3.
20 *Satis Cognitum*, LA 16 (1896) 161: 'Complexio copulatioque earum duarum velut partium (visibilis et invisibilis) prorsus est ad veram Ecclesiam necessaria, sic fere ut ad naturam humanam intima animae corporisque coniunctio'.

NOTES

21 *La Elevatezza*, AAS 38 (1946) 143.
22 Cf. CHARLES JOURNET, *L'Eglise du Verbe Incarné* II, Bruges 1951, pp. 934-49.
23 *Circondati dal Concorso*, AAS 34 (1942) 157.
24 *Satis Cognitum*, LA 16 (1896) 169.
25 *ibid.*, p. 170: 'Unam esse fidem debere, qui se profitentur christianos, vulgo assentiuntur'.
26 *ibid.*: 'Quaerendo statuendoque qualem in fide unitatem Jesus Christus esse praeceperit'.
27 *Mystici Corporis*, AAS 35 (1943) 228.
28 Cf. *Summa Theol.* II-II, 1, 1.
29 *Mortalium Animos*, AAS 20 (1928) 11: 'Utrumque Christi praeceptum, quod non impleri non potest, alterum scilicet docendi, alterum credendi ad aeternae adeptionem salutis, ne intellegi quidem potest, nisi Ecclesia evangelicam doctrinam proponat integram ac perspicuam sitque in ea proponenda a quovis errandi periculo immunis'.
30 According to the doctrine of the Vatican Council (*Denz.* no 1792), 'Fide divina et catholica ea omnia credenda sunt, quae in verbo Dei scripto vel tradito continentur et ab Ecclesia sive solemni iudicio sive ordinario et universali magisterio tamquam divinitus revelata credenda proponuntur'. But what is absolutely necessary for divine faith is 'ut revelata veritas propter auctoritatem Dei revelantis credatur' (*Denz.* no 1811). Cf. also *Denz.* no 1789.
31 Report of Section I at the Evanston Assembly: *The Evanston Report*, London 1955, p. 87. That they are responsible for one another and for the unity of the Church is a relatively new discovery among Protestant Christians, for which they bless the Ecumenical Movement; see Amsterdam Assembly, Report of Section I, §VI (*The Official Report*, London 1949, pp. 56-7).
32 *Satis Cognitum*, LA 16 (1896) 184: 'Iamvero nulla hominum cogitari potest vera ac perfecta societas, quin potestate aliqua summa regatur'.
33 *ibid.*, p. 185.
34 *Mystici Corporis*, AAS 35 (1943) 210: '. . . Siquidem, ut sapientissimus erat, constitutum ab se sociale Ecclesiae corpus nequaquam sine conspicuo capite relinquere poterat'. The same reference to the positive will of Christ is found in *Praeclara Gratulationis* when Leo XIII defends the jurisdiction of the Church (LA 14 [1894] 206): 'For by the will and ordinance of God her Founder, the Church is a society perfect in its kind . . . . Therefore it is endowed with a living power and efficacy which is not derived from any external source (civil governments) but from the intention of God and the constitution which he gave to her'.

35 *The Report*, London 1952, p. 14.
36 *Satis Cognitum*, LA 16 (1896) 197: 'Si Petri eiusque successorum plena ac summa potestas est, ea tamen esse ne putetur sola. Nam qui Petrum Ecclesiae fundamentum posuit, idem "elegit duodecim . . . quos et apostolos nominavit". Quo modo Petri auctoritatem in romano Pontifice perpetuam permanere necesse est, sic Episcopi, quod succedunt Apostolis, horum potestatem ordinariam hereditate capiunt; ita ut intimam Ecclesiae constitutionem ordo episcoporum necessario attingat. Quamquam vero neque plenam neque universalem ii, neque summam obtinent auctoritatem, non tamen vicarii romanorum pontificum putandi, quia potestatem sibi gerunt propriam, verissimeque populorum, quos regunt, antistites ordinarii dicuntur'. For the same doctrine at the Vatican Council, see *Denz.* no 1828.
37 *ibid.*, p. 198: 'Excidere episcopos iure ac potestate regendi, si a Petro eiusve successoribus scientes secesserint'.
38 See Vatican Council, *Denz.* no 1828.
39 'Notes sur les mots "Confession", "Eglise" et "Communion" ', *Irénikon*, 23 (1950) 27.
40 *Dacché Piacque*, AAS 37 (1945) 259.
41 *Immortale Dei*, LA 5 (1885) 128: 'Quidquid igitur est in rebus humanis quoquo modo sacrum, quidquid ad salutem animarum cultumve Dei pertinet, sive tale illud sit natura sua, sive rursus tale intelligatur propter causam ad quam refertur, id est omne in potestate arbitrioque Ecclesiae: cetera vero . . .' The quotation is also found in *Denz.* no 1866.
42 *Praeclara Gratulationis*, LA 14 (1894) 206: 'Non enim potentiam consectatur Ecclesia'.
43 *La Elevatezza*, AAS 38 (1946) 143: 'Being sent to preach and to gain for the gospel every creature, the Church is not an empire. . . . She develops first of all in depth, then in extension and amplitude. Her work is accomplished in the heart of man and, from thence exercises an influence on his whole life and indeed on all human activity'.
44 *Sapientiae Christianae*, LA 10 (1890) 22: 'Futurum sane Jesus Christus significavit, ut quam ipse offensionem hominum invidiamque prior excepit, in eandem pari modo opus a se institutum incurreret; . . . Quare voluit non alumnos dumtaxat instituere disciplinae suae, sed hos ipsos . . . societate coniungere; . . . Hoc ei est inditum ab Auctore suo ut debeat pro salute generis humani contendere "ut castorum acies ordinata" '.
45 In the eyes of Leo XIII, the promise of Christ that the gates of hell shall not prevail against the Church or her rock foundation 'expresses and confirms' that there is jurisdiction in the Church

NOTES

and that it is meant to be a power against the attacks of the enemies; see *Satis Cognitum*, LA (1896) 187–8.

46 *Immortale Dei*, LA 5 (1885) 125.
47 Cf. the address of Archbishop CUSHING of Boston to the Canon Law Society of America on charity as the fulfilment of the law, reported in *Herder-Korrespondenz*, 9 (1954–55) 110–11. In a similar vein, ecclesiastical law is treated by THOMAS SARTORY in his book *Die ökumenische Bewegung und die Einheit der Kirche*, Meitingen bei Augsburg 1955, pp. 178–83.
48 *Satis Cognitum*, LA 16 (1896) 168: 'Quicumque seorsum eant, aberrant a voluntate et praescriptione Christi Domini, relictoque salutis itinere, ad interitum digrediuntur'.
49 *Mystici Corporis*, AAS 35 (1943) 226: 'Quo autem nobilior est finis, ad quem haec (omnium membrorum) conspiratio contendit, quo divinior est fons ex quo eadem procedit, eo excelsior procul dubio evadit unitas'.
50 *Mit Brennender Sorge*, AAS 29 (1937) 153. In *Mystici Corporis*, AAS 35 (1943) 203, we read that because the Church on earth is still on pilgrimage, a member who loses the gift of charity does not thereby cease to belong to her. Nevertheless charity belongs essentially to the Church's unity. In *Orientalis Ecclesiae* Pius XII defines unity as the divine gift to men by which they are made one in mind, action, and heart, that is, as the gift of faith, obedience to the hierarchy—and charity. Pope Pius writes, AAS 36 (1944) 132, 'Tria eiusmodi vincula . . . ita sunt necessaria, ut quodlibet ex eis desit, vera in Ecclesia Christi unitas et concordia ne intelligi quidem possit'.
51 *Lux Veritatis*, AAS 23 (1931) 510: 'Personalis Christi unitas arcanum exsistit exemplar, ad quod ipsemet unam christianae societatis compagem conformare voluit'.
52 See *Divinum Illud*, LA 17 (1897) 133 and *Mystici Corporis*, AAS 35 (1943) 204–5.
53 *Mystici Corporis*, AAS 35 (1943) 199: 'unum quiddam et indivisum'.
54 *ibid.*, p. 205.
55 *ibid.*, pp. 198–9: 'Pendens e Cruce Christus Jesus non modo violatam resarsit Aeterni Patris iustitiam, sed ineffabilem nobis consanguineis gratiarum copiam promeruit. Quam directo per se ipse universo humano generi dilargiri potuerat; voluit tamen per adspectabilem, in quam homines coalescerent Ecclesiam . . .'.
56 *ibid.*, p. 213: 'Dum enim in Cruce emoriens, immensum Redemptionis thesaurum Ecclesiae suae, nihil ea conferente, dilargitus est; . . .'.
57 *ibid.*, p. 206: 'In arbore Crucis denique sibi suam acquisivit Ecclesiam, hoc est omnia mystici sui Corporis membra, quippe

quae per Baptismatis lavacrum mystico huic Corpori non coagmentarentur, nisi ex salutifera virtute Crucis, in qua quidem iam plenissimae Christi ditionis facta essent'.

58 *ibid.*, p. 217: 'Christus Dominus ex divina plenitudine sua in Ecclesiam vult ubera sua dona influant, ut eadem sibimet ipsi quam maxime adsimuletur'.

59 *ibid.*, p. 246: 'Nos baptismate factos esse Crucifixi carnem'. See Leo the Great, *Serm.* 63.6 and 66.3 (Migne P.L. 54, 357 and 366).

60 *ibid.*, p. 218: 'Servator noster bona maxime sibi propria . . . cum Ecclesia sua communicat'.

61 *Mortalium Animos*, AAS 20 (1928) 15: 'Quisquis igitur cum eo (Corpore) non copulatur . . . non cum Capite Christo cohaeret'.

62 *Satis Cognitum*, LA 16 (1896) 166: 'Dispersa membra atque seiuncta non possunt eodem cum capite, unum simul effectura corpus, cohaerere'.

63 *ibid.*, pp. 166–7.

64 *Mystici Corporis*, AAS 35 (1943) 207: 'Pretiosae suae mortis hora Ecclesiam suam uberioribus Paracliti muneribus ditatam voluit'. Cf. also *ibid.* p. 248: 'Spiritus iam in Cruce datus'. For a patristic documentation of this doctrine, see S. TROMP, *Textus et Documenta Encyclicae* 'Mystici Corporis', Rome 1948, pp. 98–101.

65 *Mystici Corporis*, AAS 35 (1943) 219: 'Ille est, qui licet per se ipse in omnibus membris habeatur, in iisdemque divinitus agat, in inferioribus tamen etiam per superiorum ministerium operatur'. It was Christ who appointed the apostles and who sent the Holy Ghost, so that there can be no opposition or incompatibility between the invisible mission of the Holy Ghost and the juridical powers of appointed pastors; cf. *ibid.* p. 224.

66 *ibid.*, p. 206: 'E Crucis virtute Servator noster, etsi iam in utero Virginis Caput totius humanae familiae constitutus, ipsum Capitis munus in Ecclesia sua plenissime exercet'.

67 *ibid.*, p. 213: 'tremendum sane mysterium ac satis numquam meditatum'.

68 *ibid.*: 'tamen non ex eius indigentia debilitateque accidit'.

69 *ibid.*: 'ipsemet ad maiorem intemeratae suae Sponsae honorem rem ita disposuit'.

70 *ibid.*: 'Dum enim in Cruce emoriens, immensum Redemptionis thesaurum Ecclesiae suae, nihil ea conferente, dilargitus est; ubi de eiusmodi thesauro distribuendo agitur, id efficiendae sanctitatis opus non modo cum intaminata sua Sponsa communicat, sed ex eius etiam opera vult quodammodo oriri'.

71 *ibid.*, p. 209: 'Ipse solummodo est qui Ecclesiam regit atque gubernat'.

72 *ibid.*, pp. 209–10: 'Sed etiam directo per se divinus Servator noster conditam ab se societatem moderatur ac dirigit. Ipse enim regnat in mentibus animisque hominum et ad beneplacitum suum vel rebelles inflectit ac compellit voluntates'.
73 *E Ormai Passato*, AAS 36 (1944) 172. The same doctrine is explained in *Mystici Corporis*, AAS 35 (1943) 211: There is but one head of the mystical Body, namely Christ, of whose headship in things visible Peter is the representative on earth. Pius XII refers to Boniface VIII's bull *Unam Sanctam* (see *Denz.* no 468).
74 *Lux Veritatis*, AAS 23 (1931) 510. The whole sentence reads: 'Nam si personalis Christi unitas arcanum exsistit exemplar, ad quod ipsemet unam christianae societatis compagem conformare voluit, id profecto non ex commentitia quadam oriri posse multorum inter se discordium coniunctione, sed ex una solummodo hierarchia, ex uno summoque magisterio, ex una credendi lege, unaque christianorum fide nemo cordatus non videat'.
75 *Mystici Corporis*, AAS 35 (1943) 211.
76 *ibid.*, p. 214: '(Adsimilatio Ecclesiae ad Christum) profecto evenit, cum ipsa, Conditoris sui vestigiis insistens, docet, regit, divinumque sacrificium immolat'.
77 It is the explicit teaching of the Vatican Council that the history of the Church, her marvelous propagation and her spiritual fecundity, make her a constant argument for the credibility of the faith; cf. *Denz.* no 1794.
78 *Mystici Corporis*, AAS 35 (1943) 230: 'Ex eadem autem Spiritus Christi communicatione efficitur, ut, cum omnia dona, virtutes et charismata, quae in Capite excellenter, uberrime efficienterque insunt, in omnia Ecclesiae membra deriventur, et in iis secundum locum quem in mystico Jesu Christi Corpore occupant, in dies perficiantur, Ecclesia veluti plenitudo constituatur et complementum Redemptoris; Christus vero quoad omnia in Ecclesia quodammodo adimpleatur'.
79 Modern exegetes are not agreed on the meaning of 'pleroma' as it is applied to the Church in Eph. i. 23. In our context, Pius XII takes it to mean the fullness or completion of the mystical Christ: as Head of the Church Christ needs the co-operation of his members to achieve his mystical consummation in the Church. According to L. CERFAUX (*La théologie de l'Eglise suivant Saint Paul*, Paris 1942, pp. 256–60), this is the interpretation which suggests itself at first sight and which has been adopted by the Fathers. Yet for Paul, the author explains, 'pleroma' is a technical term connoting primarily the fullness of God, the divine fullness which dwells in Jesus Christ and to which man has access through faith. The Church, then, is

the zone where this fullness of life and holiness is exercised. A similar view is taken by A. WIKENHAUSER (*Die Kirche als der mystische Leib Christi nach dem Apostel Paulus*, Münster 1937, pp. 187–91). 'Pleroma' in the Church must be understood passively: 'Die Kirche ist das von Christus Erfüllte'. There are also, on the other hand, modern exegetes, and not all of them Catholic, for whom 'pleroma' in the Church signifies the fulfilment and completion which Christ the Head achieves in and through his Body. This is the view taken in the commentary on Eph. i. 23 in *La Bible de Jérusalem* (P. BENOIT, vol. 7, Paris 1949), in the *Regensburger Neues Testament* (H. STAAB and J. FREUNDORFER, vol. 7, Regensburg 1950), and in the Protestant commentary *Schlatter's Erläuterungen zum Neuen Testament* (part 7, Stuttgart 1944).

80 *Mystici Corporis*, AAS 35 (1943) 217, 218.
81 *La Elevatezza*, AAS 38 (1946) 142.
82 *Negli Ultimi*, AAS 38 (1946) 18. The test refers to AUGUSTINUS, serm. 341, cap. 1: 'Christus in Scripturis dictus tribus modis . . .; tertius modus est quodam modo totus Christus, in plenitudine Ecclesiae, id est, caput et corpus, secundum plenitudinem perfecti cuiusdam viri, in quo viro singuli membra sumus' (Migne P.L. 39, 1493). Cf. also *de Dono Persev.*, cap. 7: 'Christus enim totus cum membris suis est, propter Ecclesiam, quae est corpus eius, plenitudo eius' (Migne P.L. 45, 1001).
83 It is the explicit doctrine of the popes that the Church of Christ is visible and visibly one, by the very fact that he made it his body. *Satis Cognitum*, LA 16 (1896) 160 and *Mystici Corporis*, AAS 35 (1943) 199: 'Propter eam rem quod corpus est, oculis cernitur Ecclesia'.
84 *Mystici Corporis*, AAS 35 (1943) 202: 'In Ecclesiae autem membris reapse ii soli annumerandi sunt, qui regenerationis lavacrum receperunt veramque fidem profitentur, neque a Corporis compage semet ipsos misere separarunt, vel ob gravissima admissa a legitima auctoritate seiuncti sunt'.
85 *ibid.*, p. 203: 'Qui fide vel regimine invicem dividuntur, in uno eiusmodi Corpore, atque uno eius divino Spiritu vivere nequeunt'.
86 *ibid.*, p. 243: '. . . ut internis divinae gratiae impulsionibus ultro libenterque concedentes, ab eo statu se eripere studeant, in quo de sempiterna cuiusque propria salute securi esse non possunt; quandoquidem, etiamsi inscio quodam desiderio ac voto ad mysticum Redemptoris Corpus ordinentur, tot tamen tantisque caelestibus muneribus adiumentisque carent, quibus in Catholica solummodo Ecclesia frui licet'.
87 The theological studies of Church membership, according to *Mystici Corporis*, prior to the publication of the Boston Letter

(see below), are very numerous. It would take too much space, however, to give a complete bibliography of the controversies. A short account of the principal debate is found in T. ZAPELENA, *De Ecclesia Christi* II, Rome 1954, pp. 372–8. A long, though still incomplete list of the controversial articles is appended to P. A. LIEGE's, essay 'Le Salut des Autres', itself controversial, in *Lumière et Vie*, 1954, pp. 770–1. Two more recent studies, K. ALGERMISSEN, 'Aktuelle Mitgliedschaft in der Kirche', *Theologie und Glaube*, 46 (1956) 260–75, and G. VODOPIVEC, 'Membri in re ed appartenenza in voto alla Chiesa di Cristo', *Euntes Docete*, 10 (1957) 65–104, give a more systematic treatment of the whole problem in the light of the Roman teaching. The bibliographical note attached to the latter article is very extensive.

88 *American Ecclesiastical Review*, 127 (1952) 307–15.
89 A man cannot be said to 'adhere' to the Church by a good natural disposition which actual graces occasionally and transiently orientate towards Christ. 'Adhering' to the Church implies habitual grace, or at least some permanent supernatural character.
90 Having indicated the triple mark of membership in the Church, Pius XII continues, in the same encyclical, to refer to catechumens as members (*Mystici Corporis*, AAS 35 [1943] 242).
91 Cf. the famous passage from Pius IX's encyclical *Quanto Conficiamur*, explaining how the way of salvation is open to men who are invincibly ignorant of the Christian religion (*Denz.* no 1677).

CHAPTER 2: DISSIDENT CHRISTIANS

1 We follow the definition of 'heretic' and 'schismatic' as given in the *Codex Iuris Canonici*, can. 1325 §2, which includes the 'pertinacious' refusal to hear the Church. There exists also another terminology, introduced into theology in recent centuries (see CH. JOURNET, *L'Eglise du Verbe Incarné* II, Bruges 1951, pp. 708–17), according to which all separated Christians are, independently of their intention, heretics or schismatics. This usage is also reflected in the *Codex*: v.g., can. 731 §2. However, in the papal documents of our period we never find the second terminology employed. We never read, for instance, of 'heretics in good faith'. In our study therefore, we shall follow the usage of our source documents: we shall employ the terms 'heretic' and 'schismatic' in the strict sense which includes the idea of sinful obstinacy. Cf. also p. 68.

2 We shall list the most important documents dealing with or touching upon the problem of Christian unity. On the nature of the Church: *Satis Cognitum* (1896), *Mystici Corporis* (1943). With reference to Eastern Christians: *Praeclara Gratulationis* (1894), *Ecclesiam Dei* (1923), *Rerum Orientalium* (1928), *Orientalis Ecclesiae* (1944), *Orientales Omnes Ecclesias* (1945), *Rex Sempiternus* (1951). With reference to the Christians of the West: *Amantissimae Voluntatis* (1895), *Caritatis Studium* (1898), *Mortalium Animos* (1928), the instruction *Ecclesia Catholica* (1949).

3 ROGER AUBERT, *Le saint-siège et l'union des Eglises*, Brussels 1947, pp. 153–8.

4 In our documents the word 'patrimony' is applied in a wide sense to the supernatural elements surviving among dissident Christians; with reference to the Orthodox in *Orientalis Ecclesiae*, AAS 36 (1944) 137, and in regard to Protestants in *Praeclara Gratulationis*, LA 14 (1894) 203. See pp. 36 and 53.

5 The separated Christians of the East are called 'Orthodoxi' (without quotation marks) in *Orientis Catholici*, AAS 9 (1917) 533; usually the Roman documents refer to them as 'dissidentes Orientales'.

6 *Praeclara Gratulationis*, LA 14 (1894) 199: '. . . quod non ingenti discrimine seiunguntur: imo, si pauca excipias, sic cetera consentimus, ut in ipsis catholici nominis vindiciis non raro ex doctrina, ex more, ex ritibus, quibus Orientales utuntur, testimonia atque argumenta promamus. Praecipium dissidii caput, de romani Pontificis primatu'.

7 *Rerum Orientalium*, AAS 20 (1928) 287: 'Praesertim cum apud illos populos tanta divinae Revelationis pars religiosissime asservata sit; et sincerum Christi Domini obsequium et in eius matrem intemeratam amor pietasque singularis, et ipsorum sacramentorum usus vigeat'.

8 *ibid.*, p. 284: 'pars tam conspicua dominici gregis'.

9 *Arcano Divinae Providentiae* (1868), Mansi 50, 199*: 'pars christiani populi'.

10 *ibid.*: 'pretiosissimo Salvatoris nostri sanguine redemptus et sacris baptismatis aquis in dominicum gregem adlectus'.

11 *Orientalis Ecclesiae*, AAS 36 (1944) 137: 'Aestimatione debita ea omnia amplectatur oportet, quae Orientalibus gentibus fuere, peculiare veluti patrimonium, a maioribus tradita, simul quae ad sacram Liturgiam et ad Hierarchicos Ordines spectent, simul etiam quae ad ceteras christianae vitae rationes pertineant, modo eadem cum germana religionis fide rectisque de moribus normis penitus concordent'.

12 *Paternas Caritas*, LA 8 (1888) 274, 275: 'qui Christum colunt

sed a Romana Ecclesia secesserunt'; 'per baptismum ingressi in christianae vitae societatem'.

13 To refer to the dissident Christian bodies of the East as 'Churches' is quite normal in the Roman documents. It is done without hesitation; in the encyclicals *Orientalis Ecclesiae* (1944), *Orientales Omnes Ecclesias* (1945), and *Orientales Ecclesias* (1953) they are thus called in the very titles. We find Orthodox bishops designated as 'dissidentes episcopi' (*Orientalis Ecclesiae*, AAS 36 [1944] 142) and Orthodox ministers in general as 'dissidentes ecclesiastici' (*A Dilecto Filio*, AAS 16 [1924] 327). Leo XIII can write of his 'benevolentia in clerum et populum Orientalium ecclesiarum, etiam dissidentium' (*Quum Nuper*, LA 15 [1895] 247). For a detailed investigation into the Roman usage of designating dissident Christian bodies, see YVES CONGAR, *Chrétiens désunis*, Paris 1937, Append. VI, and the continuation by the same author in *Irénikon*, 23 (1950) 22–4.

14 *Sempiternus Rex*, AAS 43 (1951) 642: 'ob virtutis constantiam et christianae fidei professionem'.

15 'Ex tot . . . martyriis', writes Pius XII (*ibid.* p. 643), there surges a great hope for Christian unity. Or again, the Churches of the East in ancient and in modern times are made red 'profuso martyrum . . . sanguine' (*Orientales Ecclesiae*, AAS 45 [1953] 5).

16 Cf. *Summa Theol.* III, 73, 3, in corp.

17 See especially *Ecclesiam Dei*, AAS 15 (1923) 581. Cf. also p. 131.

18 *Orientalis Ecclesiae*, AAS 36 (1944) 138: 'tum qui in Catholicae Ecclesiae gremio sunt nati, tum qui desiderio ac voto eidem assequendae velificantur'.

19 In the eyes of the popes, the Church of England has abandoned the Catholic faith. *Amantissimae Voluntatis*, LA 15 (1895) 142: 'primum divulsa a communione Apostolicae Sedis, dein ab ea fide sanctissima abducta est . . .'. Or again, *Gratissimas Cito*, LA 17 (1897) 280: '. . . in Anglia primum ab unitatis centro abscessum, dein a fide sanctissima descitum est'.

20 See p. 73.

21 *Ecumenical Review*, 4 (1951–2) 261.

22 For a collection of ecclesiastical pronouncements on Church membership conferred through baptism, see YVES CONGAR, *Chrétiens désunis*, Paris 1937, p. 288.

23 *Mystici Corporis*, AAS 35 (1943) 201.

24 Cf. the doctrine on baptism of the Council of Trent, *Denz.* no 860. In the brief *Singulari Nobis* (1749) Benedict XIV writes: 'Eum qui ab haeretico baptisma rite suscepit, illius vi Ecclesiae Catholicae membrum esse docemus' (cited by T. ZAPELENA, *De Ecclesia Christi* II, Rome 1954, p. 379).

25 *Summa Theol.* III, 68, 9, ad 3.
26 *Annum Sacrum*, LA 19 (1899) 72–3 and *Quas Primas*, AAS 17 (1925) 601: '(Ii) qui sacro baptimate rite abluti (sunt) utique ad Ecclesiam, si spectetur ius, pertinent, quamvis vel error opinionum devios agat, vel dissensio a caritate seiungat'.
27 *Sempiternus Rex*, AAS 43 (1951) 642.
28 Cf. J. GIBLET, 'Le baptême, sacrement de l'incorporation à l'Eglise selon saint Paul', *Lumière et Vie*, 1956, pp. 53–80.
29 The interpretation of this canon has given rise to a recent controversy between K. Mörsdorf and Karl Rahner on the possibility of Church membership in several grades; for an account of the controverted issue and the bibliographical references, see THOMAS SARTORY, *Die ökumenische Bewegung und die Einheit der Kirche*, Meitingen bei Augsburg 1955, pp. 137–8. Th. Sartory concludes, against the position of K. Rahner, that even from the legal point of view the Church recognizes various degrees of membership (*ibid.*, pp. 138–40).
30 Concerning the legislation of the Church on sacramental intercommunion with Oriental dissidents, see YVES CONGAR, art. 'schisme', *Dict. Théol. Cath.* 14, col. 1310–11. In particular we refer to a decision of the Holy Office, July 20, 1898 (cited in P. PRUEMMER, *Manuale Theologiae Moralis* I, 9th ed., Freiburg 1940, p. 365) according to which sacramental absolution may be given to a dissident Christian in danger of death, provided there is no likelihood of scandal.
31 AUGUSTINUS GIBBON, *De Luthero-Calvinismo*, Erfurt 1663, pp. 17–19.
32 See pp. 30–31.
33 *Sapientiae Christianae*, LA 10 (1890) 24. Pope Leo is quoting from the Vatican Council; here is the complete sentence (*Denz.* no. 1789): 'Hanc vero fidem, quae "humanae salutis initium est", Ecclesia catholica profitetur, virtutem esse supernaturalem, qua, Dei aspirante et adiuvante gratia, ab eo revelata vera esse credimus, non propter intrinsecam rerum veritatem naturali rationis lumine perspectam, sed propter auctoritatem ipsius Dei revelantis, qui nec falli nec fallere potest'.
34 *Sapientiae Christianae*, LA 10 (1890) 24: 'Statuere vero quae sint doctrinae divinitus traditae, Ecclesiae docentis est, cui custodiam interpretationemque Deus eloquiorum suorum commisit'.
35 Cf. *Denz.* nos 1812, 1813.
36 *Denz.* no 1790: '. . . voluit Deus cum internis Spiritus Sancti auxiliis externa iungi revelationis suae argumenta, facta scilicet divina, atque imprimis miracula et prophetias, quae . . . divinae revelationis signa sunt certissima et omnium intelligentiae accommodata'.

NOTES

37 *Aeterni Patris*, LA 1 (1879) 261: 'Ideo (propter mirabilia quaedam signa tamquam certa revelatae veritatis argumenta) omnes, qui Evangelio fidem adiungunt, non temere adiungere, tamquam doctas fabulas secutos, sed rationabili prorsus obsequio intelligentiam et iudicium suum divinae subiicere auctoritati'.

38 *Denz.* no 1794: 'Ad solam enim catholicam Ecclesiam ea pertinent omnia, quae ad evidentem fidei christianae credibilitatem tam multa tam mira divinitus sunt disposita'.

39 *Denz.* no 1793.

40 The Boston Letter; see p. 31.

41 *Wie Hätten Wir*, AAS 40 (1948) 419: '. . . der Gott weiss wie viele von ihnen ohne persönliche Schuld fernstehen'.

42 *Amantissimae Voluntatis*, LA 15 (1895) 149: 'animi ita (ad uberioris gratiae munera) affecti'.

43 *Longinqua Oceani*, LA 15 (1895) 20: '. . . quorum non paucos quis neget hereditate magis, quam voluntate dissentire'.

44 *Missam In Vobis*, AAS 3 (1911) 564: 'Cum sint acatholici (oves deviae) Canadenses, iique magnam partem, conscientiae bonae, . . .'.

45 English translations of the official Roman documents are sometimes quite 'timid'. Often they prefer a literal rendering in bad English to an interpretative translation of the text. Thus the participial nouns 'separati' and 'devulsi' offer a difficulty. The translators frequently dare not write 'separated brethren', because they sense the positive judgment implied in the expression and do not know if this is Roman enough. Consequently they simply write 'the separated', which is either un-English or insulting. However in the English translations printed in the AAS, we find no such hesitation. 'Eos quoque invitamus, quos Mater Ecclesia a se divulsos deflet' (*Sertum Laetitiae*, AAS 31 [1939] 644) is translated by 'We invite those, too, whom Mother Church laments as separated brethren' (*ibid.*, p. 655).

46 *Caritatis Studium*, LA 18 (1898) 109–10.

47 *Annum Ingressi*, LA 22 (1902) 66.

48 *Ubi Arcano Dei*, AAS 14 (1922) 696.

49 *Rerum Orientalium*, AAS 20 (1928) 288.

50 *ibid.*, p. 286: 'non manca sed integra et aperta fidei professio'.

51 *Caritatis Studium*, LA 18 (1898) 101: '. . . quibus christianae fidei abest integritas'.

52 *Amantissimae Voluntatis*, LA 15 (1895) 150: 'ut liceat (eis) . . . doctrinae eius plene dispicere veritatem, eiusdemque misericordiae consilia fidelissime amplecti'.

53 *Iam Vos Omnes* (1868), Mansi 50, 203*: 'qui etiamsi eundem Christum Jesum veluti Redemptorem agnoscant et in christiano nomine glorientur . . .'.

54 *Longinqua Oceani*, LA 15 (1895) 21: 'christianis initiati sacris'.
55 *Annum Sacrum*, LA 19 (1899) 73: '(non) christianae fidei expertes'.
56 *Praeclara Gratulationis*, LA 14 (1894) 196: 'christiano initiata nomine'.
57 *Satis Cognitum*, LA 16 (1896) 206: 'Jesum Christum Filium Dei eundemque Servatorem generis humani agnoscunt et fatentur'.
58 *Lux Veritatis*, AAS 23 (1931) 510: 'asseclae Christi ... qui in ipso cum singulorum, tum humanae consortionis spem salutemque reponunt'.
59 *Non Mai Forse*, AAS 42 (1950) 126: 'gli adoratori di Cristo'; 'credenti in Gesù Cristo'.
60 *Summi Pontificatus*, AAS 31 (1939) 542.
61 *Nell'alba*, AAS 34 (1942) 21: 'sono a Noi vicini per la fede in Dio e in Gesù Cristo'.
62 *Caritatis Studium*, LA 18 (1898) 109: 'Scotorum nobiscum de fide dissidentium complures Christi nomen ex animo diligunt, eiusque et disciplinam assequi et exempla sanctissima persequi imitando nituntur'.
63 *Amantissimae Voluntatis*, LA 15 (1895) 144: '. . . illi praeclare consulunt qui non timide complectuntur atque etiam asserunt summa Dei et Christi eius iura, leges, documenta; his namque divinum in terris regnum consistit'. And *ibid.*, p. 149: 'in qua intuemur crebriora et manifestiora indicia divinae gratiae'.
64 *Ad Beatissimi Apostolorum*, AAS 6 (1914) 577.
65 *Rerum Orientalium*, AAS 20 (1928) 287: 'longe a recto tramite dudum aberrantes'.
66 *Sempiternus Rex*, AAS 43 (1951) 640-1: 'ab unitate mystici Corporis Christi ... longam per saeculorum seriem misere abscesserunt'.
67 *Orientales Omnes*, AAS 38 (1946) 58: ' ... hac (Christi) plenitudine is profecto frui nequit qui ab Ecclesia "quae est corpus ipsius" seiunctus sit'.
68 *Lux Veritatis*, AAS 23 (1931) 515: '. . . ut ab Ecclesiae unitate adeoque a Filio ... aberrent'.
69 *Properante ad Exitum*, LA 19 (1899) 64: 'Quanta pars christianorum, sentiendi cogitandique licentia deliniti, malarum doctrinarum veneno sitienter hausto, fidei divinae in se ipsi grande munus quotidie corrumpant'.
70 Cf. *Summa Theol.* II–II, 39, 2.
71 Cf. St JEROME, *Comm. ad Titum*, III, 10: 'Nullum schisma non sibi aliquam confingit haeresim, ut recte ab Ecclesia recessisse videatur' (Migne P.L. 26, 598). St AUGUSTINE, *Contra Cresconium*, II, 7: '. . . schisma esse recens congregationis ex aliqua sententiarum diversitate dissensio . . .; haeresis autem, schisma inveteratum' (Migne P.L. 43, 471).

NOTES

72 It has been remarked that in all his letters Leo XIII never refers to the dissention of the Eastern Churches by the term 'schisma'; see CH. JOURNET, *L'Eglise du Verbe Incarné* II, Bruges 1951, pp. 759–60.
73 *Arcano Divinae Providentiae* (1868), Mansi 50, 199*: 'per nefarias illius artes . . . qui primum schisma excitavit in caelo'.
74 *Inscrutabili*, LA 1 (1878) 49.
75 *Praeclara Gratulationis*, LA 14 (1894) 200.
76 *ibid.*, p. 199.
77 *Rerum Orientalium*, AAS 20 (1928) 277: 'Siquidem noverant et complura antehac mala et miserrimum illud discidium quod tam multas easque florentissimas olim Ecclesias ab radice unitatis abstraxerat, cum ex mutua imprimis populorum ignoratione et despicientia, tum ex praeiudicatis opinionibus, quas diuturna animorum alienatio consecuta est, necessario exstitisse'. This mutual 'alienatio' or *estrangement* is the key-concept about which YVES CONGAR centres his phenomenology of the rift between the Churches of East and West ('Neuf cents ans après', in *L'Eglise et les Eglises* I, Chévetogne 1954, pp. 3–95).
78 *Orientales Omnes*, AAS 38 (1946) 39.
79 *Ecclesiam Dei*, AAS 15 (1923) 580: '. . . neque in Ecclesiam Romanam privatorum culpas conferant, quas ipsa quidem et damnat et emendare connititur'.
80 *Sempre Bella*, AAS 14 (1922) 345. This passage is a faint echo of the famous statement of Pope Hadrian VI (1522) admitting Catholic and papal guilt in preparing the Reformation; see YVES CONGAR, *Chrétiens désunis*, Paris 1937, Append. II.
81 *Militantis Ecclesiae*, LA 17 (1897) 249.
82 *Annum Ingressi*, LA 22 (1902) 58: 'Quo facto discidio illuc necessitate evasere, quo fortasse non spectarant (novatores), ut christiani nominis vix umbram retinerent, rem fere exuerent'.
83 *Ecclesia Catholica*, AAS 42 (1950) 144.
84 *In Hac Tanta*, AAS 11 (1919) 217.
85 *Antequam Ordinem*, AAS 11 (1919) 97.
86 *Inscrutabili*, LA 1 (1878) 49.
87 *Mit Brennender Sorge*, AAS 29 (1937) 156.
88 *Orientales Omnes*, AAS 38 (1946) 36.
89 Leo XIII's judgment on the consequences of the Protestant Reformation was rather severe. See *Immortale Dei*, LA 5 (1885) 133; *Iam Pridem*, LA 6 (1886) 13; *Providentissimus Deus*, LA 13 (1893) 339; *Praeclara Gratulationis*, LA 14 (1894) 203; *Militantis Ecclesiae*, LA 17 (1897) 248–59; *Annum Ingressi*, LA 22 (1902) 57–8.

90 Leo XIII's interpretation of the principle of private judgment is perhaps influenced by certain Protestant writers of the last century. Usually Protestant theologians teach differently on the freedom of choice before the revealed Word of God. MAX THURIAN writes in 'Orientations actuelles de la spiritualité protestante', *Irénikon*, 22 (1949) 376: 'The doctrine of free examination has never been received in orthodox Protestantism and does not derive its foundation from the Reformers of the 16th century; it has had some fortune in the liberal theologies of the 19th century. The doctrine has bit by bit destroyed the true spirit of Protestantism'.

91 *Praeclara Gratulationis*, LA 14 (1894) 203.

92 *Ecclesia Catholica*, AAS 42 (1950) 142: 'In pluribus orbis partibus, quum ex variis exterius eventibus et animorum mutationibus, tum maxime ex communibus fidelium orationibus, afflante quidem Spiritus Sancti gratia, in multorum animis ab Ecclesia Catholica dissidentium desiderium in dies excrevit ut ad unitatem omnium redeatur, qui in Christum Dominum credunt. Quod profecto filiis Ecclesiae verae est causa sanctae in Domino laetitiae'.

93 Cf. *Già Fin Dagli*, LA 20 (1900) 238–243 and *Une Douce Emotion*, LA 21 (1901) 190.

94 *Orientales Omnes*, AAS 38 (1946) 43. In this connection we note the reference of Benedict XV, later quoted by Pius XI, to 'those who are spreading error', probably meaning Protestant missionaries; see *Maximum Illud*, AAS 11 (1919) 453 and *Decessor Noster*, AAS 21 (1929) 342.

95 'Le théologien catholique, envisageant ce problème dans une perspective oecuménique, ne valorisera les éléments communs *aux dépens* des ensembles respectifs, mais valorisera au contraire la partie *en fonction* du tout' (JEROME HAMER, 'Mission de l'oecuménisme catholique', *Lumière et Vie*, 1955, p. 70).

96 *E Ormai Passato*, AAS 36 (1944) 171.

97 Cf. *Summa Theol.* II–II, 2, 5. Protestant theologians generally do not admit that a true act of faith can be made implicitly in the readiness to receive the whole of divine revelation; see S. HARENT, art. 'foi', *Dict. Théol. Cath.* 6, col. 343–8.

98 Faith may also vary with respect to its formal motive. We speak of one man having greater faith than another, by which we mean that the former is more surrendered to God in his faith. It is clear, however, that variations of faith with respect to its object are by no means proportional to variations with respect to its motive. A man with an undeveloped faith may cling to God more firmly than another who holds the full Catholic creed.

99 *Summa Theol.* II–II, 1, 3, ad 3.

NOTES

100 *Summa Theol.* III, 27, 2.
101 *Mystici Corporis*, AAS 35 (1943) 203; see note 85 of chapter 1.
102 For complete quotation, see note 84 of chapter 1.
103 Cf. LUCIEN CERFAUX, 'L'Unité du Corps Apostolique dans le Nouveau Testament', *L'Eglise et Les Eglises*, I, Chévetogne 1954, pp. 99–110.
104 *Mystici Corporis*, AAS 35 (1943) 243: 'ab eo statu se eripere studeant, in quo de sempiterna cuiusque propria salute securi esse non possunt'. Cf. Pius IX, *Iam Vos Omnes*, Mansi 50, 205*.
105 *Mystici Corporis* AAS 35 (1943) 243: '. . . tot tantisque caelestibus muneribus adiumentisque carent, quibus in Catholica solummodo Ecclesia frui licet'.

CHAPTER 3: DISSIDENT CHURCHES

1 This is the explicit teaching of *Satis Cognitum* (1896), *Mortalium Animos* (1928) and *Mystici Corporis* (1943), and hence of the Roman *magisterium ordinarium*. The theologians setting up the preparatory *schema* 'de Ecclesia Christi' for the Vatican Council meant to integrate a very strong expression of this doctrine in the conciliar definition: '(Ecclesiam) ita plane in sua constitutione esse determinatam, ut quaecumque societates a fidei unitate vel a communione unius corporis seiunctae nullo modo pars eius aut membrum dici possint' (cap. 5, *Mansi* 51, 541).
2 *Ad Quosdam Puseistas Anglicos*, AAS 11 (1919) 315: 'Coetus prorsus ab externa visibilique communione et obedientia Romani Pontificis separatos, esse non posse Ecclesiam Christi, neque ad Ecclesiam Christi quomodolibet pertinere'.
3 In the art. 'ecumenismo', *Enciclopedia Cattolica*, Vatican City, vol. 5, col. 65, Yves Congar is severely criticized for conceding, in his book *Chrètiens désunis*, Paris 1937, that dissident Churches are in some sense elements of the true Church. While we admit that Fr. Congar's excellent book contains some ambiguous formulations, we do not think that he is here teaching the doctrine that is ascribed to him. On pp. 301–2 of his book he writes tentatively, 'On ne peut dire des Chrétientés dissidentes qu'elles soient des membres de l'Una Sancta, on peut cependant, nous semble-t-il, dire d'elles qu'elles sont à des degrès divers d'ailleurs, des éléments de l'Eglise'. Explaining this sentence (pp. 302-7), the author intends to say nothing more than that dissident Churches have retained a heritage, incomplete but supernatural, from the Church of Christ, and that in passing it on they do not save in spite of themselves, but rather on account of part of themselves, that is, on account of the Christian patrimony which is truly

theirs without ceasing thereby to belong to the Catholic Church in a more proper sense.

4 For a detailed description of this recovery within a separated Church, see CHARLES JOURNET, *L'Eglise du Verbe Incarné* II, Bruges 1951, pp. 720–2.

5 There is one notable exception to this rule: the two letters of the Holy Office *Ad Omnes Angliae Episcopos* and *Ad Quosdam Puseistas Anglicos*. These letters however do not properly belong to the period which we are studying. They were written in the years 1864–5, and even though they were reprinted in the AAS of 1919 (pp. 310–16), they present Catholic doctrine in a vocabulary and with an emphasis for which we have no parallel in the documents of our period. In these two letters we find the frequent use of the adjectives 'heretical' and 'schismatic' applied to individuals as well as to religious societies. We have noted in chapter 2, note 1, that in the Roman documents belonging to our period these adjectives are employed only to describe a wilful and therefore sinful situation.

6 The dissident Christian bodies of the East are usually, though not always, called 'Churches' in our documents; see note 13 of chapter 2. In some contexts they are referred to as 'societies' to make clear that they are not Churches in the full and proper sense.

7 Pp. 13–14.

8 We assume in this paragraph that the faith professed by the Orthodox Churches is, apart from the denial of Roman primacy, reconcilable with the faith of the Catholic Church. Is this a reasonable assumption? There are certainly doctrinal divergences. The papal writings, however, seem more optimistic than many evaluations on the part of Catholic theologians. There is, to be sure, no direct statement in the Roman documents. 'With few exceptions', writes Leo XIII without further specification, 'we are entirely at one . . . The principal contention is the primacy of the Roman Pontiff'. (For full quotation, see note 6 of chapter 2.) The Church always recalls the unions of former centuries where the differences in belief did not present insurmountable obstacles. For a discussion of the doctrinal divergences between the Orthodox Churches and the Catholic Church, see YVES CONGAR, *Chrétiens désunis*, Paris 1937, pp. 359–65; MARTIN JUGIE, *Le schisme byzantin*, Paris 1941, pp. 359–98; PIERRE DUMONT, 'Les croyances de l'Orthodoxie', *Qu'est ce que l'Orthodoxie*, Brussels 1944, pp. 137–72.

9 The promise that the Eastern Churches can keep their traditional ecclesiastical institutions is constantly repeated in the Roman documents. *Praeclara Gratulationis* begins the series: 'There is no reason for you to fear that We or any of our

Successors will ever diminish your rights, the privileges of your patriarchs, or the established customs of any of your Churches' (LA 14 [1894] 201). Such a promise is, in our eyes, the Roman acknowledgment of the structural integrity of the dissident apostolic communities of the East; there is only one way for them to return, and that is as Churches. This is the foundation of the guarantee that 'they shall lose nothing of their dignity, nor of the splendour of their liturgies, nor of the sacred patrimony of laws handed down to them from their forefathers; rather shall they gain in security and renown' (*Alacre Studium*, AAS 47 [1955] 600).

10 For quotation see note 7 of chapter 2.
11 *Satis Cognitum*, LA 16 (1896) 198: 'Excidere episcopos iure ac potestate regendi, si a Petro eiusve successoribus scientes secesserint'.
12 A bibliography of the studies up to 1930 is given by YVES CONGAR, art. 'schisme', *Dict. Théol. Cath.* 14, col. 1310. For a more recent treatment, see CHARLES JOURNET, *L'Eglise du Verbe Incarné* I, Bruges (2nd ed.) 1955, pp. 654–8. The most critical study, which nevertheless comes to a positive conclusion, is that of A. COUSSA, *opus citatum* in note 15 below.
13 The Holy Office has recognized, in certain particular cases, the validity of sacraments demanding jurisdiction which were administered in an Orthodox Church. When Oriental dissidents are reconciled with the Holy See, there is never a repetition of confirmation or the demand for a general confession. For more detailed references, see CHARLES JOURNET, the pages cited in the last note.
14 Christ has founded his Church to perpetuate his redemptive mission on earth. This perpetuation is the purpose also of ecclesiastical jurisdiction. Would it be reasonable to suppose that the popes want to deprive a large part of the Christian world, a part to whom collectively they ascribe good faith, of a healthy sacramental life? Such a reflex principle has certainly been applied in the evaluation of the Western Schism of the 14th century. There we had Western Christianity split up between pope and anti-pope into two contesting parties, and because pope and anti-pope solemnly and repeatedly excommunicated each other and each other's following, half of the Christian West was apparently cut off from ecclesiastical life. But theologians claim that the papal excommunications were incapable of removing all jurisdiction from the schismatic Churches, since the true pope could not reasonably want (*rationabiliter invitus*) to exclude half of Europe from the gifts of Christ for a guiltless error concerning the lawful heir of papal authority. In spite of all excommunications, the anti-pope

is judged to have participated in true papal jurisdiction; by reason of the good faith of his followers, the ecclesiastical life which proceeded from his initiative was valid and authentic. (See L. Salembier, art. 'Schisme d'Occident', *Dict. Apol. Foi Cath.*, vol. 4, col. 1237–8). We admit, of course, that the so-called Western Schism is hardly comparable to the cleavage between East and West; since both parties professed obedience to the Roman Pontiff, the Western Schism was no true schism at all. (See JEAN LECLERCQ, 'Point de vue sur le Grand Schisme d'Occident', *L'Eglise et les Eglises* II, Chévetogne 1955, pp. 223–40.) It is significant, nevertheless, to see how an objective jurisdiction can be established on a legal title which is none other than a multitude in good faith.

15 ACACIUS COUSSA (*Epitome Praelectionum de Iure Ecclesiastico Orientali* I, Cryptaeferratae 1948, pp. 20–7) treats the question from the canonical point of view. The author teaches as certain that the dissident hierarchy has a borrowed jurisdiction for the *forum internum;* according to him, they have no jurisdiction whatever for the *forum externum*.

16 In a letter to the Copts, *Christi Domini*, Leo XIII had occasion to remind dissident Christians that the Catholic hierarchy of their rite is the lawful heir of apostolic authority (LA 15 [1895] 409).

17 Art. 'Eglise', *Catholicisme*, vol. 3, col. 1426: 'L'Eglise parle des "Eglises d'Orient"—ce sont pour elle des Eglises "blessées", mais qui restent des Eglises'.

18 'Note sur les mots "Confession", "Eglise" et "Communion" ', *Irénikon*, 23 (1950) 28: 'Qu'il suffise pour notre propos de marquer qu'il peut y avoir des communautés chrétiennes vérifiant la qualité d'Eglise locale, mais d'une façon imparfaite faute de communion aux principes institués par le Seigneur pour structurer l'Eglise totale. Telle m'apparaît être la situation des Eglises Orthodoxes.'

19 *Amantissimae Voluntatis*, LA 15 (1895) 144–5.

20 *ibid.*, p. 144: 'Prudentes viri extimescunt rationalismi et materialismi pestes . . ., quarum contagione quidquid usquam est in religione tollitur . . . vel admodum infirmatur'. And 'non timide complectuntur atque etiam asserunt summa Dei et Christi eius iura'.

21 See p. 53.

22 For full quotation, see note 92 of chapter 2.

23 LA 16 (1896) 267.

24 A renewed appreciation of our Lady is particularly noticeable in German Lutheranism, where the veneration of Mary had never completely disappeared; cf. R. SCHIMMELPFENNIG *Die Geschichte der Marienverehrung im deutschen Protestantismus*, Paderborn

1952. The Lutheran General Synod of Germany (VELKD) meeting at Braunschweig in 1954 incorporated three feasts of our Lady into the Church calendar, on February 2, March 25, and July 2; see *Herder-Korrespondenz* 9 (1954–5) 166–8.
25 *Lux Veritatis*, AAS 23 (1931) 513.
26 *Orientalium Dignitas*, LA (14 (1894) 361.
27 In the early Church it was emphatically denied that anyone outside the Church could be considered a martyr, even if he died for the name of Christ. St CYPRIAN, *De Unit. Eccl.*, 14: 'Tales (qui extra Ecclesiam colliguntur) etiamsi occisi in confessione nominis fuerint, macula ista nec sanguine abluitur . . . Esse martyr non potest qui in Ecclesia non est' (Migne P.L. 4, 510). St AUGUSTINE writes to a Donatist priest, *Epist.* 173, 6: 'Foris ab Ecclesia constitutus, et separatus a compagine unitatis et vinculo caritatis, aeterno supplicio punireris, etiamsi pro Christi nomine vivus incendereris' (Migne P.L. 33, 756). Do these verdicts necessarily presume bad faith? It seems that they were also meant to condemn the practice, not uncommon among schismatics, of seeking martyrdom enthusiastically. Cf. PAUL ALLARD, art. 'martyre', *Dict. Apol. Foi Cath.*, vol. 3, col. 339–42. Modern theologians have not resolved the problem.
28 AAS 42 (1950) 144: '(non) . . . redeuntes aliquid substantiale afferre ad Ecclesiam, quod in ipsa hactenus defuerit'.
29 In this paragraph we follow the thought and the terminology of CHARLES JOURNET, *L'Eglise du Verbe Incarné* II, Bruges 1951, pp. 1215–22.

CHAPTER: 4: CATHOLIC ECUMENISM: ITS FOUNDATION

1 *Denz.* no 1821. For Latin text, see note 8 of chapter 1.
2 *Rerum Ecclesiae*, AAS 18 (1926) 65: 'Neque enim ad aliud nata Ecclesia est, nisi ut, regno Christi ubique terrarum dilatando, universos homines salutaris redemptionis participes efficiat'.
3 *ibid*. Cf. also ANDRE RETIF, *Introduction à la doctrine pontificale des missions*, Paris 1953, p. 23.
4 W. A. VISSER'T HOOFT, 'The Word Ecumenical—Its History and Use', *A History of the Ecumenical Movement*, Philadelphia 1954, p. 735. According to a more detailed study by the same author, *The Meaning of 'Ecumenical'*, London 1950, 'ecumenical' is occasionally used by modern writers in ways which, on account of their ecclesiological implications, are unacceptable from the Catholic viewpoint.
5 See GUSTAVE THILS, *Histoire doctrinale du mouvement oecuménique*, Louvain 1955, p. 167.
6 TH. GRENTRUP, *Jus Missionarium*, Steyl 1925, pp. 6–7.

7 ANDRE SEUMOIS, *Vers une définition de l'activité missionaire*, Schöneck/Beckenried 1948, p. 22. The same author, in his *Introduction à la missiologie*, Schöneck/Beckenried 1952, draws up a detailed plan for a theology of missions (pp. 207–37) which is to include the concerns of Christian unity. CHARLES JOURNET (*L'Eglise du Verbe Incarné* II, Bruges 1951, p. 1247) also reckons dissident Christianity as part of the mission field of the Church.

8 The main encyclicals on missions are *Maximum Illud* (1919), *Rerum Ecclesiae* (1926), and *Evangelii Praecones* (1951). In the AAS we also find a host of shorter missionary documents, including letters, speeches, and official statements. For convenient collections, see *Documenta de Re Missionaria*, Rome 1938, and *Documents sur l'activité missionaire de SS. Pie XI*, fasc. II: Principaux textes missionaires, Namur, no date. The same silence about matters ecumenical in ANDRE RETIF, *Introduction à la doctrine pontificale des missions*, Paris 1953.

9 *Evangelii Praecones*, AAS 43 (1951) 506, 526.

10 We shall cite the entire passage defining both proximate and final end of missionary action. 'Eo autem, ut omnes norunt, haec sacrae expeditiones primo loco spectant, ut christianae veritatis lumen novis gentibus luculentius affulgeat, utque novi habeantur christiani. Ad illud tamen, extremam veluti metam, contendant necesse est . . ., ut nempe Ecclesia apud alios populos firmiter constabiliatur, eidemque propria, ex indigenis delecta, tribuatur Hierarchia' (AAS 43 [1951] 507).

11 Cf. *Perlibenti Quidem*, AAS 42 (1950) 727: '. . . esse finem expeditionum sacrarum, Ecclesiam in locis infidelium firmiter constituere adeo ut, radices altius agendo, per se ipsa vivere et efflorescere queat sine Missionalium Operum adiumento, quod proinde, suimet ipsius ibi ratio desit, cessare debet'.

12 For the principal encyclicals dealing with Christian unity, see note 2 of chapter 2. There is a passage in the writings of Leo XIII where the Church's missions are explicitly contradistinguished from the 'work for Christian unity'; see *Christi Nomen*, LA 14 (1894) 406.

13 In actual practice, however, this Congregation has not always kept to the limits of this division. It has, to give an example, contributed to the support of the Catholic ministry among Canadian Indians and to organizations dealing with non-Christian overseas students in Europe, though according to the C.I.C. these undertakings cannot be considered as belonging to the field assigned to the *Propaganda Fide*.

14 A Motu Proprio *Dei Providentis*, AAS 9 (1917) 529–31, established a special Congregation for Oriental Catholics. It was on this occasion that Benedict XV, wishing to dispel a false impression, wrote the oft-cited words: 'In the Church of

Jesus Christ, which is neither Latin nor Greek nor Slavonic, but Catholic, there can be no distinction among members. They all, whether Latin, Greek, or of other nations, have exactly the same place in the eyes of the Apostolic See' (p. 530).

15 *Annum ingressi*, LA 22 (1902) 54: '. . . neque ad filios modo catholicae unitatis feliciter compotes, sed etiam ad eos qui Nobiscum de fide dissident, vel qui ab ipsa plane sunt alieni'. Considering the people still outside the Church, the popes usually speak of two distinct groups, of 'those who are in complete ignorance of the gospel, and those who dissent from the Catholic faith, although initiated into Christianity' (*Praeclara Gratulationis*, LA 14 [1894] 196). Or again: 'There are many who are in complete ignorance of Christ, and many who have not preserved the true and integral doctrine or the commanded unity' (*Ubi Arcano Dei*, AAS 14 [1922] 696–7).

16 *Annum Sacrum*, LA 19 (1899) 72–3 and *Quas Primas*, AAS 17 (1925) 600–1: 'Imperium eius non est tantummodo in gentes catholici nominis, aut in eos solum, qui sacro baptismate rite abluti, utique ad Ecclesiam, si spectetur ius, pertinent, quamvis vel error opinionum devios agat, vel dissensio a caritate seiungat; sed complectitur etiam quotquot numerantur christianae fidei expertes, ita ut verissime in potestate Jesu Christi sit universitas generis humani'.

17 To schematize the reign of Christ according to the New Testament witness, OSCAR CULLMAN (*Christus und die Zeit*, Zurich 1946, p. 166) draws two concentric circles, standing for the Church and for the world surrounding it.

18 In this context we have left out of consideration the Jews. They belong to the 'world' only with great qualifications. In his radio talk *Non Mai Forse*, Piux XII addresses the Jews as a group theologically distinct from non-believers and Christians (AAS 42 [1950] 126).

19 *Epistola ad Quosdam Puseistas Anglicos* (1865), AAS 11 (1919) 313: 'Ecclesia Christi propter summam, quam per omnes gentes et in omne tempus diffusa firmissime retinet, fidei communionisque unitatem catholica est et dicitur'.

20 *Ab Ipsis Pontificatus*, 18 (1926) 304.
21 *Satis Cognitum*, LA 16 (1896) 172, 174.
22 *ibid.*, p. 164.
23 *Mystici Corporis*, AAS 35 (1943) 239–40.
24 *Evangelii Praecones*, AAS 43 (1951) 521.
25 *ibid.*, p. 523. The sentence is a quotation from *Summi Pontificatus*, AAS 31 (1939) 429.
26 *Mit Brennender Sorge*, AAS 29 (1937) 152.
27 *Ad Beatissimi Apostolorum*, AAS 6 (1914) 565.

28 *Mystici Corporis*, AAS 35 (1943) 206. For Latin text, see note 57 of chapter 1.
29 *Negli Ultimi*, AAS 38 (1946) 20.
30 Error of Quesnel condemned: 'Extra Ecclesiam nulla conceditur gratia' (*Denz.* no 1379).
31 *Negli Ultimi*, AAS 38 (1946) 18–9.
32 In a critique of the various attempts to define the dogmatic motive of missionary action, ANDRÉ SEUMOIS concludes with Louis Capéran and others, that this formal foundation must be sought in the nature of the Church itself and, more precisely, that the property which motivates the expansive drive of the Church is her catholicity (*Vers une définition de l'activité missionaire*, Schöneck/Beckenried 1948, p. 34.) This view is widely accepted; cf. PAUL BROUTIN, *Mysterium Ecclesiae*, Paris 1947, p. 177, CHARLES JOURNET, *L'Eglise du Verbe Incarné* II, Bruges 1951, pp. 1207–8. The properties of the Church, however, are so mysteriously interrelated that there is no reason why, from a different point of view, the missionary action of the Church could not be motivated by her apostolicity, her unity, or her holiness.
33 The distinction which we have made between the formal principles of missionary and ecumenical activities (catholicity towards nature and towards grace) is a theological abstraction, albeit a legitimate one. In the concrete order of history the Church meets much that is of grace in her mission field, and she must face unredeemed natural elements in her work among Christians. We do not speak of two different catholicities, but of one catholicity possessing two distinct aspects.
34 *Ecclesiam Dei*, AAS 15 (1923) 573, 574, 576, 579, 581. See also *Ex Quo Proximum*, ibid., p. 608, and *Libenti Sane*, AAS 18 (1926) 7.
35 *Audistis Venerabilis*, AAS 31 (1939) 598.
36 *Negli Ultimi*, AAS 38 (1946) 18.
37 The Church is mother in a real sense with respect to non-Christians who have been justified by a faith invisibly communicated; even in this case, God wanted to bestow grace through the Church's intercession and on account of her divine office.
38 From the texts on the Church's maternal function, we single out two longer passages, *In Questa Vibrante*, AAS 32 (1940) 493–4, and *Mystici Corporis*, AAS 35 (1943) 240–6.
39 *Mystici Corporis*, ibid., p. 194: '. . . Ecclesiae Matris, cui post Deum omnia debemus'.
40 *Mortalium Animos*, AAS 20 (1928) 15: 'Mater universorum Christi fidelium et magistra'. This is a quotation from the 4th

Lateran Council (see *Denz.* no 436), and is applied in the encyclical also to dissident Christians.
41 *Longinqua Oceani*, LA 15 (1895) 20: 'communis omnium mater'. The reference is to the dissident Christians of America.
42 *Spiritus Paraclitus*, AAS 12 (1920) 403.
43 *Mystici Corporis*, AAS 35 (1943) 243.
44 *ibid.*, p. 199: 'Quam (copiam gratiarum) directo per se ipse universo humano generi dilargiri potuerat; voluit tamen per adspectabilem . . . Ecclesiam'.
45 *Tametsi Futura*, LA 20 (1900) 304: 'Praesidia salutis humanae in eam omnia contulisset'.
46 *Mystici Corporis*, AAS 35 (1943) 201.
47 See pp. 39–40.
48 *Divinum Illud*, LA 17 (1897) 134, 135. The conclusion reads in Latin: 'Quae ita cumsint, nequaquam comminisci et expectare licet aliam ullam ampliorem uberioremque divini Spiritus manifestationem et ostensionem, quae enim nunc in Ecclesia habetur'.
49 *Providentissimus Deus*, LA 13 (1893) 326–7. We shall quote the complete sentence from the Vatican Council: 'Eos (libros) vero Ecclesia pro sacris et canonicis habet, non ideo, quod sola humana industria concinnati, sua deinde auctoritate sintapprobati; nec ideo dumtaxat, quod revelationem sine errore contineant; sed propterea, quod Spiritu Sancto inspirante conscripti Deum habent auctorem, atque ut tales ipsi Ecclesiae traditi sunt' (*Denz.* no 1787).
50 *Providentissimus Deus*, LA 13 (1893) 348.
51 *Divino Afflante Spiritu*, AAS 35 (1943) 297: 'Sancta Ecclesia hunc e caelo datum thesaurum, quem doctrinae de fide et moribus pretiosissimum habet fontem divinamque normam, . . ex manibus Apostolorum accepit'.
52 'Nous ne disons pas que l'Eglise soit juge de la parole de Dieu, mais nous assurons qu'elle est juge des diverses interprétations que les hommes donnent à la sainte Parole de Dieu.' Bossuet, *Réfutation du catéchisme du Sieur Paul Ferry*, part ii, chap. 4 (*Oeuvres Complètes*, ed. Lachat, Paris 1863, vol. 13, p. 476).
53 *Caritatis Studium*, LA 18 (1898) 105.
54 *Providentissimus Deus*, LA 13 (1893) 338.
55 Cf. the interesting article of Pierre-Yves Emery, 'La Réforme du XVIe siècle et les Conciles Oecuméniques', *L'Eglise et les Eglises* II, Chévetogne 1955, pp. 263–81.
56 *Romanorum Pontificum*, AAS 9 (1917) 61.
57 For the doctrine of Mary's spiritual maternity, see especially Piux X's encyclical *Ad Diem Illum* (1904). 'Universi ergo, quotquot cum Christo iungimur, quique, ut ait Apostolus, "membra sumus corporis eius, de carne eius et de ossibus eius"

(Eph. v. 30), de Mariae utero egressi sumus, tamquam corporis instar coherentis cum capite. Unde, spiritali quidem ratione ac mystica, et Mariae filii nos dicimur, et ipsa nostrum omnium mater est' (*Pii X Pontifici Maximi Acta*, vol. 1, Rome 1905, pp. 152-3).

58 For references to the Marian piety of Orientals as a link to the Catholic Church, see *Adiutricem Populi*, LA 15 (1895) 308, 312; *Ecclesiam Dei*, AAS 15 (1923) 581; *Rerum Orientalium*, AAS 20 (1928) 287; *Lux Veritatis*, AAS 23 (1931) 515; *Fulgens Corona*, AAS 45 (1953) 581-2; *Je Me Suis*, AAS 46 (1954) 656. The popes are also aware of the religious motives which impel Protestants to object to our veneration of Mary; see *Lux Veritatis*, AAS 23 (1931) 513; *Fulgens Corona* 45 (1953) 581-2.

59 At the occasion of a liturgical congress (at Vicence in 1954) having as subject the Marian liturgy, Pius XII appointed Mgr Montini to encourage the work and the aim of the congress by a letter from the Holy See. There we read, 'The liturgy is not only a chair of doctrinal truth, it is also and above all a school of holiness and the most proper means of incorporating men into Christ. The studies at your congress will therefore be especially directed towards this end in respect to Marian liturgy. Being led back to its authentic purpose the liturgy of Mary will fulfill its essential destination, that is, to be the way which takes us to Christ by a transformation of the old man into the new. Every form of Marian devotion which neglects this aspect becomes necessarily defective . . . By thus finding its true aim, our devotion to Mary will not spend itself in a superficial sentimentalism nor in a selfish search for temporal favours; it will be marked by maturity and depth which is the guarantee of a lasting and fruitful spiritual life'. See 'Document du saint-siège relatif à la piété mariale', *Irénikon*, 27 (1954) 327-8.

60 For the reaction of the non-Catholic world to the new dogma, see the extensive collection of essays, quotations, and references published in two full numbers of HEILER's *Oekumenische Einheit*, 2 (1951), pp. 1-225.

61 *Munificentissimus Deus*, AAS 42 (1950) 769.

62 For references to Mary's intercession for Christian unity, see *Amantissimae Voluntatis*, LA 15 (1895) 153; *Adiutricem Populi*, ibid., pp. 301, 305-10; *Fidentem Piumque*, LA 16 (1896) 286; *Mortalium Animos*, AAS 20 (1928) 16; *Ephesinam Synodum*, AAS 23 (1931) 11; *Lux Veritatis*, ibid., p. 513; *Mystici Corporis*, AAS 35 (1943) 247-8; *Munificentissimus Deus*, AAS 42 (1950) 769; *Fulgens Corona*, AAS 45 (1953) 591.

63 *Adiutricem Populi*, LA 15 (1895) 306.

64 ibid., pp. 309-10.

NOTES

65 *Apostolicae Curae*, LA 16 (1896) 260: '. . . nihil non experiri quod videtur quoquo modo conducere ad animarum vel avertenda damna vel utilitates fovendas'.
66 We have defined ecumenism and its field of action primarily with regard to dissident Christians. But since Christians outside the Church in bad faith (schismatics and heretics) are also heirs of a Christian patrimony, they are not excluded from the ecumenical concern of the Church.
67 *Praeclara Gratulationis*, LA 14 (1894) 199.
68 For examples of this usage, see *Missam A Vobis*, AAS 3 (1911) 564; *Conditam Abhinc*, AAS 15 (1923) 207; *Nostis Qua Praecipue*, AAS 16 (1924) 491.
69 *Ecclesiae Fastos*, AAS 46 (1954) 354; 'iter illud'.
70 *Quinquagesimo Ante Anno*, AAS 21 (1929) 714: 'ad pristinam communionem gradatim revocare'.
71 *Lux Veritatis*, AAS 23 (1931) 510; 'ut firmius et arctius Romanae Ecclesiae adhereant'.
72 *Munificentissimus Deus*, AAS 42 (1950) 769.
73 Terms such as 'maturare', 'provehere', 'faciliorem reddere', or 'preparare unitatem' are constantly used to describe Catholic ecumenical action.
74 *Sie Haben*, AAS 47 (1955) 597.
75 'Notre travail pour l'Union', *Irénikon*, 7 (1930) 393.
76 D. C. LIALINE, considering the ordination of dissidentChristianity towards the Catholic Church writes, 'Au mouvement unioniste Catholique d'activer cette ordination' ('Une étape en ecclésiologie: Réflexions sur l'encyclique "Mystici Corporis" ', *Irénikon*, 20 [1947] 52).
77 *Conditam Abhinc*, AAS 15 (1923) 208: 'Cavere enim debetis potissimum, ne usquam, improvido abrepti studio, id audeatis, unde acatholicorum (from the context: German Protestants) offensio cum animorum detrimento magis augeatur quam minuatur'.
78 *Paternas Caritas*, LA 8 (1888) 269: '. . . parentem ab se digressos diuque expectatos liberos revocare domum, imo occurrere . . .'.
79 *Conditam Abhinc*, AAS 15 (1923) 207.
80 *Ecclesia Catholica*, AAS 42 (1950) 143.
81 *ibid.*, p. 143 (see note 42, chapter 5) and p. 145.

CHAPTER 5: CATHOLIC ECUMENISM: ITS EXERCISE

1 This question has frequently been studied; see W. H. VAN DE POL, *The Christian Dilemma*, London 1952, pp.262–84; GUSTAVE THILS, *Histoire doctrinale du mouvement oecuménique*,

Louvain 1955, pp. 180–3. Cf. also ROBERT ROUQUETTE, 'Rome et les mouvements oecuméniques', *Etudes*, 265 (1950) 240–9; C. J. DUMONT, 'L'Eglise romaine et le mouvement oecuménique', *La Vie Intellectuelle*, 18'1 (1950) 433–40; G. DEJAIFVE, 'Oecuménisme et Catholica', *Nouv. Rev. Théol*, 75 (1953) 1038–52 and 76 (1954) 24–43.

2   AAS 11 (1919) 310–6.
3   AAS 20 (1928) 9.
4   'The World Council of Churches is a fellowship of Churches which accept our Lord Jesus Christ as God and Saviour.' This basis, taken over from the Faith-and-Order movement, was adopted and accepted at the Utrecht Conference of 1938 for the projected World Council; it was confirmed at the first General Assembly at Amsterdam (see W. A. VISSER'T HOOFT, 'The Genesis of the World Council of Churches', *A History of the Ecumenical Movement*, Philadelphia 1954, pp. 704–5, 720). The faith in Christ as 'God and Saviour' is professed at the very beginning of the Message of Amsterdam, and in Christ as 'true God and true Man' in the Message of Evanston.
5   'The Toronto Statement of the Central Committee 1950' is reprinted in the *Ecum. Rev.*, 3 (1950–1) 47–53; we shall cite from it, however, by referring to its numbered paragraphs: III : 3, 4, 5 and IV : 4.
6   *ibid.*, III : 5. Apart from this verbal citation from Pius XII, the Toronto Statement contains another direct reference to Catholic doctrine: it is claimed, and rightly so, that even the Church of Rome recognizes the existence of members 'extra muros', of members which 'aliquo modo' belong to the Church (IV : 3).
7   Cf. *ibid.*, III : 1, 'The World Council of Churches is not and must never become a Super-Church'. This has been the constant attitude of the Council in all of its documents.
8   Amsterdam Assembly, *The Official Report*, London 1949, p. 66.
9   *ibid.*
10 Report of the Advisory Commission on the Main Theme of the Second Assembly, *Ecum. Rev.*, 6 (1953–4) 446.
11 In the Report of Section I at the Evanston Assembly we read a striking sentence confirming our interpretation. 'In this way we may think of the Church as we think of the individual believer, who may be said at one and the same time to be a justified man and a sinner' (*The Evanston Report*, London 1955, p. 84).
12 'The Toronto Statement of the Central Committee 1950', III : 5; see note 5 above.
13 This is certainly the opinion of the influential *Herder-Korrespondenz*, whose judgment however is sometimes severe. In a more reserved way these observations are confirmed by

THOMAS SARTORY, *Die ökumenische Bewegung und die Einheit der Kirche*, Meitingen bei Augsburg 1955, pp. 74–5. Concerning a shift of theological emphasis within the Council, see also 'Das Glaubensbewusstsein der "ökumenischen Christenheit" ', *Der Grosse Herder*, vol. 10, Freiburg in Br. 1953, col. 1464–5.

14   Message to the Churches, Faith-and-Order Conference, New Zealand, 1955. (We have only seen a mimeographed copy which was kindly put at our disposal by the Library of the World Council of Churches, Geneva.)
15   *The Evanston Report*, London 1955, pp. 92–5, 329–31.
16   *ibid.*, p. 93.
17   *Ecclesia Catholica*, AAS 42 (1950) 142. For the full quotation, see note 92 of chapter 2.
18   *The Evanston Report*, London 1955, pp. 27–8.
19   It is not an exaggeration to speak of a 'movement' since the efforts of Pius XI were continuous and systematic, and their aim is perpetuated by the schools and institutions which he created. For a detailed account of Pius XI's reunion efforts, see ROGER AUBERT, *Le saint-siège et l'union des Eglises*, Brussels 1947, pp. 99–128, in a chapter which the author calls 'Le pontificat de Pie XI et la mise au point de la méthode irénique'.
20   Sincere benevolence towards the Churches of the East was a guiding principle of Pius XI's ecumenical method. Taking up this key-word, Pius XII probably refers to his immediate predecessor when he writes: 'The greatest help of all—with the guidance of God—for promoting the reconciliation of dissident Christians with the Church of Rome is undoubtedly a sincere and practical good will (benevolentia). This benevolent attitude fosters a mutual understanding, for the increase and deepening of which Our Predecessors have done so much . . .'. (*Orientalis Ecclesiae*, AAS 36 [1944] 137.)
21   From Pius XI's speech of January 11, 1927, cited in *Irénikon*, 3 (1927) 20.
22   Cf. the *C.I.C.* on the prohibition of books, especially can. 1399, nos 2 and 4.
23   *Ecce Ego*, AAS 47 (1955) 25.
24   *Humani Generis*, AAS 42 (1950) 564.
25   *Ecclesia Catholica*, *ibid.*, p. 143.
26   Cf. p. 97.
27   Cf. *Rerum Orientalium*, AAS 20 (1928) 283–4.
28   Cf. *Lux Veritatis*, AAS 23 (1931) 513. In a similar vein, the popes recommend to Protestants the study of the Fathers of the Church. Thus in an apostolic letter written shortly before the opening of the Evanston Assembly, Pius XII suggests that 'To study with great attention the writings of St Augustine will also be useful to those who, while hungry and thirsty for

the truth, still wander off the path of Catholic doctrine' (*Quamquam*, AAS 46 [1954] 515).
29 *Tametsi Futura*, LA 20 (1900) 296.
30 *ibid.*, p. 305: 'Amoto Jesu, destituitur sibi humana ratio, maximo orbata praesidio et lumine'.
31 *ibid.*, p. 310: 'Non quod praecepta naturae dispicere ac servare recta ratione homo plura non queat; sed omnia quamvis dispiceret et sine ulla offensione in omni vita servaret, quod nisi opitulante Redemptoris gratia non potest, tamen frustra quisquam, expers fidei, de salute sempiterna confideret'.
32 *ibid.*, p. 312: 'Quotquot ubique sunt, christianos obtestamur dare velint operam, quoad quisque potest, Redemptorem suum ut noscant qualis est'.
33 *Caritatis Studium*, LA 18 (1898) 105.
34 *Rerum Orientalium*, AAS 20 (1928) 277: '. . . nec posse, nisi ea impedimenta (scl. mutua ignoratio, dispicientia et praeiudicatae opiniones) amoverentur, tot malis medicina adhiberi'. For a partial citation of this phrase, see *Quod Catholicis*, AAS 22 (1930) 146.
35 *Nostis Qua Praecipue*, AAS 16 (1924) 491: '. . . nisi depositâ hinc eâ, quam saeculorum decursu combiberat vulgus de Orientis Ecclesiarum doctrinis institutisque, vanitate opinionum, exploratâque illinc interius Patrum suorum cum latinis in unam eandemque fidem consensione'.
36 In some Protestant ecumenical circles to-day Catholic literature is being read; the *Ecumenical Review* always includes Catholic publications in their book reports. However the attitude of ERNST KINDER, *Ecum. Rev.* 7 (1954–5) 338–46, who considers the ecumenical encounter with Catholics a necessary thing, is by no means widely accepted. For another very positive opinion, see ROGER SCHUTZ, 'Résultats théologiques et spirituels des rencontres oecuméniques avec les catholiques romains', *Verbum Caro*, 10 (1956) 16–22.
37 Apart from the encyclical *Rerum Orientalium*, the main documents of Pius XI on Oriental studies are: *Amplissimum Consessum*, AAS 16 (1924) 123–24, and *Nostis Qua Praecipue*, *ibid.* pp. 490–2, sections of two consistorial addresses; *A dilecto Filio*, *ibid.*, pp. 326–7, *Libenti Sane*, AAS 18 (1926) 7–8, and *Laeto Iucundoque*, AAS 25 (1933) 23–4, three letters preparing theological congresses. For a longer analysis of Pius XI's encouragement of Eastern studies, see R. AUBERT, *Le saint-siège et l'union des Eglises*, Brussels 1947, pp. 99–128. In this chapter we find the full citation (pp. 110-12) of the letter *Equidem Verba* (March 21, 1924), not contained in the AAS, which Pius XI wrote to Fidelis of Stotzingen, then Primate of the Benedictine Order; the letter suggests the foundation of a

monastery in charge of reunion work and describes the ecumenical importance of study and research. Pius XI's wish was heeded; the monastery founded was the Benedictine Priory of Amay, since 1939 at Chévetogne, Belgium, which is well known as the editor of the union review *Irénikon*.

38 *Rerum Orientalium*, AAS 20 (1928) 283, 284. Two years later the Congregation of Seminaries and Universities issued a letter, *Quod Catholicis*, AAS 22 (1930) 146–8, prescribing Oriental studies and outlining their importance for Catholic seminaries.

39 *Rerum Orientalium*, AAS 20 (1928) 281: 'ad caritatem mutuamque aestimationem fovendam'.

40 See note 49 below.

41 *Ecclesiam Dei*, AAS 15 (1923) 580: '. . . ex recta rerum cognitione aequam hominum existimationem itemque sinceram benevolentiam efflorescere, quae, Christi caritate coniuncta, religiosae unitati quam maxime est, Dei munere, profutura'.

42 AAS 42 (1950) 143: 'Plane perspecta habere debent (episcopi) quaecumque in suis diocesibus per illam "Motionem" (Oecumenicam) constituta sunt ac geruntur. Ad hoc sacerdotes idoneos designabunt, qui, iuxta doctrinam et normas a Sancta Sede perscriptas, . . . omnia ad "Motionem" attingentia sedulo attendent'.

43 *Humani Generis*, AAS 42 (1950) 563–4.

44 *Ecclesia Catholica*, *ibid*., pp. 143–4; *Humani Generis*, *ibid*., pp. 564–5.

45 *Ecclesia Catholica*, *ibid*., p. 144. Cf. also the warning of Leo XIII in his letter on true and false 'Americanism' in religion, *Testem Benevolentiae*, LA 19 (1899) 8–9.

46 *Mystici Corporis*, AAS 35 (1943) 197.

47 *Ecclesia Catholica*, AAS 42 (1950) 144.

48 *Humani Generis*, *ibid*., p. 568.

49 *Rerum Orientalium*, AAS 20 (1928) 284: '. . . uberiorem exinde catholicae theologiae latinaeque disciplinae cognitionem haurire'.

50 Cf. pp. 121–22 below. Lest we remain purely in general terms, we shall give a simple example that the ecumenical contact poses problems to Catholic theology which cannot be solved by consulting a manual, but which demand a new inquiry. Sacraments not only produce grace, they also announce the faith; they are signs proclaiming salvation until the Lord returns. This aspect of the sacraments is emphasized greatly in Protestantism. What is, in Catholic theology, the kerygmatical value of the sacraments?

51 See Pius XI's speech of Dec. 21, 1924, opening the Mission Exhibition at the Vatican, *Documents sur l'activité missionaire de*

S.S. *Pie XI*, fasc. II: 'Principaux textes missionaires', Namur, no date, p. 18.
52 *Le saint-siège et l'union des Eglises*, Brussels 1947, p. 155.
53 *Orientales Omnes*, AAS 38 (1946) 34: 'Quandoquidem ex plena perfectaque christianorum omnium unitate mysticum Jesu Christi corpus eiusque singula membra magnum incrementum non consequi non possunt'.
54 *Orientalis Ecclesiae*, AAS 36 (1944) 138.
55 *Sempiternus Rex*, AAS 43 (1951) 642.
56 *Cum Catholicae Ecclesiae*, AAS 8 (1916) 137.
57 *Romanorum Pontificum*, AAS 9 (1917) 61: 'In unitate enim fidei praecipua enitit Ecclesiae veritatis nota . . . Iucundo igitur accepimus animo . . . preces compositas esse . . ., ut hic unitatis finis a Domino impetraretur'.
58 Cf. YVES CONGAR, *Chrétiens désunis*, Paris 1937, pp. 316–9; CHARLES JOURNET, *L'Eglise du Verbe Incarné* II, Bruges 1951, pp. 1221–3; KARL RAHNER, 'Ueber Konversionen', *Hochland*, 46 (1953–4) 119–26.
59 AAS 15 (1923) 580: 'Ita hac et singulorum hominum et populorum conciliatione perfecta, coniunctio simul perficietur Ecclesiae, in eiusdem sinum redeuntibus omnibus, quotquot, quavis de causa, sint ab ea seiuncti'.
60 P. 76.
61 *Orientales Omnes*, AAS 38 (1946) 33: '. . . certum exploratumque est ex eiusmodi coniunctione, redintegrata feliciter, cum rei christianae universae, tum peculiari modo Orientalibus ipsis uberrimos fructus ortum iri'.
62 Through a letter written by Card. Gasparri, Benedict XV encouraged the ecumenical efforts of American Protestants, and wished them success in finding the true nature of the Church '*ut mysticum Christi Corpus distrahi et discerpi non ultra sinatur*'. The whole correspondence of the years 1914–5 between Robert Gardiner, Secretary of the American Commission for the World Conference of Christian Churches, and Card. Gasparri, Papal Secretary of State, is reprinted in MAX PRIBILLA, *Um Kirchliche Einheit*, Freiburg i. Br. 1929, pp. 314–8. For the above quotation, see *ibid.*, p. 315. Excerpts from this correspondence, which are of interest because of Pope Benedict's encouragement of Protestant ecumenical endeavours, can be found in *Rome and Reunion*, ed. by E. C. Messenger, London 1934, pp. 105–7.
63 In the terminology of the Roman Missal, the prayers for Christian unity ask God 'for the unity of the Church'; see p. 128 below.
64 The terrible word 'absorb' which is sometimes used by non-Catholics to characterize the Roman idea of reunion is not as unfounded as one would wish; there are Catholic writers who

NOTES

do give such an impression. To absorb human beings, however, does not correspond to the intention of the Church, not even with regard to unbelievers whom she seeks to convert. Says Pius XII: 'All men, nations and individuals, are called to come into the Church. But the word "to come" suggests no idea of emigration or expatriation . . ., it does not imply the giving up of holy traditions and venerable customs . . . But, in the words of St Augustine, "they shall come, not by emigrating from their homes, but by having the faith in their own midst" ' (*La Elevatezza*, AAS 38 [1946] 146-7). See St Augustine, *Epist.* 199, cap. 12, no. 47 (Migne P.L. 33, 922).

65 *Ecclesia Catholica*, AAS 42 (1950) 144: 'Hii (dissidentes) edoceantur se ad Ecclesiam redeuntes nihil perdituros eius boni, quod gratia Dei in ipsis huc usque est natum, sed per reditum id potius completum atque absolutum iri'.

66 Referring to an Eastern nation which returned to the Catholic Church, Pius XII writes, 'Per eiusmodi nempe coagmentationem nobilissima haec gens Catholicae Ecclesiae conserta est, cuius proinde vitam vivit, cuius veritate collustratur, cuius gratia fit particeps' (*Orientales Omnes*, AAS 38 [1946] 50).

67 See *Orientalium Dignitas*, LA 14 (1894) 369; *Antequam Ordinem*, AAS 11 (1919) 98.

68 Jerome HAMER considers it to be the task of the ecumenical theologian to discover what elements of the Church can be found beyond her walls, and to demonstrate that these elements cannot achieve completion except in the Church ('Mission de l'oecuménisme catholique', *Lumière et Vie*, 1955, p. 79).

69 Cf. G. DEJAIFVE, 'Sobornost ou papauté?', *Nouv. Rev. Théol.*, 74 (1952) 355-71, 466-84.

70 *A Dilecto Filio*, AAS 16 (1924) 327. Cf. also note 35 of this chapter.

71 *Rerum Orientalium*, AAS 20 (1928) 287.

72 Art. 'ecumenismo', *Enciclopedia Cattolica*, Vatican City, vol. 5, col. 65.

73 *Amplissimum Consessum*, AAS 16 (1924) 124.

74 *Longinqua Oceani*, LA 15 (1895) 20.

75 *Paternas Caritas*, LA 8 (1888) 269.

76 *Tametsi Futura*, LA 20 (1900) 304: 'ideoque via homini Christus, via item Ecclesia'. We recall the remarkable sentence from the Faith-and-Order Conference at Lund: 'The Church is called to continue the mission of Jesus Christ to the world, so that the way of Christ is the way of the Church' (*The Report*, London 1952, p. 8).

77 *Mystici Corporis*, AAS 35 (1943) 199: 'Sicut enim Dei Verbum, ut doloribus cruciatibusque suis homines redimeret, nostra voluit natura uti, eodem fere modo per saeculorum decursum

utitur Ecclesia sua, ut inceptum opus perennet'.
78 Having the quality of Christ or of Church, can no longer be expressed by the adjectives 'Christian' or 'ecclesiastical', since they have acquired a different meaning. Moreover, the artificial adjectives 'christique' and 'ecclésial' which theological authors have created to fill the gap in French, are not good usage when transliterated into English.
79 Do we have an explicit statement of the Roman magisterium that the Church is necessary for salvation not simply because of a divine command, but even by the divine counsel to make her the unique instrument of grace? We do not find a clear formulation of the doctrine in *Denzinger's Enchiridion Symbolorum*. It is expressed with great precision in the preparatory *schema* 'de Ecclesia Christi' for the Vatican Council, ch. 6 (*Mansi* 51, 541), which was destined, however, never to be discussed and approved. The first explicit statement of the magisterium that the Church is the ark of salvation not only *necessitate praecepti*, but *medii*, is found in the Boston Letter; see p. 30 above and below p. 178.
80 *Ecclesiam Dei*, AAS 15 (1923) 579: 'Hi porro intelligant non tamen disputationibus aut incitamentis aliis, quam sanctae vitae exemplis officiisque hanc esse unitatem promovendam, in primis vero caritate erga Slavos fratres ceterosque Orientales'.
81 *L'Eglise du Verbe Incarné* II, Bruges 1951, p. 732.
82 S. TYSZKIEWICZ, *La sainteté de l'Eglise christoconforme*, Rome 1945, p. 185.
83 WALTER NIGG, *Grosse Heilige*, Zurich 1946, pp. 309-54.
84 ROGER SCHUTZ, 'Naissance de communauté dans les Eglises de la réforme', *Verbum Caro*, 9 (1955) 27. The sentence is a quotation from the author's *La Règle de Taizè*, introd., paragr. 2.
85 *The Official Report*, London 1949, p. 9. It is interesting to note how different the official German version of this sentence sounds: 'Wo wir ihn suchen, finden wir einander'. Here the hope for a Church (to the 'where' corresponds a 'there') is much more forcefully expressed than in English.
86 *Ecclesiam Dei*, AAS 15 (1923) 581.
87 Message to the Churches, Faith-and-Order Conference, New Zealand 1955 (mimeographed copy).
88 *Adiutricem Populi*, LA 15 (1895) 306.
89 The apostolic letter *Romanorum Pontificum* approving certain payers for Christian unity is entitled, 'Preces quaedam ad Ecclesiae unitatem a Domino impetrandam indulgentiis ditantur' (AAS 9 [1917] 61).
90 What is the exact meaning of the terms 'adunare' and 'coadunare Ecclesiam' as they are daily used in the Roman mass? Do they express a prayer for social concord among Catholics,

or are they properly speaking prayers for Christian unity? According to a remark of Pius XI in *Ecclesiam Dei*, AAS 15 (1923) 581, they represent the Church's intercession for the reunion of Christendom. This holds true also for the other liturgical formulas in which we pray for the unity of the Church. Thus, for instance, we pray in the Secret of the mass for Corpus Christi, 'Ecclesiae tuae, quaesumus, unitatis et pacis dona concede', and in the Collect of the mass For the Removal of Schism, 'super populum christianum tuae unionis gratiam clementer infunde'.

91   In the restored Liturgy of Good Friday, the public intercessions for the return of 'heretics and schismatics' are entitled *Pro unitate Ecclesiae*.
92   *Mortalium Animos*, AAS 20 (1928) 9.
93   *Ecclesiam Dei*, AAS 15 (1923) 576: '. . . usque dum promissum illud Christi . . . eveniat: "et fiet unum ovile et unus Pastor" '.
94   *Sempiternus Rex*, AAS 43 (1951) 641-2.
95   See p. 120 above.
96   *Circondati Dal Concorso*, AAS 34 (1942) 161.
97   See note 90 of this chapter. On the concern for Christian unity in the liturgical year, cf. C.-J. DUMONT, *Les voies de l'unité chrétienne*, Paris 1954, pp. 15-68.
98   *Mediator Dei*, AAS 39 (1947) 528: 'non alio contendit ac spectat, nisi ut magis in dies amplificetur ac coagmentetur'.
99   *Providae Matris*, LA 15 (1895) 184-6; *Divinum Illud*, LA 17 (1897) 147.
100 Cf. *Adiutricem Populi*, LA 15 (1895) 301; *Ad Fovendum*, LA 22 (1902) 98-100.
101 There has been a controversy about the origin of the Octave. Some writers have held Spencer Jones, an Anglican clergyman, to be its author. Yet in a letter, dated February 6, 1928, the latter explains that not he, but Paul Watson was responsible for the Church Unity Octave. Cf. D. GANNON, *Father Paul of Graymoor*, New York 1952, pp. 145-6.
102 In 1909 Pius X approved the Octave (D. GANNON, *op. cit.*, p. 256); in 1916 Benedict XV proposed it to the universal Church and conceded indulgences (*Romanorum Pontificum*, AAS 9 (1917) 61-2; and in 1946 Pius XII renewed the indulgences attached to it (D. GANNON, *op. cit.*, p. 259).
103 *Supremi Apostolatus*, LA 3 (1883) 280-9.
104 LA 15 (1895) 301; 16 (1896) 286.
105 *Fidentem Piumque*, LA 16 (1896) 287.
106 *Summa Theol.* III, 73, 3, in corp.
107 See *Mirae Caritatis*, LA 22 (1902) 127-8 and *Mystici Corporis*, AAS 35 (1943) 232-3. The encyclical *Mediator Dei* (1947) considers the entire worship of the Church as in and through

Christ the Mediator, so that every prayer and every sacrament is understood as building up the Body of Christ.
108 *Infinità Dei*, AAS 16 (1924) 211.
109 *Ecclesiam Dei*, AAS 15 (1923) 581: 'Eucharistiae Sacramentum percolamus, pignus causamque praecipuam unitatis'.
110 *ibid.*
111 In the Report of Section I at the Amsterdam Assembly, *The Official Report*, London 1949, p. 56.
112 *The Evanston Report*, London 1955, p. 91.
113 *Amantissimae Voluntatis*, LA 15 (1895) 139.
114 *ibid.*, p. 138.
115 *ibid.*, p. 148.
116 *ibid.*, p. 149.
117 *ibid.*, p. 149.
118 *ibid.*, p. 155.
119 To further the 'bonum christianae unitatis' is practically a technical term in the letters of Leo XIII to designate the common effort for the reunion of Christendom. For examples, see *Amantissimae Voluntatis*, LA 15 (1895) 138; *Unitatis Christianae, ibid.* p. 229; *Compertum Est Omnibus*, LA 17 (1897) 265; *Gratissimas Cito, ibid.*, p. 281. In *Ad Fovendum*, LA 22 (1902) 99, the expression appears in inverted commas as the accepted term.
120 See p. 130 above. On the origin of the Octave, cf. D. GANNON, *Father Paul of Graymoor*, New York 1952, pp. 136-49, 256-83.
121 See YVES CONGAR, *Chrétiens désunis*, Paris 1937, p. i (préface).
122 The Octave was recommended at the Lund Conference (*The Report*, London 1952, p. 24) and again at Evanston (*The Evanston Report*, London 1955, p. 91).
123 The apostolic letter *Romanorum Pontificum*, AAS 9 (1917) 61-2, approves the Octave prayers 'ad Ecclesiae unitatem a Domino impetrandam': 'That they may all be one as thou, Father, in me and I in thee; that they also may be one in us; that the world may believe that thou hast sent me (John xvii. 21)./I say unto thee, thou art Peter, and upon this rock I will build my Church (Matthew xvi. 18)./O Lord Jesus Christ, who hast said to thy apostles, Peace I leave with you, my peace I give unto you; look not upon my sins, but upon the faith of thy Church, and deign to grant her peace and unity according to thy will (Roman mass)'.
124 *Ecclesia Catholica*, AAS 42 (1950) 146.
125 *Orientalis Ecclesiae*, AAS 36 (1944) 142: 'qua precibus, qua scriptis, qua alloquiis'.
126 *Christi Nomen*, LA 14 (1894) 407.
127 From Leo XIII's speech of March 9, 1895, quoted in ROGER AUBERT, *Le saint-siège et l'union des Eglises*, Brussels 1947,

pp. 57–8. In this context Leo XIII refers to the reunion with Oriental Christianity, but the motive which he gives holds equally for ecumenical action in Western Christianity: 'Living in the gospel' the Pontiff says 'we have the sweet and certain promise of the Saviour that "there shall be one fold and one Shepherd". And one would want the Vicar of Christ to cease working with untiring devotion to make this promise come true? God forbid!'

BIBLIOGRAPHY

A. *The (recent) documents of the Holy See cited or referred to in this study:*

Leo XIII

Inscrutabili	encyclical	April	21, 1878
Aeterni Patris	encyclical	Aug.	4, 1879
Supremi Apostolatus	encyclical	Sept.	1, 1883
Immortale Dei	encyclical	Nov.	1, 1885
Iampridem Nobis	encyclical	Jan.	6, 1886
Paternas Caritas	encyclical	July	25, 1888
Sapientiae Christianae	encyclical	Jan.	10, 1890
Providentissimus Deus	encyclical	Nov.	18, 1893
Praeclara Gratulationis	apost. letter	June	20, 1894
Orientalium Dignitas	apost. letter	Nov.	30, 1894
Christi Nomen	encyclical	Dec.	24, 1894
Longinqua Oceani	encyclical	Jan.	6, 1895
Amantissimae Voluntatis	apost. letter	April	14, 1895
Provida Matris	apost. letter	May	5, 1895
Unitatis Christianae	apost. letter	June	11, 1895
Quum Nuper	letter	July	1, 1895
Adiutricem Populi	encyclical	Sept.	5, 1895
Christi Domini	apost. letter	Nov.	26, 1895
Satis Cognitum	encyclical	June	29, 1896
Apostolicae Curae	apost. letter	Sept.	13, 1896
Fidentem Piumque	encyclical	Sept.	20, 1896
Divinum Illud	encyclical	May	9, 1897
Militantis Ecclesiae	encyclical	Aug.	1, 1897
Compertum Est	apost. letter	Aug.	22, 1897
Gratissimas Cito	letter	Aug.	30, 1897
Caritatis Studium	encyclical	July	25, 1898
Testem Benevolentiae	apost. letter	Jan.	22, 1899
Properante Ad Exitum	apost. bull	May	11, 1899
Annum Sacrum	encyclical	May	25, 1899
Già Fin Dagli	letter	Aug.	19, 1900
Tametsi Futura	encyclical	Nov.	1, 1900
Une Douce Emotion	allocution	Jan.	8, 1901
Annum Ingressi	apost. letter	March	19, 1902
Ad Fovendum	circular letter	April	18, 1902
Mirae Caritatis	encyclical	May	28, 1902

BIBLIOGRAPHY

Pius X

Ad Diem Illum	encyclical	Feb.	11, 1904
Missam A Vobis	letter	July	10, 1911

Benedict XV

Ad Beatissimi Apostolorum	encyclical	Nov.	1, 1914
Romanorum Pontificum	apost. letter	Feb.	25, 1916
Cum Catholicae Ecclesiae	apost. letter	April	15, 1916
Dei Providentis	motu proprio	May	1, 1917
Orientis Catholici	motu proprio	Oct.	15, 1917
Antequam Ordinem	allocution	March	10, 1919
In Hac Tanta	encyclical	May	14, 1919
Ad Omnes Angliae Episcopos (1864)	letter of Holy Office	(July	11, 1919)
Ad Quosdam Puseistas Anglios (1865)	letter of Holy Office	(July	11, 1919)
Maximum Illud	apost. letter	Nov.	30, 1919
Spiritus Paraclitus	encyclical	Sept.	15, 1920

Pius XI

Sempre Bella	homily	June	4, 1922
Ubi Arcano Dei	encyclical	Dec.	23, 1922
Conditam Abhinc	letter	Feb.	24, 1923
Ecclesiam Dei	encyclical	Nov.	12, 1923
Ex Quo Proximum	allocution	Dec.	20, 1923
Amplissimum Consessum	allocution	March	24, 1924
Infinita Dei	proclamation	May	29, 1924
A Dilecto Filio	letter	June	21, 1924
Nostis Qua Praecipue	allocution	Dec.	18, 1924
Quas Primas	encyclical	Dec.	11, 1925
Rerum Ecclesiae	encyclical	Feb.	28, 1926
Ab Ipsis Pontificatus	letter	June	15, 1926
Libenti Sane	letter	June	29, 1926
Mortalium Animos	encyclical	Jan.	6, 1928
Rerum Orientalium	encyclical	Sept.	8, 1928
Decessor Noster	motu proprio	June	24, 1929
Quinquagesimo ante	encyclical	Dec.	23, 1929
Quod Catholicis	letter	Aug.	28, 1930
Ephesinam Synodum	letter	Dec.	25, 1930
Lux Veritatis	encyclical	Dec.	25, 1931
Laeto Jucundoque	letter	Jan.	6, 1933
Mit Brennender Sorge	encyclical	March	14, 1937

PIUS XII

Summi Pontificatus	encyclical	Oct.	20, 1939
Audistis Venerabilis	homily	Oct.	29, 1939
Sertum Laetitiae	encyclical	Nov.	1, 1939
In Questa Vibrante	allocution	Nov.	10, 1940
Nell'alba	radio message	Dec.	24, 1941
Circondati Dal Concorso	radio message	May	13, 1942
Mystici Corporis	encyclical	June	29, 1943
Divino Afflante Spiritu	encyclical	Sept.	30, 1943
Orientalis Ecclesiae	encyclical	April	9, 1944
E Ormai Passato	allocution	June	2, 1944
Dacché Piacque	allocution	Oct.	2, 1945
Orientales Omnes	encyclical	Dec.	23, 1945
Negli Ultimi	allocution	Dec.	24, 1945
La Elevatezza	allocution	Feb.	20, 1946
Mediator Dei	encyclical	Nov.	20, 1947
Wie Hätten Wir	allocution	Sept.	5, 1948
Ecclesia Catholica	instruction	Dec.	20, 1949
Non Mai Forse	radio message	Dec.	23, 1949
Perlibenti Quidem	letter	Aug.	9, 1950
Humani Generis	encyclical	Aug.	12, 1950
Munificentissimus Deus	encyclical	Nov.	1, 1950
Evangelii Praecones	encyclical	June	2, 1951
Sempiternus Rex	encyclical	Sept.	8, 1951
Orientales Ecclesias	encyclical	Dec.	15, 1952
Fulgens Corona	encyclical	Sept.	8, 1953
Ecclesiae Fastos	encyclical	June	5, 1954
Quamquam	apost. letter	July	25, 1954
Je Me Suis	letter	Oct.	18, 1954
Ecce Ego	radio message	Dec.	24, 1954
Sie Haben	letter	June	27, 1955
Alacre Studium	letter	June	30, 1955

Apart from these documents contained in the official collections, we quote the following pronouncements:

A speech of Leo XIII of March 9, 1895.

The letters of Card. Gasparri (1914-5) written on behalf of Benedict XV to the Ecumenical Secretary Robert Gardiner.

The letter *Equidem Verba* of Pius XI dated March 21, 1924.

A speech of Pius XI of December 21, 1924.

A speech of Pius XI of January 10, 1927.

The Dogmatic Letter of the Holy Office dated August 8, 1949, to Archbishop Cushing of Boston, U.S.A.

BIBLIOGRAPHY

B. Since ecumenical literature is too vast to be completely catalogued here, we refer the reader to some of the published bibliographies, even if these are by no means exhaustive. To keep up with the ever growing literature on Christian unity, one cannot do without ecumenical reviews, such as, for instance, *Ecumenical Review, Herder-Korrespondenz, Irénikon, Istina,* and *Verbum Caro.*

Bibliographies:

HENRY BRANDRETH, *Unity and Reunion*, 2nd edit. + suppl., London 1948.
MAX THURIAN, 'Bibliographie des principaux ouvrages, revues et articles oecuméniques parus en langue française', *Verbum Caro*, 2 (1948) 190–202.
A. A. E. ROMERO, 'Nota informativo-bibliographica sobre el Ecumenismo', *Revista Espanola Teologià*, 1952, pp. 153–73, 395–431.
'Bibliography', *A History of the Ecumenical Movement*, ed. by RUTH HOUSE and STEPHAN C. NEILL, Philadelphia 1954, pp. 745–86.

C. *Books dealing either wholly or in part with the precise subject of this study, the Roman view of Christian unity:*

ROGER AUBERT, *Le saint-siège et l'union des Eglises*, Brussels 1947.
YVES CONGAR, *Chrétiens désunis*, Paris 1937.
EDWARD HANAHOE, *Catholic Ecumenism*, Washington 1953.
W. H. VAN DE POL, *The Christian Dilemma*, London 1952.
MAX PRIBILLA, *Um kirchliche Einheit: Stockholm Lausanne, Rom*, Freiburg i. Br. 1929.
THOMAS SARTORY, *Die Oekumenische Bewegung und die Einheit der Kirche*, Meitingen bei Augsburg 1955.
KRISTEN SKYDSGAARD, 'The Roman Catholic Church and the Ecumenical Movement', *The Church Universal in God's Design*, London 1949.
GEORGES TAVARD, *A la rencontre du protestantisme*, Paris 1954.
GUSTAVE THILS, *Histoire doctrinale du mouvement oecuménique*, Louvain 1955.
OLIVER S. TOMKINS, 'The Roman Catholic Church and the Ecumenical Movement', *A History of the Ecumenical Movement*, Philadelphia 1954, pp. 677–97.
'Das Glaubensbewusstsein der "ökumenischen Christenheit" ', *Der Grosse Herder*, vol. 10, Freiburg i. Br. 1953, col. 1425–86.

D. *The more important books employed in this study, related to the subject in a wide sense:*

PAUL BROUTIN, *Mysterium Ecclesiae*, Paris 1947.
YVES CONGAR, *Esquisses du mystère de l'Eglise*, Paris 1941.
NEWTON FLEW (edit.), *The Nature of the Church*, London 1952.
N. GOODALL (edit.), *Missions under the Cross*, London 1953.
ROBERT GROSCHE, *Pilgernde Kirche*, Freiburg i. Br. 1938.
CHARLES JOURNET, *L'Eglise du Verbe Incarné*, vol. 1, 2; Bruges 1941-51.
HENRI DE LUBAC, *Catholicisme*, Paris 1938.
HENRI DE LUBAC, *Méditation sur l'Eglise*, Paris 1953.
ALBERT MICHEL, art. 'Unité de l'Eglise', *Dict. Théol. Cath.*, vol. 15, col. 2172-230.
ALBERT MITTERER, *Geheimnisvoller Leib Christi*, Vienna 1950.
JOHANN ADAM MOEHLER, *Symbolik*, 7th ed., Ratisbon 1909.
WILLIAM NICHOLS, *Ecumenism and Catholicity*, London 1952.
ANDRE RETIF, *Introduction à la doctrine pontificale des missions*, Paris 1953.
ANDRE SEUMOIS, *Introduction à la missiologie*, Schöneck/Beckenried 1952.
HERMANN TUECHLE (edit.), *Die Eine Kirche*, Paderborn 1939.
S. TYSZKIEWICZ, *La sainteté de l'Eglise christoconforme*, Rome 1945.
W. A. VISSER'T HOOFT, *The Kingship of Christ*, London 1948.
W. A. VISSER'T HOOFT, *Le renouveau de l'Eglise*, Geneva 1956.
TIMOTHEUS ZAPELENA, *De Ecclesia Christi*, vol. 2, Rome 1954.
A History of the Ecumenical Movement, ed. by RUTH HOUSE and STEPHAN C. NEILL, Philadelphia 1954.
Collection IRENIKON, *L'Eglise et les Eglises:* 1054-1954, vol. 1, 2; Chévetogne 1955.
La Sainte Eglise Universelle, Cahiers théologiques de l'actualité protestante, Neuchâtel 1948.

THE BOSTON LETTER

THE MEANING OF THE DICTUM: NO SALVATION OUTSIDE THE CHURCH

The doctrinal part of the letter from the Holy Office, dated August 8, 1949, addressed to Archbishop Cushing of Boston, U.S.A.:

The Official English Translation

We are bound by divine and Catholic faith to believe all those things which are contained in the word of God, whether it be Scripture or Tradition, and are proposed by the Church to be believed as divinely revealed, not only through solemn judgment but also through the ordinary and universal teaching office (*Denz.* no 1792).

Now, among those things which the Church has always preached and will never cease to preach is contained also that infallible statement by which we are taught that there is no salvation outside the Church.

However, this dogma must be understood in that sense in which the Church herself understands it. For, it was not to private judgments that Our Saviour gave for explanation those things that are contained in the deposit of faith, but to the teaching authority of the Church.

Now, in the first place, the Church teaches that in this matter there is question of a most strict command of Jesus Christ. For He explicitly enjoined on His apostles to teach all nations to observe all things whatsoever He Himself had commanded (Matthew xxviii. 19-20).

Now, among the commandments of Christ, that one holds not the least place, by which we are commanded to be incorporated by Baptism into the Mystical Body of Christ, which is the Church, and to remain united to Christ and to His Vicar, through whom He Himself in a visible manner governs the Church on earth.

Therefore, no one will be saved who, knowing the Church to have been divinely established by Christ, nevertheless refuses to submit to the Church or withholds obedience to the Roman Pontiff, the Vicar of Christ on earth.

Not only did the Saviour command that all nations should enter the Church, but He also decreed the Church to be a means of salvation, without which no one can enter the kingdom of eternal glory.

In His infinite mercy God has willed that the effects, necessary for one to be saved, of those helps to salvation which are directed towards man's final end not by intrinsic necessity but only by divine institution, can also be obtained in certain circumstances when those helps are used only by *desire* and *longing*. This we see clearly stated in the Sacred Council of Trent, both in reference to the Sacrament of Regeneration and in reference to the Sacrament of Penance (*Denz.* no 796, 807).

The same in its own degree must be asserted of the Church, in as far as she is the general help to salvation. Therefore, that one may obtain eternal salvation, it is not always required that he be incorporated into the Church *actually* as a member, but it is necessary that at least he be united to her by *desire* and *longing*.

However, this desire need not always be explicit, as it is in catechumens; but when a person is involved in invincible ignorance, God accepts also an *implicit desire*, so called because it is included in that good disposition of soul whereby a person wishes his will to be conformed to the will of God.

These things are clearly taught in that dogmatic letter which was issued by the Sovereign Pontiff, Pope Pius XII, on June 29, 1943, 'On the Mystical Body of Jesus Christ'. For in this letter the Sovereign Pontiff clearly distinguishes between those who are *actually* incorporated into the Church as members, and those who are united to the Church only *by desire*.

Discussing the members of which the Mystical Body is composed here on earth, the same August Pontiff says: 'Actually only those are to be included as members of the Church who have been baptized and profess the true faith, and who have not been so unfortunate as to separate themselves from the unity of the Body, or been excluded by legitimate authority for grave faults committed'.

Towards the end of this same Encyclical Letter, when most affectionately inviting to unity those who do not belong to the body of the Catholic Church, he mentions those who 'are related to the Mystical Body of the Redeemer by a certain unconscious *yearning* and *desire*', and these he by no means excludes from eternal salvation, but on the other hand states that they are in a condition 'in which they cannot be sure of their salvation' since 'they still remain deprived of those many heavenly gifts and helps which can only be enjoyed in the Catholic Church' (AAS 35 [1943] 243).

With these wise words he reproves both those who exclude from eternal salvation all united to the Church *only by implicit desire*, and those who falsely assert that men can be saved equally well in every religion (cf. Pius IX's 'Singulari quadam,' *Denz.* no 1642 ff, and 'Quanto conficiamur moerore', *Denz.* no 1677).

But it must not be thought that any kind of desire of entering the Church suffices that one may be saved. It is necessary that the desire by which one is related to the Church be animated by perfect charity. Nor can an implicit desire produce its effect, unless a person has supernatural faith: 'For he who comes to God must believe that God exists and is a rewarder of those who seek Him' (Hebr. xi. 6). The Council of Trent declares (Session VI, chap. 8): 'Faith is the beginning of man's salvation, the foundation and root of all justification, without which it is impossible to please God and attain to the fellowship of His children' (*Denz.* no 801).

(Copied from *The American Ecclesiastical Review*, 127 (1952) 312-4).

INDEX

adunare Ecclesiam, 128
ALGERMISSEN, K., 143
ALLARD, P., 155
Amsterdam Assembly, 127, 135, 137, 162, 170
AUBERT, R., ix, 34, 117, 163, 164, 170
AUGUSTINE, St., 25, 142, 148, 155, 163, 167

Baptism, 38–40, 67, 72, 90
BEAUDUIN, L., 99
Bible in the Church, 42–43, 91–93
BOSSUET, 159
Boston Letter, 29–32, 177–79
BROUTIN, P., 158

Catholicity, 73, 75, 82–88, 107, 120, 157
CERFAUX, L., 141, 151
Charity, bond of unity, 16, 24, 123, 124
Christian, defined, viii
Church: as mystical Christ, 16, 24–25; as social body, 4, 6–8, 11–12, 75, 84; as family of Churches, 14, 69
Codex Juris Canonici, 39–40, 80, 132, 143, 163
Common prayer, 131–34
Communio in sacris, 40, 55, 132
CONGAR, Y., 14, 72, 145, 149, 151, 166, 170
COUSSA, A., 71, 154
CULLMANN, O., 157
CYPRIAN, St., 155

DEJAIFVE, G., 162, 167
Dissident Christians, defined, 34
Dissident spiritualities, 119–20, 121–22
Disunity: effect on the Catholic Church, 117–19
DUMONT, C.-J., 162, 169
DUMONT, P., 152

Eastern Schism, 49–50
Ecumenical: the word, 78, 88; the definition, 97–98, 101
Ecumenical Movement, 2, 54, 74, 101, 103–08, 119
Ecumenical theology, 115–17, 122
EMERY, P.-Y., 159

Eschatological hope, 7–8, 15, 27, 62, 106, 122
Eucharist, 36–37, 90, 131
Evanston Assembly, 3, 10, 107, 108, 132, 137, 162, 170
Extra Ecclesiam nulla salus, 16, 18–19, 27, 29–31

Faith of Protestants: its possibility, 40–44; its nature, 57–59; its genesis, 91–93
Freedom in the Church, 84, 122

GANNON, D., 169, 170
GIBBON, A., 40
GIBLET, J., 146
Good faith of Protestants, 44–46
GORDILLO, M., 123
GRENTRUP, T., 155

HAMER, J., 150, 167
HARENT, S., 150
HERDER-KORRESPONDENZ, 139, 155, 162
Heresy, heretics, 33, 48, 54–55, 68, 80, 109, 161
Holiness: in the Church, 105–06, 121, 124–26; in dissident Christianity, 46, 55, 120, 126–27
Holy Spirit, 19, 60, 128

Implicity faith, 57

January Octave of prayer, 130, 133
JEROME, St., 148
JOURNET, Ch., 126, 137, 143, 149, 152, 153, 155, 156, 158, 166
JUGIE, M., 152
Jurisdictional power: in the Church, 12–15, 22–23; of the Orthodox clergy, 71

KINDER, E., 164
Kingship of Christ, 11, 22, 81

LECLERCQ, J., 154
LE GUILLOU, M.-J., 72
LEO THE GREAT, St., 18
LIALINE, D., 161
LIÉGÉ, P.-A., 143
Liturgies of the East, 36, 70, 75, 153
Local Churches, 13–14, 69
Lund, Faith-and-Order Conference, 3, 5, 12, 135, 170

INDEX

Martyrdom of dissidents, 36, 75
Mary: her relation to dissidents, 94–97, 130; her veneration by dissidents, 36, 74, 95, 154–55; sentimental devotion, 160
Mediation of the Church, 3–4, 18, 20–21, 84, 89, 125
Membership: in the Church, 27-31, 82; of dissidents, 37, 39, 63–64
Missions, 78–80, 86–87, 117, 119
MOERSDORF, K., 146

New Testament on dissident Christians, 61–62, 81–82
New Zealand, Faith-and-Order Conference, 107, 128
NIGG, W., 127

Oriental studies, 113–14, 122
Orthodox Christianity, Orthodox Christians, 35–37, 49–50, 51–52, 75, 91, 107, 110, 121
Orthodox Churches, 36, 69–72, 145

Pentecostal Novena, 129, 133
Pilgrimage of the Church, 5, 7–8, 15, 27, 106
pleroma, 24, 141–42
POL, W. van de, 161
Prejudices, 49, 113–14
PRIBILLA, M., 166
Private judgement, 10–11, 53
Proselytism rejected, 98–99, 111–13
Protestantism, Protestants, 37–47, 50–51, 52–54, 57–59, 74, 93, 110, 113, 122, 127
Protestant studies, 114–15
PRUEMMER, P., 146

RAHNER, KARL, 146, 166

Reformation, Reformers, 50–51, 53, 93
RETIF, A., 155
ROUQUETTE, R., 162

SALEMBIER, L., 154
Salvation of pagans, 31, 43–44, 84
SARTORY, T., 139, 146, 163
SCHIMMELPFENNIG, R., 154
Schism, schismatics, 33, 48, 54, 67–68, 80, 109
SCHUTZ, R., 127, 164
SEUMOIS, A., 156, 158
Sin in the Church, 50, 105–06
SPICQ, C., 135

Teaching office of the Church, 10–11 42, 91, 93
THILS, G., 155, 161
THOMAS AQUINAS, St., 58, 131
THOMKINS, O., 38
THURIAN, M., 150
Toronto Statement, 104, 106-07
TROMP, S., 140
TYSZKIEWICZ, S., 7, 126

ut omnes unum sint, 128–29

Vatican Council: the constitution 'Pastor Aeternus', 13, 41–42, 77, 137, 138, 141, 146, 147, 159
VISSER'T HOOFT, W., 78, 108, 162
VODOPIVEC, G., 143

Western Schism, 153–54
WIKENHAUSER, A., 142
World Council of Churches, viii, 3, 10, 103–08, 128, 131

ZAPELENA, T., 143, 145